Men's Health Advisor 1997

Essential New Strategies to Stay Young and Look Great

Edited by **Michael Lafavore, Men'sHealth Magazine**

Rodale Press, Inc.
Emmaus, Pennsylvania

Notice

This book is intended as a reference volume only, not as a medical manual. The information given here is designed to help you make informed decisions about your health. It is not intended as a substitute for any treatment that may have been prescribed by your doctor. If you suspect that you have a medical problem, we urge you to seek competent medical help.

—— OUR PURPOSE ——

*"We inspire and enable people to improve
their lives and the world around them."*

Men's Health Advisor 1997 Editorial Staff

Executive Editor, *Men's Health* Magazine: **Michael Lafavore**
Senior Managing Editor, *Men's Health* Books: **Neil Wertheimer**
Editor: **John D. Reeser**
Writers: **Adam Bean, Stefan Bechtel, David Brill, Brian Chichester, Warren Christopher, Tim Dowling, Martin Dugard, Stephen C. George, Mark Golin, Greg Gutfeld, Bill Heavey, David Hume, Joe Kita, Richard Laliberte, Jennifer Lynch, Rob Medich, P. Myatt Murphy, Dick Noel, Hugh O'Neill, Stephen Perrine,John Poppy, Joe Queenan, Mark Roman, Hal Rubenstein, Carrie Silberman, Laurence R. Stains, Russell Wild, Jack Wolfe**
Researchers: **Jan Eickmeier, Jane Unger Hahn, Deborah Pedron, Sally A. Reith**
Permissions: **Sally A. Reith**
Copy Editor: **David R. Umla**
Book and Cover Designer: **Lynn N. Gano**
Cover Photographers: **Angelo Caggiano, John P. Hamel, Ed Landrock, Sally Shenk Ullman, Kurt Wilson**
Photo Editor: **Susan Pollack**
Illustrator: **John R. Nelson**
Studio Manager: **Joe Golden**
Layout Designer: **Mary Brundage**
Research Chief, *Men's Health* Magazine: **Melissa Gotthardt**
Director, Book Manufacturing: **Helen Clogston**
Manufacturing Coordinator: **Patrick T. Smith**
Office Staff: **Roberta Mulliner, Julie Kehs, Bernadette Sauerwine, Mary Lou Stephen**
Office Manager, *Men's Health* Magazine: **Susan M. Campbell**

Rodale Health and Fitness Books

Vice-President and Editorial Director: **Debora T. Yost**
Art Director: **Jane Colby Knutila**
Research Manager: **Ann Gossy Yermish**
Copy Manager: **Lisa D. Andruscavage**

Contents

Introduction
The Respected Man viii

1. Eating Right

Top Ten: Eating Trends 2

Fix-It Menus
Meal Plans to Shed Flab, Gain Muscle and Live Longer . . 3

Guilt-Free Eating
Bad Foods That Really Are Good 11

An Ounce of Prevention
Powerful New Compounds That May Ward
Off Disease 20

A Beer Drinker's Paradise
Quaff These Suds without Sweating the Calories 25

Eating by the Clock
A Meal Plan to Energize Your Workouts 32

2. Youthful Living

Top Ten: Oldest Professional Athletes 40

Stay Alert
Twelve Ways to Sharpen Your Senses 41

Survival Strategies
Deal with Life by Simplifying It 49

Minor Maladies
Quick Fixes for Everyday Pains 60

Do You Measure Up?
Compare Yourself to the Average Guy 69

3. Muscle Mastery

Top Ten: 1996 Olympic Records 78

No More Excuses
Overcoming Obstacles to Workouts 79

Precise Moves
How to Correctly Use Exercise Machines 90

Cogs in the Machine
Take Care of These Small but Important Muscles 96

Visible Results
Have Something to Show from Your Workouts 103

Fitness Challenges
Can You Handle These Feats of Athleticism? 112

4. Disease-Free
Top Ten: Hot Health Facts 124

Pre-launch Checklist
Get Your Day off to a Healthy Start 125

The Truth about Teeth
Answers to Common Dental Questions 130

Listen to Your Body
The Right Way to Treat Symptoms 136

Nature's Medicines
Herbs You Should Take Notice Of 142

5. Women and Sex
Top Ten: Recent Sex Books for Men 150

Super Sex
Earth-Shaking Orgasms Can Be Yours, Too 151

Kiss and Tell
Sizzling Secrets from Some Regular Guys 155

Fantasies Explained
Sexual Daydreaming Is Nothing
to Feel Guilty About 164

New Set of Rules
Men Should Have a Say in Relationships 176

Hot Spots
Follow This Map to Better Sex 184

6. Looking Good

Top Ten: Fashion Trends 190

Casual Days
Dress Right When Your Company Dresses Down . . . 191

A Man of Style
Simple Steps to Sharper Dressing 195

The Face of Youth
Get a Healthier Look with This Advice 204

Grooming through the Ages
Look Your Best at Any Time 207

7. Man to Man

Top Ten: Movies That Make You Proud to Be a Man . . 218

Fatherly Advice
Salvage Your Kids' Love and Your Self-Respect 219

Command Respect
Tips to Make You the Envy of Others 223

Male Bonding
Name-Calling Is What Friends Do 237

Dads' Wisdom
There Is Much to Learn from Their Experiences 242

8. Men at Work

Top Ten: Business Etiquette Faux Pas 252

Bridging the Gender Gap
Overcoming Miscommunication Mishaps
with Women 253

Balancing Act
A Guide to Getting It All Done 262

Backstabbing Protection
Steering Clear of Friendly Traitors 270

Stress Busters
Call on These Tips to Ease Your Woes 275

Cool Careers
Check Out These Great Ways to Earn a Living 281

9. Men at Play

Top Ten: Mail-Order Fun 288

Mentally Tough
Training Your Mind to Give You an Edge 289

Smarter Golf
How a Busy Man Can Lower His Links Score 298

Best Vacation Ever
How to Really Relax When You Get Away 302

10. Ask *Men's Health*

Top Ten: Recent Headlines from Women's Magazines . . 312

Ask *Men's Health*
Answers to Your Top 20 Questions 313

Credits 329

Index 330

Introduction

The Respected Man

What information teaches, amuses and inspires men to lead better lives? Our survival here at *Men's Health* magazine and books lies in always knowing the answer. So we do a whole lot of research and experimenting to find out.

No insult to the research industry, but for us, the best method is usually the simplest: Ask. Every now and then we gather groups of men and talk to them for a few hours. We recently did just that, organizing discussions on both U.S. coasts.

You were probably represented. There were guys in their twenties who felt that they were physically and mentally invincible. Some were in their thirties and forties and were starting to experience the vagaries of age and wanted to slow that process. Others were more mature, with very specific and serious health concerns.

Many commonalities and insights emerged from these discussions, but one in particular has been ringing loud bells around here. Here's the setup: We asked the men to pick 3 adjectives from a list of 30 that best described how they wanted to be seen by others. The list was evenly weighted with physical and mental characteristics and had words such as good-looking, intelligent, hardworking, strong, sensitive, clever and well-dressed.

Amazingly, not a single physical adjective made it into the top ten. In fact, if we added up every physical attribute mentioned by these guys, the combined total would still have placed just third, barely edging out "sensitive" and "successful."

So what came on top? Respect. More than anything else, these men wanted to be respected by their wives and children, co-workers and bosses, friends and family.

Although we were surprised at first by how often the word "respected" came up (it was on 60 percent of the men's lists), it really does fit. Who doesn't want to hear "That guy has his act together!" said about himself?

We've been probing deeply into this issue of respect. Like, what does the word mean? For many men, it's reliability, resourcefulness, the ability to handle every and any situation. It also means never missing a day. Wasting time in bed because of sickness or injury is the worst thing that could happen to the men we talked with. As one said, "My family needs to eat, whether I'm sick in bed or not." If we're not holding up our responsibilities—be they to our families, employers or communities—in our minds, the respect that we so desire doesn't deserve to be there.

To not miss a day of life, though, means being in good health. And to be in good health takes action. It means eating well, exercising, managing stress. It means taking good care of yourself.

Boiled down, to earn respect, you first have to respect yourself.

We are pleased to report that more men are realizing this. There is much evidence that men are taking significant steps to improve their health. Of course, many are acting off the top of their heads. To be worthy of respect, a man needs to know when he no longer has all the answers and, more important, where to get the right advice.

We built this book with that in mind. *Men's Health Advisor 1997* is the perfect road map to good health and a lifestyle worthy of respect. Yes, we have a chapter entitled "Command Respect" that tells you 48 ways to get respect. But not a single chapter in this book doesn't touch on the subject in some way. You'll learn about the latest foods to keep disease away; how to craft a super workout routine; new, fiery sex techniques; and how to excel in your career.

Read this book and you'll know how to become healthier, stronger and tougher. You'll discover the actions, programs and attitudes necessary to keep you on your feet, energized and alert, every single day of your long life. And you'll find that it's far easier than you think.

So get out there and start earning some respect. You'll be a better man for it.

Michael Lafavore
Executive Editor, *Men's Health* Magazine

PART 1

Eating
Right

Eating Trends

Here are some of the top food and eating trends that nutritionists predict will last through the end of the decade.

1. Microwave magic disappearing. Although the majority of homes have a microwave, only 30% of consumers use it for anything other than reheating food.

2. Energy-enhancing foods. Energy bars and sports drinks used to be eaten only by athletes. Now, they're becoming mainstream items in supermarkets.

3. More meatless meals. This is less about becoming a vegetarian and more about focusing on pasta, vegetables and beans—with meat as an accompaniment.

4. Adventurous fish. As more Americans discover the appeal of well-prepared, truly fresh fish, we've grown more willing to try the oddball fish that are finding their way to the market.

5. Coffee. The recent proliferation of coffeehouses suggests that people are serious about the beverage.

6. Taste is tops. As a result, expect interest in spicy foods, gourmet foods and multicultural cuisines to grow.

7. Great breads. Cottony white bread is dead. We're increasingly willing to pay what it costs to buy real, crusty breads, the kinds made with premium flours.

8. Food as drugs. Increasingly, foods, ingredients and supplements will be used to prevent disease.

9. Fresh food. According to a recent survey, "fresh" is the most desirable label claim, even ahead of "fat-free."

10. Old-fashioned vegetables. We're talking about roots, among them parsnips, turnips, carrots, beets and rutabagas.

Fix-It Menus

*Meal Plans to Shed Flab, Gain Muscle
and Live Longer*

When you have a problem you can't solve, you pay someone to fix it for you. You call a plumber for the backed-up kitchen sink and a mechanic when the car breaks down. And when your golf game is suffering, you call a retired congressman. He'll have time on his hands.

Now consider your diet. Sure, it would be great to have a nutrition troubleshooter drop by, inspect your fridge contents, teach you to make smart nutritional choices and leave without uttering the word "tofu." But experts like that cost money and, really, you don't want to be seen at a Jenny Craig seminar. So we asked a top nutritionist, Cheryl Hartsough, R.D., from PGA National Resort and Spa in Palm Beach Gardens, Florida, to redesign the eating strategies of three average men to meet their varying health goals. Whether you want to lose a belly roll, add muscle or extend your life, you'll identify with one of these guys. Read on: The weight that you save may be your own.

Losing That Gut

Frank Mancuso, age 30, weighs about 175 pounds, 20 pounds more than his five-foot-six body should carry. He's a sales executive, a professional schmoozer who entertains clients in restaurants where no meal is complete without goose liver, rack of lamb and the Heimlich maneuver. "I try to eat light, but dining out all the time makes it tough," he says. Plus, most meals are accompanied by a salesman's tool of persuasion—alcohol. Although Mancuso has no history of health problems in his family, and he exercises a few times a week, his high life has led to a lowly physique.

The old menu: At breakfast, Mancuso grabs an English muffin with cream cheese and two cups of coffee with cream. Lunch and dinner are more lavish affairs. His restaurant lunches include creamy soups, large crusty sandwiches, petite steaks or swordfish fillets. Dinner always involves rich appetizers, followed by a heavily sauced meat dish. He'll wash it down with a handful of drinks. "In between, I'm always snacking on nuts because I'm always at bars with clients," he says. And dessert is—what else?—crème brûlée.

"Mancuso eats rich, fattening foods. It's no wonder he's overweight," says Hartsough. "We can't change his lifestyle, but we can scale down the more extravagant aspects of it."

The new menu: Here's the menu she devised.

Breakfast: Whole-grain, high-fiber cereal with low-fat milk, toast with apple butter, orange juice, coffee with low-fat milk.

Snack: An apple, a bagel or a cup of low-fat yogurt.

Lunch: A cup of brothy soup (such as minestrone, Manhattan clam chowder, bean or lentil) and a lean turkey, chicken or beef sandwich with lettuce and tomato on whole-grain bread, with mustard, not mayo. And for dessert, a piece of fruit.

Snack: An apple, a bagel or a cup of low-fat yogurt—whichever he didn't have in the morning.

Dinner: Start with a salad (with dressing on the side—preferably a light vinaigrette or a flavored vinegar like balsamic or raspberry). For the entrée, broiled seafood or chicken, or pasta with clam or marinara sauce, instead of the steaks or chops. Allow two glasses of vino to wash it down. We know it's tough, Mancuso, but skip the brûlée. Fresh fruit for you, pal.

The fat-fighting strategy: Here are the methods behind Mancuso's new menu.

Fill up on a smart breakfast. On an average day, Mancuso gets 42 to 47 percent of his calories from fat. According to the American Heart Association, the optimal level is below 30 percent. "By exchanging the cream cheese for apple butter, he'll knock ten grams of fat off his daily intake," Hartsough says. Switching to 1 percent milk instead of cream will further reduce his fat. "And because fiber helps with weight loss by pulling more fat through the intestine, Mancuso needs whole-grain, high-fiber cereal." This will also make him feel fuller at lunchtime, so he'll be less inclined to pig out.

Go easy on the sauce. In a typical night out with clients, Mancuso might have two martinis, a glass of champagne and a light beer, adding up to roughly 680 calories, which quickly converts to fat. He might do this twice a week. "If Mancuso doesn't drink on one of those nights each week, he could lose ten pounds in one year," says Hartsough. He might start by having a nonalcoholic beverage between every drink or waiting until the meal arrives before imbibing.

Nosh before mealtime. "An apple, bagel or a cup of yogurt will help curb his appetite, so he'll be less likely to indulge at the restaurant," says Hartsough. "And it might also keep him from inhaling the nuts, crackers and chips at the bar."

Favor clear, brothy soups. "They're lower in fat than creamy soups," says Hartsough. "And warm fluids sit in the stomach longer, so he'll feel fuller and go easier on the main course."

Trim the fat. By skipping the heavy chops and steaks in favor of broiled chicken and fish, Mancuso is making another dent in his fat intake. The same goes for having the clam and marinara sauces instead of the Alfredo sauces. Says Hartsough: "A frequent diner like Mancuso should be on good terms with a few restaurant managers and chefs so that he can talk to them about serving healthier dishes or lightening up his favorite meals."

Drink more water. Water is a necessity for weight loss. Mancuso drinks four to five eight-ounce glasses a day, but he should be taking in close to ten. Water will keep his metabolism running high, which helps prevent fat deposits from forming.

Say good-bye to the country club. Mancuso plays tennis and golf and calls it exercise. Hartsough is not impressed: "There are a lot of fat golfers and tennis players, so you know those activities aren't best for weight loss." Mancuso needs to burn fat through aerobic conditioning—45 minutes of jogging or cycling four or five times a week will do it.

Building Muscles

Keith Jackson, 28, an assistant office manager at a publishing company, is a skinny guy who dreams of bigger arms, a wider chest and, most of all, some beefy legs. "I'm as imposing as a broomstick," he says. His hectic job forces him to dine on the run, so he indulges in high-fat fast food. "I would think that this junk would add some bulk to my frame, but I'm still thin," he complains.

The old menu: A typical day in Jackson's culinary life reads like a truck-stop menu: two coffee cakes and a soda for breakfast, a couple of Snickers bars as a late-morning snack, a big cheesesteak for lunch and another steak (accompanied by potato chips) for dinner. (What, no Spam shake?)

"Keith, like many skinny guys, knows he needs to gain weight, so he'll eat just about anything," says Hartsough. "But since the food is low in nutrition, he isn't going to get bigger, just unhealthier."

The new menu: Here's a meal plan that will help Jackson add good, lean muscle.

Breakfast: Make it big, with one stack of buckwheat pancakes, toast with two tablespoons of peanut butter and cranberry juice. Or make a hefty egg-white omelet, accompanied by a bagel with light cream cheese and jam, fruit and nonfat milk.

Lunch: Have two lean turkey, ham or chicken sandwiches, with a side of rice or pasta. Snack on pretzels, low-fat cookies, frozen yogurt, fruit juices, dried fruit or energy bars.

Dinner: Pasta, rice or potatoes with lean meat such as chicken or top round, plenty of vegetables, whole-wheat bread and nonfat milk.

Snack: Cereal with a banana and nonfat milk.

The muscle-adding strategy: "If Jackson wants to add weight by building muscle, he has to eat a lot while still eating right," says Hartsough. Here's the game plan.

Help protein do its job. Protein is needed to build muscle, and Jackson already eats more than enough. But his lack of carbohydrates keeps him from growing. "Carbohydrates are needed as fuel, and without them, the body burns protein instead," says Hartsough. "Guys like Jackson overdo the protein because they think it will build more muscle—shortchanging themselves on carbohydrates." Increase carbohydrates, says Hartsough, and protein is available to build muscle. "Right now, Jackson only gets 40 percent of his total calories from carbohydrates; he needs to increase that to 60 percent." He should load up on pancakes at breakfast and have pasta, rice and bread with lunch and dinner.

Load up a cooler. When he's in a hurry, Jackson tends to eat whatever's in front of him, so Hartsough suggests that he fill a cooler with lean beef and turkey sandwiches and take it to work. "Also, stock it with healthy calories in the form of fruit, yogurt, ready-to-eat cereal, energy bars, fig bars, graham crackers, trail mix and gingersnaps," she says. All are high in calories and low in fat.

Frequent Mel's Diner. "Because of his high metabolism, Jackson can eat without the consequence of getting fat," says Hartsough. "But instead of relying on fast-food joints, he should eat at home-style diners and order the full platters." These places—the ones with the vinyl booths and rotating pie carousels—are where Jackson will find a well-rounded meal: meat (like broiled chicken or meat loaf) surrounded by the healthful side orders he skips at the drive-through—potatoes, rice, corn and green beans.

Get juiced. Hartsough wants Jackson to replace his usual morning soft drink with cranberry juice. The juice is higher in calories, and unlike solid fruit, it's not going to fill him up. So he can eat and drink more.

Eat egg whites. "When athletes want to build muscle, they eat egg whites—probably the best protein supplier," Hartsough says. "Make an egg-white omelet in the morning or fold it into a sandwich. Throw in some tomatoes, onions and low-fat cheese, too."

Eat breakfast at midnight. "Having a few extra bowls of whole-grain or bran cereal in the evening adds calories, and none of it's junk," says Hartsough.

Shape up. If Jackson wants to put muscle onto his meager frame, he's going to have to start pushing some weight around. "He'll need a good stretching program first, then some weight training," says Hartsough. She advises a beginner's program consisting of three workouts a week, including two or three sets of exercises that target major muscle groups in the chest, back and legs. "If he wants a bigger, more muscular frame, nutrition is only half the equation," she says.

Living Longer and Healthier

Jim Policelli, a 51-year-old environmental engineer, wouldn't mind enjoying a longer life. Right now, though, he's headed down the wrong track. His family history is rife with heart disease, and his own cholesterol level is outperforming the stock market. Although he skis in the winter and windsurfs in the summer, that's not enough to keep his weight under control and his heart in good shape.

The old menu: Policelli's diet contains more junk than Fred Sanford's front yard. For breakfast: milk and cookies or doughnuts. He

---

JUST THE FACTS

To lose one pound a week, it's recommended that you decrease your food intake by 250 calories a day and burn 350 more calories a day through exercise.

skips lunch entirely, opting to shovel down more cookies. At dinner, he jumps into a heavy pile of cheese-laden pasta. "I figure since I don't eat much in the day, I can have all I want at night," he says. "But, really, I know my diet is a mess."

"Policelli is laying the groundwork for a heart attack," says Hartsough. "If he wants to live longer, he'll have to make some changes."

The new menu: Here's Hartsough's menu makeover for Policelli.

Breakfast: A slice of whole-wheat toast with nonfat apple butter; three-quarters cup of whole-grain, high-fiber cereal with 1 percent milk; orange juice and a multivitamin.

Snack: Gingersnaps, graham crackers or low-fat string cheese.

Lunch: A turkey-breast or turkey-pastrami sandwich with lettuce and tomato, a tablespoon of low-fat salad dressing and mustard.

Snack: Gingersnaps, graham crackers or low-fat string cheese.

Dinner: Switch the cheesy pastas for spaghetti with marinara sauce, or have a vegetable stir-fry.

The live-longer strategy: To help Policelli avoid his heartsick family legacy, Hartsough recommends radical surgery on his lifestyle.

Redo the eating schedule. "Because he skimps on breakfast and skips lunch, he's ravenous at night," says Hartsough. "So he eats a ton, which keeps him up at night. The next day, he eats sugary, fattening cookies to stay alert." The big breakfast Hartsough added to Policelli's menu will give him more energy during the day so that he won't snack on junk. "He also needs a medium-size lunch and a smaller dinner," she says. "He'll have more energy in the day, and the lighter dinner will help him sleep better."

Slip in the good stuff. Policelli's nutrient intake lacks depth. He's eating too many calories without nutritional value. "He's totally deficient," says Hartsough. "And that translates into lowered immunity, which makes him vulnerable to illness." The cereal in the morning helps solve the problem. "That should give him plenty of zinc and vitamin B. As men age, they need more zinc for their metabolisms, to preserve their senses and sex drives," says Hartsough. "Zinc helps counter decreasing testosterone levels." And the bag of veggies mixed into pasta or a stir-fry at dinner contains antioxidants such as vitamin C and beta-carotene (which may lower risk for heart disease) as well as folate (found in leafy vegetables), which studies suggest may reduce risk for heart disease and stroke by 40 percent.

Do a check on the vitamins. To his credit, Policelli takes a multivitamin. The problem is that it may not be doing him much good. "The one he currently takes doesn't break down in time to be absorbed properly," says Hartsough. If a vitamin doesn't break down within 20 to 30 minutes, it will bypass the first part of the small intestine, where most nutrients are absorbed. To see how well a vitamin is absorbed, drop it in a glass of vinegar. "If it doesn't break down in 30 minutes, try another brand," she says. And because Policelli is at risk for heart disease and sometimes lacks important nutrients in food that are known to reduce the risk, Hartsough also suggests taking vitamins C and E and selenium supplements. "With his family health history, he could use more protection," she says.

Trade the Oreos and cheese for low-fat alternatives. "Policelli eats 80 grams of fat each day," Hartsough notes, "about 25 grams too much. And most of that is saturated fat, which raises cholesterol and increases risk for heart disease. By switching from Oreos to gingersnaps, he drops from 3 grams to 1 gram per serving." She also suggests that Policelli switch to nonfat ricotta cheese on his pasta, with a bit of Romano sprinkled in to add some extra flavor. "He can add herbs, garlic and onion to enhance the flavor." He can also snack on part-skim mozzarella string cheese.

Clear those arteries. "Any man with heart disease in his family should be increasing his HDL cholesterol, the good stuff that helps clear arteries," says Hartsough. "The only way to do that is through aerobic exercise. He should start slowly, with a walking program of 15 minutes a day, three times a week, then build up to 45 minutes a day, four times a week."

Guilt-Free Eating

Bad Foods That Really Are Good

Grab a napkin. We can see you drooling from here.

You've been waiting for a story like this, haven't you? One that breaks through that jungle of leafy, green vegetables and carrot sticks and tells you how to eat real beef stew, macaroni and cheese and a banana split with whipped cream—without gaining a single ounce. Well, here it is.

Our extensive research, which involved hours of nutritional testing, day-long marathons of data calculation and several late-night staff gatherings punctuated by unseemly displays of unabashed gluttony, has revealed a joyous truth: When it comes to the conventional wisdom about what's good for you, and what's bad, most of us have been misguided. Misinformed. Led astray. Duped.

Somewhere, somehow, while we were cruising along the food court of life, we were taught that the good-tasting stuff crowding the shelves is terribly fattening and chock-full of calories. We're talking about a lot of those greasy, gooey, cheesy and meaty meals that you crave following a Saturday afternoon of touch football.

Well, not all of it is that bad for you. Thanks to food science and some creative fiddling in the kitchen, there are loads of foods out there, from instant meals to snacks to full-blown recipes, that you'll swear are just laden with vats of fat—but aren't.

For example, you can eat real beef hot dogs, lobster and Italian sausage and peppers and not gunk up your arteries. No lie. Nothing on our list of foods gets more than 30 percent of its calories from fat, the percentage many dietitians recommend for heart-healthy eating.

Dig in.

Banana split with chocolate syrup and whipped cream. Sometimes, laziness is a virtue. For example, let's say that you take the time to make your own whipped cream. What you've just whipped up is as many as 22 grams of fat. But if you're lazy like us and buy one of the commercial whipped toppings, such as Cool Whip or the ones that come in squirt cans, you're only getting a few fat grams. Now use it to make a banana split that looks like it would harden your arteries but is actually healthy for you: Plop two scoops of low-fat ice cream or yogurt in a dish and sandwich them between the halves of a banana. Top with fresh cherries, strawberries, pineapple and kiwifruit chunks. Finish with whipped topping and chocolate syrup (also naturally low in fat). Total fat grams: 9. That's about half of what you'd get from a regular split.

Kraft Macaroni and Cheese. You lived on this stuff in college, remember? And you loved it. But you haven't touched it since you read the box and found out that one serving packs more than 16 grams of fat. Well, here's a way to prepare a low-fat bowl of the creamy noodles without giving up any flavor: Simply leave out the three tablespoons of margarine you're instructed to use. That orange powdered stuff, or cheese sauce mix, as Kraft describes it, is so potent that you won't need the margarine for flavoring. And now you're down to just 4.5 grams of fat.

Fudge. Go ahead. Indulge. One ounce (a good-size cube to you) has 112 calories and 3.4 grams of fat. That's 10 grams less than a Snickers bar.

Shrimp. A serving of steamed or baked shrimp, a great source of protein, has only 84 calories and less than a gram of fat. Here's our favorite shrimp recipe: Combine a pound of peeled shrimp with 2 tablespoons lime juice, 1 tablespoon Worcestershire sauce, 1 teaspoon hot-pepper sauce, 2 teaspoons olive oil, and 1/2 teaspoon each of thyme, oregano and ground black pepper. Cook in a baking dish at 400°, stirring occasionally, for about 15 minutes. Top with plum tomatoes, sweet peppers and chives. Serve over pasta or rice.

Potato skins with melted cheese. Prick a few baking potatoes with a fork and bake them at 425° for 45 minutes, or until tender. Now cut the potatoes lengthwise into quarters and scoop out three-fourths of the potato pulp. (Save it to make hash browns for breakfast.) Place the skins on a baking sheet coated with no-stick spray and bake at 425° for 10 to 15 minutes, or until crisp. Sprinkle some low-fat Monterey Jack and Cheddar cheese on the potato skins, then bake 2 minutes more or until the cheese is melted. Sprinkle with chopped green onions or fresh chives. Each skin has only 42 calories and 1 gram of fat.

Chocolate milk. Nestlé Quik delivers only a half-gram of fat per 2 tablespoons. The key is to use skim or 1 percent milk instead of whole milk. Chocolate syrup is just as low in fat.

Beef stew. Some stews pack nearly 40 grams of fat into one serving. This recipe gets only 9 grams per serving, or 24 percent of its calories from fat.

12 ounces boneless beef round roast, cut into 1″ cubes
1/2 cup chopped onions
1 green pepper, chopped
2 cloves garlic, minced
2 medium potatoes, peeled and diced
4 carrots, sliced
1 can (14 ounces) beef broth, defatted
1/4 cup evaporated skim milk
1 teaspoon paprika
2 tablespoons cornstarch
2 tablespoons dry sherry, dry red wine or non-alcoholic red wine

Heat a frying pan coated with no-stick spray over medium-high heat. Add the beef, onions, peppers and garlic. Stir occasionally, until the meat is browned. Stir in the potatoes, carrots and broth. Bring to a boil, then reduce the heat. Cover and simmer for 30 minutes on low until the meat is tender. Mix in the milk and paprika. In a small bowl, stir together the cornstarch and sherry or wine. Then pour the mixture into the frying pan. Cook until thick and bubbling. Stir, then cook for 2 minutes more.

Bacon, lettuce and tomato sandwich. Here's how to keep that smoky flavor and lose 16 grams of the fat: Use two slices of turkey bacon (a remarkable substitute for pork), low-fat mayonnaise, lettuce and tomatoes on a toasted whole-grain roll or bread.

Onion rings. The trick to making crispy onion rings that won't drip grease on your khakis is to keep them out of that deep fryer. Bake them: In a large bowl, beat 2 egg whites until foamy. Cut 2 peeled sweet onions crosswise into ¼″-thick slices. Separate the rings and toss them with the egg whites to coat. Roll the coated rings in a mixture of 2 cups cornflake crumbs and 1 teaspoon chili powder, and place them on a baking sheet coated with no-stick spray. Bake at 375° for 15 minutes. Only 94 calories, and 2 percent calories from fat, per 5 rings.

Twinkies. Have you tried the new low-fat version? We did, and we loved them. They're almost as creamy as their classic counterparts, but two have only 2.5 grams of fat, as opposed to 9 grams. Hostess also makes low-fat cupcakes and brownies.

Italian ice. What you're tasting is the sugary syrup. There's no fat. A cup carries only 247 calories. Ice pops are nonfat, too.

Oscar Mayer Fat-Free Bologna. We couldn't believe that this stuff had no fat and just 20 calories per slice. It tasted like the real thing between two slices of white bread. Oscar Mayer's Healthy Favorites Honey Ham, with 1.5 grams of fat per four slices, also scored well in our taste test.

Sausage-and-peppers sandwich. It's better-tasting than the kind you get at the ballpark and a lot less fatty. In fact, each sandwich delivers just 344 calories and 5 grams of fat.

> ¾ pound spicy Italian turkey sausage
> ½ cup water
> 1 cup chopped onions
> 3 cloves garlic, minced
> 2 sweet peppers, chopped
> 1 can (28 ounces) Italian tomatoes, cut up
> 2 teaspoons dried basil
> 1 teaspoon dried oregano
> ½ teaspoon freshly ground black pepper

In a large pot, bring the sausage and water to boil over high heat. Reduce the heat, cover and simmer for 8 minutes. Uncover the pot and cook the sausage until the water evaporates. After cooking, on a cutting board slice the links into sandwich-size lengths.

Coat the same pot with no-stick spray and warm it over medium-high heat for 1 minute. Stir-fry the onions and garlic for 2 minutes. Stir in the sweet peppers. After 2 minutes, mix in the tomatoes, basil, oregano, black pepper and sausage and bring to a boil. Reduce heat. Cover the pot and simmer, stirring occasionally, for 30 minutes. Take the lid off the pot and cook for another 10 minutes, or until the sauce has thickened. Serve on Italian rolls. Save the leftover sauce and sausage to spoon over hot pasta tomorrow night.

Oscar Mayer Free and Hormel Low-Fat Hot Dogs. Hot dogs. The worst of the fatty foods. A typical hot dog contains nearly 15 grams of fat. But Oscar Mayer and Hormel have created nonfat and low-fat franks, respectively, that taste more than semiauthentic. Oscar Mayer's nonfat hot dogs are made of a mixture of beef and turkey, but they taste surprisingly like all-beef franks, though the skin is a bit rubbery. We liked the Hormel low-fat beef franks better, though, because, with 2 grams per hot dog, you still get a little taste of grease.

Garlic bread. The kind they serve down at your local Italian spot is usually soaked with a butter spread. When eating out, ask for your bread served plain with a little olive oil in a dish on the side, and sprinkle some garlic salt on top. At home, make your own: Mix 3 tablespoons olive oil with 4 cloves minced garlic and then brush the mixture on both halves of a loaf of

French or Italian bread. Sprinkle each half with Parmesan cheese and toast under the broiler for 3 to 4 minutes.

Chef Boyardee Beef Ravioli. It's Italian, it has beef in it and it comes in a can. You'd swear it had to be fatty. Not in this case. Chef Boyardee's Cheese Ravioli, Beef Ravioli, Beefaroni and Tortellini all get less than 25 percent of their calories from fat.

Clams, oysters and lobster. You always thought that these foods from the sea were bad for you, right? That's because you usually see them swimming in a sea of drawn butter. Keep them out of the dip, and they are low in fat, registering between one and two grams per serving. Instead, use cocktail sauce or a drop of hot-pepper sauce on each bite. If you're planning to dump your clams over pasta, prepare a light tomato sauce instead of the fatty oil-and-clam-juice white sauce.

Sardines. They come canned in oil, but that doesn't mean you have to use a straw. Pour the oil out, then rinse them under the tap to reduce the fat, calorie and sodium content. A can eaten this way delivers just three grams of fat.

Low-Fat Pop-Tarts. The low-fat strawberry Pop-Tarts we tried were sweet and flaky, and whether you choose one with icing or not, you still get a low-fat treat. Each one contains three grams of fat.

Breakfast sandwich. If you stop at your local fry pit for an egg, bacon and cheese sandwich, you'll start your day having bagged more than half of your recommended daily intake of fat. Now, if, on the other hand, you take the time to make one of those sandwiches yourself, you can save 20 grams of fat. Simply fry three egg whites in a pan coated with no-stick spray instead of butter. Serve them on a toasted English muffin with Canadian bacon and low-fat American cheese.

JUST THE FACTS

Percentage of decrease in your risk for lung, colon, stomach, esophageal and oral cancers if you eat at least five fruits and vegetables a day (compared with people who eat two or fewer a day): 40

Pizza. Whether you make it at home or order takeout, you can trim eight grams of fat and more than 100 calories by using less cheese. When you place your order, ask them to make the pizza with one-third less cheese.

Potato chips and hot beer dip. Sound like the recipe for a heart attack? Not fixed our way. First, make your own low-fat potato chips by cutting potatoes into thin slices and microwaving 10 at a time on a rack for about 4 minutes.

To make hot beer dip that contains only 1 gram of fat: Coat an unheated saucepan with no-stick spray. Add ¼ cup chopped green onions and 1 clove minced garlic. Stir over medium heat for about 3 minutes. Meanwhile, in a separate bowl, combine 1 cup shredded nonfat Cheddar cheese with 1 cup shredded reduced-fat sharp Cheddar cheese, then sprinkle in 1 teaspoon cornstarch. Stir ¾ cup nonalcoholic beer into the saucepan and bring to a low boil. Slowly add the cheese mixture. Stir until melted. Remove from heat and blend in 1 cup nonfat yogurt. It's ready for dipping.

Aunt Jemima Low-Fat Waffles. Try the low-fat version. Two of these waffles have 18 fewer grams of fat than the ones you make from powdered mix, and they take a lot less time to prepare. Just pop them into your toaster. Look for Aunt Jemima low-fat pancakes and French toast, too.

Barbecued ribs. A plate of country-style ribs or spareribs can weigh in with more than 50 grams of fat. But you can make a lean boneless rib dinner by using pork loin or a boneless chop and slicing off the visible fat. Cut it into thick strips and slather it with all the barbecue sauce you want. A quarter-cup has only a gram of fat. Roast the ribs over hot coals for 20 minutes, turning occasionally.

For oriental ribs, mix a few pounds of meat with 1 tablespoon each of onion powder, garlic powder, dry mustard, ground ginger and ground red pepper. Add also 1 teaspoon five-spice powder and 1½ teaspoons black pepper. Grill as above.

Crab cakes. Sure, if you fry them in a half-inch of oil, they're fatty. But they don't have to be. By using no-stick cooking spray instead of oil, and egg whites instead of whole eggs, you can cut the fat from 12 to 2 grams per serving.

To make them, spray an unheated frying pan with no-stick spray and add 1 stalk chopped celery, ¼ cup chopped onions and 1 tablespoon parsley. Stir over medium heat until tender. Remove from the heat.

In a separate bowl, beat 6 egg whites. Add ¾ cup plain bread crumbs, 2 teaspoons Worcestershire sauce and 1 teaspoon dry mustard. Stir in the celery mixture and 12 ounces drained crabmeat. Shape into ½"-thick patties and coat with bread crumbs. Spray the pan and cook the patties over medium heat until brown. Turn and cook 3 minutes more.

For a low-fat tartar sauce, combine nonfat mayonnaise or yogurt, chopped pimentos and minced garlic to taste. Puree until smooth. Stir in red-pepper flakes to taste.

Veal Parmesan. Although veal is a relatively lean cut of meat, preparing it Parmesan-style is what gives it its hefty reputation. Instead of frying the breaded patties in oil, simply bake them. Coat a veal cutlet with egg white, then bread crumbs. Top with spaghetti sauce, oregano, black pepper and reduced-fat mozzarella cheese. Bake at 350° for 30 minutes. This version gets less than 30 percent of its calories from fat.

Refried beans. For some reason, we tend to think that all refried beans are made with lard. That might be the case across the Rio Grande, but it's not true for most canned beans. A half-cup of refried beans has only 135 calories and 1.5 grams of fat. For a lean but filling taco, spoon some beans, chopped tomatoes, lettuce, salsa and nonfat sour cream into a soft flour tortilla.

Vanilla milk shake. Providing it's vanilla, a milk shake from a fast-food restaurant gets only about 24 percent of its calories from fat. If you go where they make their own from scratch, you can get the shake even leaner by asking them to make it with 1 percent milk and low-fat ice cream or frozen yogurt.

Parmesan cheese. A tablespoon has less than 2 grams of fat. If that's not low enough for you, Kraft makes one that's nonfat, but it's not nearly as good as the freshly grated version.

Frog's legs. Like everything else that's cooked down on the bayou, they're fatty, right? Not so. A serving of frog's legs contains less than a gram of fat. To prepare, sprinkle them with seasoned flour, then sauté for 2 to 3 minutes in a pan lightly coated with olive oil.

Chicken nuggets. You can cut 12 grams of fat from the McDonald's variety by making your own. Cut up chunks of chicken breast and roll them in bread crumbs seasoned with ground red pepper, herbs and Italian seasoning or taco seasoning. Add the coated chicken nuggets to a heated frying pan coated with no-stick spray. Flip them around until the bread crumbs are brown and the chicken is fully cooked.

Pudding. Rice and tapioca puddings only look bad for you because they're so thick and rich. But 1 serving of either contains less than 5 grams of fat and less than 200 calories.

Candy corn. Dress your kids up like giant Oreo cookies, then send them out to beg for food. When they come home, steal their candy corn. Thirty kernels have only 1 gram of fat. Isn't adulthood great?

An Ounce
of Prevention

*Powerful New Compounds
That May Ward Off Disease*

What is it about the supermarket produce aisle that makes men zoom past it? Is it the humbling size of the cucumbers, the fear that you'll start squeezing melons and won't be able to stop or the threat of humiliation at not being able to get one of those plastic bags on a roll to open? No one knows for sure, but if good health is high on your shopping list, then you'd better overcome your vegetable phobia and learn to linger awhile among the fresh foods.

Especially now, since researchers have discovered a bunch of compounds buried in broccoli, onions, tomatoes and other common fruits and vegetables that could be the most potent heart-protectors and cancer-fighters yet.

They're called phytochemicals or, in an attempt to make them more palatable and popular, phytomins. Basically, they're compounds that act as a plant's police force. According to Herbert Pierson, Ph.D., vice-president of Preventive Nutrition Consultants, in Woodinville, Washington, a former project director with the National Cancer Institute and one of the leading experts in this emerging field, phytomins help plants repel bacteria, viruses, fungi and insects; defend against dehydration and harmful ultraviolet rays and stimulate chlorophyll production.

Once inside you, these compounds stay just as busy, explains Dr. Pierson. They may help keep arteries clear of cholesterol, bolster resistance to cancer, neutralize toxins, reduce inflammation and even prevent premature aging.

There's already a long list of identified phytomins (only a few of which we can pronounce after two beers), but given their potential, they could become household words in the next few years. So here's a look at some of the most promising ones, including how they work and, most important, how you can easily get more of them into your diet.

Flavonoids

These compounds, of which there are approximately 4,000, have been getting a lot of attention lately because they supposedly explain why those pâté-gobbling, butter-loving, wine-guzzling Frenchmen have a death rate from heart disease that's 2.5 times lower than the rate for Americans. Researchers used to think that it was the alcohol, but now they're saying that it's the flavonoids present in grape skins. When allowed to steep, these skins impart their dark purple color to wine, along with their powerful nutrients. These, in turn, keep blood cells from clotting and causing a heart attack. White wine and mixed drinks don't have as pronounced an effect.

But while the French may love their wine, they also eat more fruits and vegetables than we do, and these are also full of flavonoids. Onions, kale, green beans, apples, broccoli, endive, celery, cranberries and citrus fruit (especially the peel and pulp) have the most, as do grape juice, green and black teas and naturally dark beer such as Guinness Stout.

"This is a very important class of compounds," says Elliot Middleton, Jr., M.D., professor of medicine at the State University of New York at Buffalo. "There are no data yet on whether flavonoids could be as essential as diet and exercise in lowering heart disease risk, but it may be that if we consume these compounds on a regular basis, we'll have a reduced likelihood of heart disease."

Indeed, Dutch scientists studied 805 men for five years and found that those eating the most of five essential flavonoids were

32 percent less likely to die of heart disease. Their daily diets included four cups of tea, an apple (with skin) and about a quarter-cup of onions. Likewise, in seven countries around the world where flavonoid intake was high, the national rates of death from heart disease were correspondingly low.

Although preliminary studies with humans are mixed, these flavonoids might have cancer-fighting qualities as well. For instance, tea drinkers in China have lower rates of throat cancer.

"I do think that the anti-cancer effects of flavonoids exist," says Michael Wargovich, Ph.D., a researcher at the M. D. Anderson Cancer Center in Houston, "but possibly only in synergy with a lot of other compounds that are present in the same fruits and vegetables."

Carotenoids

The long-standing chief of this group of phytomins is beta-carotene. It's the most abundant carotenoid in the foods we eat and the one most efficiently converted to vitamin A. Plus, it's a powerful antioxidant, which means it counters cell damage that could lead to widespread cancer and heart disease.

But there are more than 600 other carotenoids, and research is proving that some of them have similar disease-fighting properties. For example, scientists found that people in northern Italy who ate seven or more servings of raw tomatoes every week had 60 percent less chance of developing colon, rectal and stomach cancer than those who ate two servings or less. In fact, eating tomatoes may lower your risk of cancer even more than eating fruits or green vegetables.

Tomatoes are one of the few foods rich in a carotenoid called lycopene. And since it survives heating and processing, it's still present in tomato paste, sauce, juice, even ketchup and pizza. Other sources include watermelon, pink and red grapefruit, guava and sweet red peppers.

Other carotenoids meriting study are canthaxanthin (we warned you that this was going to get multisyllabic) and lutein. The former is found in certain mushrooms and is used as a food coloring in cheese. When it was fed to lab rats, they developed 65 percent fewer cancers. The latter is found with beta-carotene in vegetables such as spinach and kale. Besides possibly protecting against cataracts, it, too, is being investigated for potential cancer-fighting properties.

Genistein, Daidzein and Saponins

No, this isn't some slick Manhattan law firm, but come to think of it, this trio can forcefully represent you in the battle against high cholesterol and prostate and colon cancer.

All three of these phytomins are present in soybeans—a staple food in Pacific Rim diets. Genistein and daidzein are reported to inhibit cancer growth in early stages and also short-circuit its spread. Meanwhile, more than 40 clinical studies have shown that saponins can lower blood cholesterol.

Some painless (relatively) ways to get soy products into your diet: Mix tofu into tuna salad or throw some chunks of it onto your greens. Dice it up and add it to chili or hearty soups. Stir-fry it. Add it into your favorite lasagne recipe or hide some inside your manicotti. But be sure to get it into your diet somehow.

"We're coming into a new era where precise questions can be asked about precise nutrients," says Dr. Wargovich. "We hope that someday we'll have a dietary prescription for foods that protect health."

For now, our best advice is to pack your shopping cart with a variety of fresh fruits and vegetables—enough for at least five servings a day.

JUST THE FACTS

A croissant has more than nine times as much fat as a plain English muffin.

The Top Sources

You'll never remember the names of all these nutrients, and fortunately, you don't have to. We took a spin around the produce department and compiled this top-ten list of the most potent phytomin foods.

1. Broccoli
2. Soy
3. Garlic (always crush or slice cloves finely to release phytochemicals)
4. Onions (eat white, yellow and red for a variety of flavonoids)
5. Tomatoes
6. Citrus fruit (flavonoids cluster in the peel and white, pulpy parts)
7. Cabbage
8. Cantaloupe or watermelon
9. Beans—kidney, pinto and so on
10. Tea—green or black (use tea bags instead of loose leaves, and steep for five to ten minutes)

Major contenders: most greens, such as spinach, collards, kale, endive, fennel, bok choy and Chinese cabbage; carrots; apples (leave the skin on); grapes, grape juice and red wine; cauliflower; sweet potatoes; celery; and flaxseed (can be baked into bread).

A Beer Drinker's Paradise

Quaff These Suds without Sweating the Calories

Say the word "beer" to a man, and you'll evoke images of grilled foods, summertime parties and delightfully dingy dive bars. Say the word "beer" to his wife, and she'll think belly. Which is too bad, considering that beer is not, in and of itself, too terribly fattening.

Oh, perhaps if you were still in college, strapping cans of beer to your head and drinking it through straws, you'd be taking in some serious calories. But nowadays your tastes are a little more sophisticated. We hope. So as your friends, as your health advisers and as a bunch of guys who, frankly, just like beer, we're going to say it loud and clear: You can have your beer and a size 34 waist, too. And not just "lite" beer. *Real* beer. Beer with flavor and body and, well, substance. In the interest of helping you enjoy your liquid refreshment more, we offer some of the finest examples of the numerous types of beer, calories included. You can take our brand suggestions or experiment down at the local brew pub. But under no circumstances should you attempt to strap any of these brews to your head. Okay?

Light Ale

Wild Goose Golden Ale

This is a smooth, light-bodied ale that's lower in calories than most "lites" and has about 20 fewer calories than a 12-ounce can of

soda. There's also plenty of flavor here. Serve at about 55°F.
Alcohol by volume: 4.1%
Calories: 125

Brown Ale

Pete's Wicked Ale

Silver medalist in the brown ale category at the World Beer Championships for the last two years, chestnut-color Pete's has a subtle roasted barley flavor and a slightly sweet edge. Most beers with this much flavor would be loaded with calories. This one isn't. We're not quite sure how they do it.
Alcohol by volume: 5%
Calories: 170

Scottish Ale

Grant's Scottish Ale

One nice thing about microbreweries such as Washington's Yakima Brewing Company, where Grant's comes from, is that their products are more nutritious than the mass-market kind. Micro-brews tend to be made with more barley malt, which is loaded with B vitamins. A 12-ounce bottle of Grant's contains 62.5 percent of the Daily Value for folate (a B vitamin), 170 percent for vitamin B_{12} and 12.7 grams of carbohydrate (about what you get from a slice of bread). As for flavor, Grant's Scottish Ale is what professional beer tasters describe as lively, meaning it takes some getting used to.
Alcohol by volume: 4.5%
Calories: 145

Old Ale

Theakston's Old Peculier

This British import is a dark, sweet ale that is so thick you can practically chew it. One bottle of old ale will give you 15.6 grams of carbohydrate, about what you'd get from three-quarters cup of oat-meal. Chill to 55°F and try it with a nice steak-and-kidney pie or something else hearty and appropriately Anglophilic.
Alcohol by volume: 5.6%
Calories: 172

Stout

Guinness Extra Stout

This black stuff used to be marketed in the United Kingdom under the slogan "Guinness is good for you." The British National Health Service has since nixed selling alcoholic products as "healthy."

Nonetheless, Guinness is a hearty beer that's not in any way unhealthy, as long as it's drunk in moderation. Many dark beers like Guinness, in fact, are loaded with micronutrients called flavonoids, which may help round up those notorious free radicals—loose oxygen molecules that damage muscle cells—hiding in your body.

Alcohol by volume: 5.8%
Calories: 181

Barley Wine Ale

Rogue Old Crustacean Barley Wine

We had to include a barley wine ale to give you an idea of the range of brews that are available these days. Located at the far end of the spectrum from, say, Wild Goose Golden Ale (see page 25), this strong, sweet stuff has twice the alcohol content and calories of regular beer.

There's an added benefit here in being able to call out to the bartender, "Make that an Old Crustacean for my lady friend." Definitely an acquired taste, and one capable of doing some damage both to brain cells and to your waistline.

Alcohol by volume: 11%
Calories: 360

Porter

Sierra Nevada Porter

A precursor to stout, porter was the most popular beer style in the United States and Britain in the eighteenth and nineteenth centuries. All but forgotten for many years, porter has been revived by companies such as Sierra Nevada. Its porter, made in Chico, California, is a fine example of the style—a medium-bodied, dark brown beer that's lighter than a stout but with a full, creamy head.

Alcohol by volume: 5.8%
Calories: 230

Home Brewing

Former President Jimmy Carter is regarded more highly today than he ever was during his administration. Is it because of his humanitarian work? His extraordinary diplomatic accomplishments? Or simply because Billy isn't around anymore?

No, for a growing number of men, it's because Carter was the man who, in 1978, signed into law a federal bill that allowed us to brew our own beer legally. Since then, more than a million people just like you have started brewing at home. It's easy, it's inexpensive and, if you're a beer drinker, it's healthier for you. That's because home brew is pure, unpasteurized and loaded with B-complex vitamins, and it has no preservatives or additives. (A 12-ounce serving of home brew will have about 10 percent of the Daily Value for riboflavin and more than 20 percent for niacin.)

To get started, here's what you need to do.

1. Start saving your empties. You'll need about two cases' worth of brown beer bottles. (Brown glass filters out sunlight, protecting your beer from spoilage.) Then rustle up a big cooking pot in which you can cook up your batch.
2. Stop by a local home-brewing supply store. (To find one, look in the phone book under "Brewing" or "Beer.") Ask about

Amber Lager

Samuel Adams Boston Lager

We've all tried it. Most of us like it. Seems as if it's been around forever, yet it's only been ten years. This American classic has made the Boston Beer Company easily the biggest microbrewery in the United States, with more than a quarter of the microbrewery market share. Similar to a mass-market beer, but with a little more color and flavor, Sam Adams beer is a good transition microbrew for those who haven't tried many of them yet.

Alcohol by volume: 4.9%

Calories: 160

a starter kit, which will get you all the supplies you need for between $35 and $150, depending on how much you want to put out. You'll need malt, yeast, hops and an instruction book. Two of the best are Charles Papazian's The New Complete Joy of Home Brewing and The Home Brewer's Companion. Both are readable and comprehensive, with the former being a tad more basic. (Papazian has also done a how-to video on the subject.) You'll also need a bottle capper and some bottle caps.

3. Now that you're ready, remember two things. First, this is going to stink up the joint, so don't do it while the ladies' auxiliary is over for tea. Second, be relentlessly finicky about sanitizing your equipment before you start. (Water and a dilute bleach solution will do fine for this.) Unclean equipment is the most frequent reason for bungled batches.

If you love it, you'll need more supplies. Try one of these top mail-order sources: Williams Brewing, P.O. Box 2195, San Leandro, CA 94577, 1-800-759-6025; The Cellar Home Brew, P.O. Box 33525, Seattle, WA 98133, 1-800-342-1871; or Beer and Wine Hobby, 180 New Boston St., Woburn, MA 01801; 1-800-523-5423.

Dark Lager

Three Finger Jack-Hefedunkel

To produce this excellent dark lager, Saxer Brewing Company brewmaster Tony Gomes uses the German *krausening* technique, which allows the unfiltered beer to finish fermenting in the bottle. The result is lots of healthful B-complex vitamins from the yeast. One bottle has 12.4 grams of carbohydrate. The beer is still not widely available in the East, but if you like dark lager, it's worth the search.

Alcohol by volume: 4.7%
Calories: 161

European Pilsner

Pilsner Urquell

A world classic, Pilsner Urquell is still brewed in the Czech town of Pilsen, which gave this beer style its name. Pilsen's brewers essentially invented the first golden-color, clear beer in the 1840s. (Until then, all of the world's beers were dark and often murky.) Medium-bodied, with a very crisp, clean flavor, Pilsner Urquell is still made from local ingredients in six miles of cool limestone caves beneath Pilsen. Let's put it another way: This stuff is damn good.

Alcohol by volume: 5.5%
Calories: 150

Bock

Paulaner Salvator

Another superb European beer, Salvator is a *doppelbock*, German for double bock, which means it is extra strong and malty. Every spring, the first barrel of Salvator is ceremonially tapped by Munich's mayor at the Paulaner's 3,500-seat beer hall. Like all doppelbocks, Salvator packs a wallop in the calories department.

Alcohol by volume: 7.5%
Calories: 273

JUST THE FACTS

Number of Americans who eat Spam regularly: 60 million

Wheat Beer

Weihenstephan

Beers made with wheat instead of barley are typically lighter-color, more carbonated and "spicier" than regular beers. Weihenstephan, like all wheat beers, should be poured into a glass, bottom-yeast sediment included. This will make the beer cloudy, which is the way it's supposed to be.

Alcohol by volume: 5.4%
Calories: 220

Steam Beer

Anchor Steam Beer

Steam beer is so named because in the original brewing process, the yeast gave off clouds of carbon dioxide. Today, the yeast is filtered out. The only beer style indigenous to the United States, it is crisp, like a lager, but with a fruitier, alelike flavor. It's an excellent choice if you want the maximum flavor for the minimum calories. San Francisco's Anchor Brewing Company invented the brew in the 1890s, but until recently, you had to go to California to get it. Now it's widely available.

Alcohol by volume: 4.7%
Calories: 154

Nonalcoholic Beer

Clausthaler

Nonalcoholic beers are limited in potential, since it's the alcohol that delivers much of the flavor. That said, this is one of the best-tasting virgin beers, and it's likely to be available at your local grocer. Nonalcoholic beers normally contain well under 100 calories per bottle, and the calories are almost entirely from carbohydrate. Microbrew enthusiasts might also look for the Minnesota Brewing Company's Pig's Eye NA, the first nonalcoholic microbrew/ale. It's mainly available in the Midwest.

Alcohol by volume: less than 0.5%
Calories: 96

Eating by the Clock

A Meal Plan to Energize Your Workouts

So you're in the gym and you feel great. No, incredible. Your arms are pumped, your mind is right and it's as though you could bench-press a week's worth of Brad Pitt's fan mail. You've never felt stronger.

Your next workout is another story altogether. You're sluggish. Your arms feel as heavy as iron beams, and your legs are as wobbly as the Cuban economy. You're bored, you're miserable, you cut your workout short and consider rechanneling your gym membership fees into overseas stock funds.

What happened? Why is it that one day you're a god and the next you're a dog?

It might be something you ate. Or more to the point, when you ate it. That's because optimal performance rests largely on eating strategies that allow you to reach your energy peak during every workout. "What you eat and when you eat it can make the difference between running on fuel and running on fumes," says Nancy Clark, R.D., director of nutrition services at Sportsmedicine Brookline in Brookline, Massachusetts, and author of *Nancy Clark's Sports Nutrition Guidebook.* Whether you want to complete a half-marathon, build a chest of Tarzanian dimensions or simply shrink the proportion of your spare tire, you can make progress faster and more efficiently by following a simple nutrition plan.

We aren't talking about reworking your entire diet. No powders. No pills. No sacks of oddly colored mixes sold only at the health food store by an emaciated guy named Coyote Starship. We're talking about a plan designed for a man who has a job, maybe some kids or at least a parakeet he has to feed, and doesn't want to spend hours skinning and boiling whole chickens or mixing protein shakes in his pajamas before bed.

We have the plan for you. Below is a low-fat menu designed to give you an added performance punch. It's geared for the man who lifts weights during his lunch hour, but if you're a morning or after-work athlete, no problem. Just see "Adjusting Your Eating Schedule" on page 34 to make simple adjustments.

7:00 A.M.: Hey, get outta bed already. Now walk to the kitchen. Turn on the tap. Grab one of those big tumblers—the one with the football logo that you got free from the gas station. Put it under the spigot until it's full. Drink. Okay, you've been told more times than you care to remember that drinking eight glasses (eight ounces each) of water a day is good for you. Unfortunately, that information is wrong. If you exercise regularly, you'll need at least two or three more glasses daily. "This is key if you're trying to enhance performance in the gym, because even mild dehydration can leave you feeling weak," says Ann Grandjean, Ed.D., director of the International Center for Sports Nutrition in Omaha, Nebraska. And when you wake up, you're already pretty dehydrated. So load up while you're still in your jammies.

8:15 A.M.: Breakfast. What you need right now is glucose, a blood sugar that your body stores in its muscles and liver as the starch called glycogen and uses for energy. And until they come out with Goofy Glycogen-Flavored Pop-Tarts, your best bet is complex carbohydrates, the high-energy foods that your body breaks down into glucose and stores as glycogen. You find them in the highest concentrations in grains such as breads and cereals. But the key is to eat carbohydrates early, because it take hours for your body to turn these nutrients into energy. What you eat now is what your body will be running on during lunchtime. "A lack of carbohydrates is the one thing that will limit you in almost any athletic performance," says Kris Clark, R.D., Ph.D., director of

Adjusting Your Eating Schedule

If you don't exercise at noon but you do at other times of the day, apply the same principles spelled out in the chapter but adjust them to fit your schedule.

If you exercise in the morning, have a larger dinner (a meat dish with a side of pasta with red sauce, bread and salad) the night before. The extra energy will carry over into the morning. Then have a small snack and plenty of water early in the morning. A piece of fruit is fine. Have a cup of coffee 30 minutes before you hit the gym, if you're so inclined. (If you have high blood pressure, check this out with your doctor first.) After the workout, have another small dose of carbohydrate (a low-fat muffin, bagel or yogurt) to replenish your energy stores.

If you exercise right after work, make sure that you have a little more protein at lunch, to provide the extra mental energy needed to get through the afternoon. But don't overdo it. Sluggishness is more common in people who eat large midday meals. These are the people you often find unconscious at their desks around 2:00 P.M. and applying for unemployment benefits shortly thereafter. Have a small snack on the way to the gym. Have a soft drink, too. It has considerably less caffeine than coffee, so it's less likely to keep you up at night, but it may pack enough of a jolt to perk you up. For dinner, cut back on the meat, because you'll be eating most of your protein at lunch. Instead, beef up the meal with carbohydrate-rich pasta.

sports nutrition at Pennsylvania State University Center for Sports Medicine in University Park.

For a power-packed breakfast, start off with one of the following combinations.

- One bagel, a piece of fruit and a bowl of cereal with skim milk.
- A bowl of grits or oatmeal. Sprinkle some wheat germ on top for some extra vitamin E.
- A stack of three pancakes, light on the butter and syrup. Pancakes get as much as 76 percent of calories from carbohydrate. Have a glass of fruit juice or some orange slices to top it off.

10:00 A.M.: Snack. By now you're at the office, and having worked tirelessly at avoiding any actual labor for the first hour, you're deep into some heady exercise that requires long division or long-winded conversation. Stop. Get up, walk to the cafeteria and grab yourself a carton of nonfat yogurt.

Here's why. Besides giving you another excuse to whittle time off your workday, taking a yogurt break will provide protein, which you need to build muscle. According to Dr. Grandjean, athletes who work out five or six times a week can safely increase protein consumption to as high as 0.7 gram of protein per pound of body weight. At that rate, a 175-pound athlete hoping to boost muscle bulk by 1 pound per week would consume about 120 grams of protein per day, the equivalent of about 1 pound of roast beef.

Now, aside from pirates, caged lions and certain conservative commentators, who would want to inhale a pound of roast beef in one sitting? "The goal of protein is not energy," says Dr. Clark. "You only need so much to perform the body's maintenance functions." The rest could well wind up being turned into body fat, and that's not the kind of bulk you need. That cup of yogurt is just what your body can handle—a small dose of protein.

11:00 A.M.: Water break. You already know that you need water to prevent fatigue. But here's another reason why you should tank up regularly: It'll help you build more muscle. That's because it takes water to use protein more effectively. Excess protein without sufficient water can put a strain on the liver and kidneys. So try to have a glass of water at every snack break and meal. Better yet, keep a large water bottle at your desk and gulp throughout the day. Think of all the extra exercise you'll get from those repeated trips to the bathroom—and all the interesting people you'll meet along the way.

On your way back, pick up a banana. Along with potatoes, bananas are among the richest sources of potassium, a mineral that's critical for keeping your body's fluid levels in balance. They're also an excellent, portable source of carbohydrates.

11:30 A.M.: Coffee break. Take time out for that cup of coffee ... or two. Research suggests that caffeine in doses of about 200 milligrams (about what you'd get from two strong cups of coffee) may help you burn more fat when you work out, says Matt Vukovich, Ph.D., assistant professor of exercise physiology for the Human Performance Lab at Wichita State University in Kansas.

Caffeine can temporarily increase the levels of fatty acids circulating in your bloodstream, which helps the body maximize the amount of fat it burns during exercise. (Caffeine, however, can also increase your blood pressure. If you have high blood pressure, check with your doctor before trying this.)

And caffeine may actually help you work harder in the gym, getting even more from your workouts. Research conducted at McMaster University in Hamilton, Ontario, indicates that this legal stimulant may decrease fatigue during low- to moderate-intensity exercise, so you can last longer than if you went javaless.

But be aware that a cup of coffee is no guarantee that you'll do better. "Some people seem to respond to it, some people don't," Dr. Vukovich says. If you're already dosing up on six to eight cups of coffee just to get through the workday, it's unlikely that any additional caffeine will help. So take this test: If there are enough coffee cups lying around your office to build a rather large replica of the Taj Mahal, another cup of joe won't do you any favors.

Noon: Workout. You should be too busy busting your butt to be eating, but to keep up with your sweat losses try to take in roughly four to six ounces of H_2O per 20 minutes of exercise. Make sure it's cool. Your body absorbs cold water much faster than warm.

1:00 P.M.: Lunch. You're finished. You've showered. You've slipped back into your corporate duds. You've packed away those smelly sneakers where no one can find them. Now grab that bag lunch you prepared the night before and whip out a pair of large soft pretzels. Or hit the cafeteria for a bowl of pasta salad, rice or baked potato or a sandwich. Any of the above give you at least 100 calories' worth of carbohydrates, which is exactly what your body needs right now. Eating carbohydrates immediately after exercise is important for boosting recovery and replenishing glycogen stores (remember, that's energy), especially for athletes who work out day after day.

"Many weight trainers may be held back because they're not getting enough carbohydrate to allow them to recover fully after a tough workout that taxes their glycogen stores," says Mike Stone, Ph.D., professor of exercise science at Appalachian State University in Boone, North Carolina. So load up now to keep your energy levels at high rev.

But you might also want to include a little protein in the mix. That may help build muscle and also keep you on your cognitive toes the rest of the day. Have turkey or chicken in that sandwich, or have a cup of low-fat cottage cheese.

4:00 P.M.: Snack. Make it a small hunk of Cheddar cheese, some skim milk or low-fat yogurt. What you're doing here is depositing a little more protein into your muscle bank. Plus the yogurt will give you an extra dose of calcium, which is necessary for enhancing muscle contractions. And do yourself a favor: Before eating it, walk out of your office, past the tacky outdoor water fountain, then sit down on a bench. Now eat. By exposing your skin to sunlight for 15 to 30 minutes a day, you'll get your body to make vitamin D, which helps build strong bones. This is also a chance to roll up your sleeves and show off your well-chiseled forearms.

6:30 P.M.: Dinner. Here's a simple two-course meal to reward yourself for all your hard work.

- Begin with a spinach salad. Toss on some sesame seeds, walnuts or sunflower seeds, and top it with a little olive oil vinaigrette. True, these toppings all add fat, but if you work them into your diet sensibly, they also offer you a healthy dose of vitamin E, an antioxidant that helps destroy free radicals, loose oxygen molecules that damage muscle cells. Vitamin E may also increase endurance and bolster the body's ability to use oxygen, particularly at higher elevations. But most important, studies suggest that vitamin E helps repair muscle tissue that you've broken down through weight lifting. (That's why we had you sprinkle wheat germ on your breakfast—it's rich in vitamin E.)

- Then add stir-fried beef with broccoli and green peppers. The beef is a prime protein source, but a three-ounce serving also supplies more than 40 percent of the Daily Value (DV) of vitamin B_{12}. This nutrient helps metabolize fats and carbohydrate and produce red blood cells, which some athletes claim can enhance endurance.

The broccoli provides 120 percent of the DV for vitamin C, and one green pepper offers 90 percent. Vitamin C is a potent antioxidant that may help reduce exercise-related inflammation, speeding up recovery after working out.

- Don't forget a potato. Whether the spud is baked, mashed or nuked, this complex carbohydrate comes jammed with nutrients, including vitamin C, potassium and iron. Make it a sweet potato and you'll add a big dose of beta-carotene, another antioxidant that helps destroy damaging free radicals.

9:00 P.M.: Snack. Call it dessert. Call it what you want. Have a fruit bar, frozen yogurt, gingersnaps, a fig bar, some graham crackers or vanilla wafers. This will bolster your carbohydrate intake and satisfy a sweet craving simultaneously.

Or have a slice of cantaloupe with a scoop of nonfat frozen yogurt on top. The yogurt gives you more calcium and protein, and the cantaloupe supplies a healthy dose of potassium, vitamin C and beta-carotene. And you'll be less likely to binge on a pint of ice cream once Letterman rolls around.

PART 2

Youthful
Living

Oldest Professional Athletes

In a profession where many don't make it past age 30, these men serve as shining examples of toughness and endurance. Of the major professional sports leagues (NFL, NBA, NHL and major league baseball), only hockey doesn't have someone in this top ten list (Joe Mullen of the Boston Bruins is the 18th oldest). All these players were active through last season.

1. Robert Parish   8/30/53   Basketball   Chicago Bulls

2. Jackie Slater   5/27/54   Football   St. Louis Rams

3. Rick Honeycutt   6/29/54   Baseball   St. Louis Cardinals

4. Dennis Eckersley   10/3/54   Baseball   St. Louis Cardinals

5. Ozzie Smith   12/26/54   Baseball   St. Louis Cardinals

6. Dennis Martinez   5/14/55   Baseball   Cleveland Indians

7. Vince Evans   6/14/55   Football   Oakland Raiders

8. James Edwards   11/22/55   Basketball   Chicago Bulls

9. Eddie Murray   2/24/56   Baseball   Baltimore Orioles

10. Clay Matthews   3/15/56   Football   Atlanta Falcons

Stay**Alert**

Twelve Ways to Sharpen Your Senses

Nothing broadcasts the fact that you're getting older quite like a little power drain in your sight and sound department.

Not even graying hair and crow's-feet tell the story as well as having to squint to see a beautiful woman across a restaurant. Or asking a buddy to repeat the punch line of a joke because you didn't hear it.

Want to keep up with those young, hyperactive go-getters that your company is hiring fresh out of grad school? Then hone your faculties, man, because when your senses get dull and sluggish, you appear dull and sluggish, even if you're one sharp hombre under that hazy veil. The problem is that nobody thinks about his senses until he, or, more likely, his partner, starts noticing them slipping away.

That's all the more reason to take some action now. Just as you can exercise biceps to grow stronger, you can strengthen your powers of perception. No, we're not saying that you can cure hearing loss or nearsightedness yourself, but there are still plenty of exercises that you can do to fine-tune your senses.

Just remember to warm up first. You don't want to pull anything, do you?

Sight

Ninety percent of all our sensory input comes through our eyes, so it makes sense to start our workout here.

"People tend to think of the eyes as a static camera. Focus and click. But there's much more to vision than that," says Paul Planer,

O.D., optometrist in Atlanta and author of *The Sports Vision Manual.* "There's night vision and peripheral vision; there's your ability to shift focus from faraway objects to close ones and to track a moving object. These are some of the components of visual ability that can be improved with a few simple techniques," Dr. Planer says. For starters:

Hone your night vision. To improve your ability to make out objects in a blackened room or the dark of night, "blink as many times as you can in the space of a couple of seconds," suggests Merrill Allen, O.D., Ph.D., professor of optometry at Indiana University in Bloomington. "Doing this stimulates the eye and helps it adjust to darkness more quickly." Also, wear sunglasses during the day. "Exposing your eyes to too much sunlight will reduce your night vision," he says. This effect on your vision is temporary. But excessive exposure to the sun's ultraviolet radiation can cause cataracts, a clouding of the eye's lens.

Overcome computer vision. People who work at a computer terminal for hours at a time often complain of blurred vision when they get up from their work. The "fine-print" sprint can bring the world back into focus: Tack a page of newsprint to a wall about eight feet from where you sit. Interrupt your work every 15 minutes or so and look at the newspaper. Bring the headlines into focus, then look at your computer screen. Do this five times, then get back to work.

Never miss an exit sign again. Having keen eyesight means being able to see as much as you can as quickly as you can, says Dr. Planer. He recommends these daily speed drills: Shift your eyes from right to left and back several times as fast as you can without moving your head. Make sure that you bring into focus the objects you see at the edges of your field of sight. This will help improve your peripheral vision. Next, try to focus on ten different objects in

---

JUST THE FACTS

Number of injuries annually in the United States involving beds, mattresses and pillows, according to the Census Bureau: 360,000

ten seconds by scanning around the room. (This time you can move your head.) Now try to name the objects and the order in which you saw them. Dr. Planer says this makes your focus more flexible by training your eyes and brain to hone in on and recognize things quickly, which can improve your reaction time for sports and driving.

Keep your eye on the ball. When focusing on a moving object, be it a pop fly or a clay pigeon, learn to track it with your eyes and chase it down by moving your head and body as one. One way to practice is to play catch with a friend using a ball or a beanbag marked with letters or numbers, each player trying to call out the last letter or number he sees before catching it.

Sound

To hear women tell it, a man's dullest sense is his hearing. Well, most of us can hear her fine; we're just ignoring what she says. Other men do have a legitimate excuse for not responding. According to the American Speech-Language-Hearing Association, more than 13 million men have significant hearing impairment, and at least 4.2 million of them are under age 45. Here are some ways to pump up the volume on your "personal stereo system."

Concentrate on hearing. Technically, you can't improve your hearing, but you can improve the way you listen, says Charles P. Kimmelman, M.D., attending physician at the Manhattan Eye, Ear and Throat Hospital. Sometimes, the best way to do this is to shut out other sensory input competing for your attention. Next time you're watching TV, close your eyes and pay attention to the voices you hear. What are the inflections in the voices telling you about what's going on? When people lose their sight, their other senses become more acute, especially hearing. That's the whole point of this exercise. By depriving yourself of sight, you are relying on your ears to provide more information and training your brain to understand it.

Closing your eyes also helps you develop a fine critical ear, says Roger Catlin, rock music critic for the *Hartford Courant* in Con-

(continued on page 46)

Equipment Problems

Your sensory organs can offer early warning signs of serious health problems. Here are some perplexing symptoms and what they may mean.

Sight

Double vision or persistent blurred vision: Sudden change in vision is worth checking out with a doctor. These symptoms may be signs of cataracts, concussion or stroke.

Blurred vision accompanied by a scratching sensation: First, check in the mirror to see if a foreign object has landed in your eye. If you don't see anything unusual, you may have a small scratch on the surface of the eyeball. Or maybe you have a mild infection. Both will disappear in a few days, says Merrill Allen, O.D., Ph.D., professor of optometry at Indiana University in Bloomington. Meanwhile, close your eyes and apply a warm, wet washcloth. The heat should speed healing. If the discomfort lasts more than two days or is so severe that you can't keep your eye open, see an ophthalmologist.

Black spots or flashes of light: These are common symptoms of a detached retina, the part of the eye that is sensitive to light. Caught early, the retina can be reattached, returning vision to normal.

Sound

Ringing in the ears: Called tinnitus, ringing can occur after long exposure to loud noise, or as a result of injury, infection or buildup of wax or fluid in the ear. If it persists more than three days, see a doctor. Tinnitus can be a symptom of Ménière's disease, a balance disorder of the inner ear that causes dizziness and vomiting. Ringing may also signal an overdose of aspirin or occur as a side effect of prescription medications such as Lasix, says Edmund Pribitkin, M.D., otolaryngologist at Thomas Jefferson University Hospital in Philadelphia.

Rumbling or shifting noises: If the sounds appear to be coming from inside your head, especially when you tilt your head or roll over in bed, you probably have wax or water trapped in your ear. The problem should go away in a few days. If it doesn't, see a doctor.

Smell

Loss of smell: Colds and sinus infections can temporarily knock out the nerve endings responsible for smell. If your sense of smell doesn't return in a week or so, or if you lose your sense of smell suddenly for no apparent reason, see a doctor. Loss of smell may indicate nasal polyps or benign growths in the nose and may also be associated with brain tumors or diseases like Parkinson's and Alzheimer's.

Strange or foul odors with no apparent source: Smelling rotten eggs, burning electrical wires or other phantom odors may be a precursor to serious conditions such as epilepsy or brain tumors. It may also be a reaction to prescription drugs, such as some thyroid and antiseizure medications. Either way, have it checked.

Taste

Loss of taste: Most people mistake a loss of smell for a loss of taste, since the two sensory organs are so closely related. To tell for sure, put a pinch of salt on your tongue. If you can taste it, then what you've lost is your sense of smell. If you can't taste the salt, see your doctor. Loss of taste can indicate a stroke or brain tumor.

Touch

Tingling, burning or numb sensation: Unless your arm has fallen asleep from lack of use, any suspicious tingling or burning sensation in your limbs, especially in your fingers and arms, could be an early warning sign of heart attack or stroke. If tingling skin is accompanied by a feeling of pressure on the chest, call for emergency help.

necticut. "When I'm listening to an album, I'll put the headset on and shut my eyes." As an exercise, he suggests trying to single out one instrument in a song—the bass guitar, for example—and follow only that instrument. Doing these exercises regularly will allow you to perceive more detail in the sounds you hear every day.

Stuff your ears. Ever spend the afternoon mowing the lawn and notice a ringing in your ears later? That's the sound of your hearing going away. A good rule of thumb: If it's loud enough that you have to shout to be heard over it, you need ear protection, says Dr. Kimmelman. Using power tools, lawn mowers and firearms and listening to rock concerts are all good opportunities to protect your hearing with earplugs.

Smell

When it comes to taste and smell, our olfactory sense is arguably the more powerful. "The nerves that govern smell are thousands of times more sensitive than the sensory cells in our taste buds. In fact, much of what we associate as the taste of something is really the smell of it," says Charles J. Wysocki, Ph.D., a researcher at the Monell Chemical Senses Center in Philadelphia. Here are some ways to enhance what your nose knows.

Sniff like a bloodhound. To appreciate a scent best, technique is everything, says Harry Fremont, a perfumer for Firmenich in New York City. As a professional "nose," Fremont has used his sense of scents to design such colognes as CK One and Polo Sport for men. "Smelling very deeply doesn't give you the best appreciation of a smell. Instead, it's better to take several small sniffs—it helps you detect the notes of an aroma better," he says.

Open your mouth. As you sniff, keep your mouth open. "You will draw the scent into your mouth, which gives an extra dimension to the smell," Fremont says.

Taste

Your taste buds recognize four basic tastes: sweet, sour, salty and bitter. But it's really your nose that sniffs out a flavor's subtleties.

The same factors that can interfere with your sense of smell—upper respiratory infections, certain medications or pollutants, aging—can play tricks on your tongue. Nonetheless, there are ways to ensure that you remain a man of good taste.

Take your time. Don't expect to appreciate the flavor of a good home-cooked meal if you're going to wolf it down. "The more you chew, the more you unlock flavors in the food," says Dr. Wysocki.

And here's a tip you can use the next time that snooty neighbor invites you over for a wine tasting: Don't gulp. Rather, hold the wine under your tongue for a moment. "There are taste sensors there as well," points out William DeWeese, director of beverage for the Waldorf-Astoria Hotel in Manhattan. This is an especially good way to savor the flavor of fine cheeses and other tasty foods as well.

Enjoy each flavor separately. Hey, you pay handsomely for a top-notch restaurant meal these days, so why not get your money's worth? Make sure that you have crackers or bread to nibble on after each course. That way your stuffed herbed guinea hen won't taste like the clove of roasted garlic you had as an appetizer. To help your taste buds pick up the flavor nuances in foods, cleanse your palate. Unsalted crackers or matzos and sips of water work best.

Touch

Your biggest sensory organ is your—uh, no, it's bigger than that; it's your skin. That's the reason why massage can be such a potent sex enhancer. No, we're not talking about the muscle-kneading kind, but about sensual massage, the gentle touching between you and your partner that goes beyond familiar erogenous zones. Not only can massage get rid of all the stressful baggage you bring to bed

but it also can leave you in a deeply relaxed state that, according to some massage therapists, makes the buildup to orgasm feel all the more intense.

Pay attention to your feelings. Good sex involves a certain degree of selfishness, so don't be afraid to focus on what you're feeling, say sex therapists. Practice sensate focusing, a technique that they've been teaching for 20 years to help men who suffer from premature ejaculation. When you touch your partner, focus on what your hand is feeling. When you kiss her, concentrate on the signals you're getting from the lips. Don't distract yourself. Forget about the genitals; concentrate on the feeling of your partner's whole body against your body. By tuning into these sensations, you'll learn ejaculatory control, which will ultimately lead to stronger orgasms.

Cover up. Want to be able to feel the nibble of a wary trout through gossamer fishing line or check your pulse after a workout well into your seventies? Then wear gloves when you're scraping the ice off your car windows. Just letting your hands get too cold can damage nerve endings in your fingertips. Even occasional exposure to intense cold can cause blood flow to be directed away from skin surfaces and result in the loss of sensation over time, says John E. Wolf, Jr., M.D., chairman of the dermatology department at Baylor College of Medicine in Houston.

Survival Strategies

Deal with Life by Simplifying It

When you were a kid, you knew how to deal with responsibility. You hid. Under the porch, in a closet, out in the woods. It was easy. No one could find you. And when you were ready, you'd reappear and resume your simple life of leisure. Until you'd have to hide again.

Now you're all grown up. You no longer have the luxury of skipping out when life becomes too demanding. There's music to face: paying the bills, placating the boss, worrying about the kids, pretending to be friendly to the in-laws, hanging the drywall, picking up the dry cleaning, keeping up on all the information that you're supposed to be keeping up on. A cumulative burden of little dilemmas, all begging for your attention.

No wonder we grown-ups want to run and hide. "It's life's small hassles that really weigh on us most," says Allen Elkin, Ph.D., program director at the Stress Management and Counseling Center in New York City. "Ironically, we respond better to major stresses, such as a death in the family or divorce, because they bring out the best in us." It's hard to rise to the occasion, though, when that occasion is a bad haircut or a dead battery. So instead, we passively absorb the daily pummeling until our bodies send us signals that enough's enough, usually in the form of headaches, irritability, fatigue, insomnia and a feeling of being constantly distracted and harried. Life's little complications soon become hazardous to our health and happiness.

What you could really use is one or two ways to eliminate these grimy little hassles. We have them right here. Whether it's the easiest way to make money or the quickest way to get out of something you don't want to do, you'll find the answer here. When you're living a complicated life, you need a few shortcuts.

Simplify Your Health

If you avoid greasy foods, visit the gym regularly and floss, you have the big issues covered. So avoid worrying about:

Mercury fillings. Remember when *60 Minutes* portrayed them as pockets of poison? Remember co-workers at the water cooler the next morning wondering aloud if their fillings should be removed? Notice how almost nobody mentions this nonsense anymore?

Food irradiation. "Many people mistakenly assume irradiation makes food radioactive," says Michael Oppenheim, M.D., a physician in private practice in Los Angeles. It doesn't, okay? Critics of irradiation often assert (in loud, grating voices) that the process destroys certain healthful properties in food. So far, these claims are unencumbered by evidence.

Food additives. Although words like "natural" and "whole" have become supermarket buzzwords, additives and preservatives get a bum rap. "It pays to remember that in the old days all the rampant diseases were caused by poorly preserved food," says Dr. Oppenheim. "Additives may not be nutritious, but they're certainly a positive health measure."

Coffee. Sure, too much makes you as jittery as Don Knotts. "But while it has been speculated that caffeine might play a role in certain illnesses, the research hasn't turned up anything," says Dr. Oppenheim. Cut back on the trips to your local coffeehouse if your doctor says so. But if it's cancer or heart disease that you're worried about, you're barking up the wrong vice.

Cleanliness. You probably know people who bathe after a dirty thought. But really, cleanliness as a health measure is overrated, say the experts. "Except socially, there is no particular reason in terms of public health to shower daily," says Dr. Oppenheim. "In fact, that Americans can bathe every day speaks highly of the tough qualities of our skin." And stop worrying about whether you'll catch anything nasty from a pay phone, toilet seat or doorknob. "The common misconception that you can get diseases like syphilis, gonorrhea, herpes or genital warts from those surfaces is just that—a misconception," says Charles Ebel, director of the Herpes Resource Center of the American Social Health Association in Research Triangle Park, North Carolina. These infections are spread through intimate skin-to-skin contact. Besides, you could take any surface in your house—the shower wall, the carpet, that dishcloth on your kitchen counter—and find all kinds of tiny pathogens. "But while we are surrounded by all that, our immune systems protect us quite well," says Ebel. If you really want to protect yourself from something that's easily spread, wash your hands. That helps against common colds.

Manage Your Career Better

You could make your job easier by quitting, but that would probably bring a whole new set of problems. There are far better ways to uncomplicate life in cubicle country.

Don't always be the go-to man. You'll get nothing done by being the guy everyone turns to for help. "One man I know liked to be thought of as the resident expert, so whenever there was a problem, he was the guy to turn to," says C. Steve Manley, Ph.D., a psychologist at the Male Health Center in Dallas. "He ended up working until midnight just to finish his own work." Stay within your boundaries and your job becomes simpler.

Keep your hands in your pockets. Have you ever heard of a task force that accomplished anything? That is why you shouldn't volunteer for them. "They're nonproductive delaying tactics that rarely solve the problem they were intended to grapple with," says Richard Stiegele, author of *Never Read a Newspaper at Your Desk: The Fundamental Principles of Business*. Be more effective and save time by working one-on-one.

Filter incoming work. If you haven't done so already, train your assistants to screen, sort and schedule your calls and mail, and run interference for unscheduled interruptions. Don't feel sorry for them—they applied for the job.

Put up the "No Visitors" sign. "We either solicit people to interfere with us or allow them to hang in our offices," says Dr. Manley. When possible, have conversations at other offices so that you can leave when the time is right. Or try this maneuver: Pick up the phone while they're talking and start dialing; then hope they get the hint before you have to fake a conversation with a dial tone.

Write a list. Don't write things to do on separate pieces of scrap. You'll create a paper trail even Columbo couldn't follow. Instead, keep a list—one list. Merge all of your daily goals onto this list, then as new goals arise, don't tack them on. Start a new list for tomorrow. Anything you didn't get to on today's list, add to tomorrow's.

Stay out of trouble. It saves a lot of aggravation in the long run. Just so we're clear:

- Don't attempt to outdrink others at office parties.
- Watch loose talk in the rest room. You never know who's reading *Outlaw Biker* in the last stall.
- Never put a heated thought into a memo or leave it on voice mail or e-mail. Write down your angry thoughts to get rid of the momentary frustration, then sit tight, and later modify them for public consumption.
- Don't sleep with anyone whom you can fire or who can fire you.

Stay Hip with Ease

In college, being a cultural maven was easy. You had time to impress stringy-haired coeds with your vast knowledge of John Waters films, obscure jazz records and where to buy cheap Indian food at 3:00 A.M. Now that you have a life, you can no longer afford to be so pretentious or so well-informed. We've simplified pretentiousness for you. Here are five ways to stay up on what's hot, even if you don't have time to read as much as you'd like or if you just feel a little behind the times.

Catch movies at Oscar time. February and March is when all the good movies nominated for big awards are re-released to capitalize on the hoopla. If you didn't have time to stand in line the first time around, now you can pop right in. No hassles, no kids. And best of all, no big hairdos to block your view. Try to avoid anything in which Harvey Keitel gets naked or Meryl Streep learns a new accent. Or vice versa.

Take advantage of the post office. Forget about fighting the crowds at Blockbuster Video. You know that they're going to be out of everything you want and you'll end up with a Steve Guttenberg movie. You can buy great movies by mail. Two good catalogs are Critic's Choice Video (1-800-367-7765) and Video Treasures (1-800-786-8777). Order the movies or just memorize their titles to impress your friends.

Enjoy books online or while you drive. Save time and money by scanning the *New York Times* book reviews online. Quote Joyce Carol Oates without ever having to read her painful prose. You can also absorb condensed books on tape. Although they're bound to lose something in the translation, most popular novels and nonfiction books are available in three- to four-hour audio versions.

Tune in to college radio. You never know what you'll get—one minute it's dueling sitars; the next, a taped collection of seal mating rituals. But you'll find out what the undergrads are listening to, which will give you a better understanding of our declining academic standards.

Establish connections in New York or Los Angeles. They may be rude and dress better than you, but at the very least they can tell you about the trendiest restaurants, the best new play or the most pretentious foreign film. You'll never have to check any of them out—just effortlessly drop their names at parties.

Get Your Paper Act Together

Take our advice and start filling your garbage can without remorse.

Chuck: Anything you can always get another copy of in an emergency. If your assistant has it or the library down the street keeps it on file, why cling to it like a winning lottery ticket?

File: Action papers. These are the biggest causes of clutter—the stuff we like to have at our fingertips and can't find it in our hearts to file because we're so attached to them. Compromise: Put those papers in an "action" file, to be kept in one spot, on your desk for easy access.

Chuck: Rough drafts of anything that's made it to final form. Don't get sentimental over past work.

File: Anything financial—receipts, warranties, pay stubs, check registers, bills, contracts. You never know when your temperamental washing machine will finally break from the wall, make its way up the street and hold up a liquor store. The warranty makes it easy to get it fixed or get a new one.

Chuck: Back issues of your favorite magazines. Why stockpile every issue of *Modern Cheerleader* when it's on microfilm at the library?

File: Any tax material. Keep medical expenses, contributions, travel expenses and other miscellaneous stuff in separate files in one spot. This makes it easy when April rolls around.

Chuck: Any item that you once thought was interesting but offers no relevance to the job at hand. Chances are that you can find something more up-to-date.

File: Ideas. Right now, you probably write them on anything within arm's reach—cocktail napkins, the backs of dollar bills, a slow-moving pet. And often they're forever lost. Instead, keep a file or notebook nearby to record your mental notes, no matter how silly they are.

Chuck: Any correspondence that may incriminate you.

File: Any correspondence that may incriminate other people.

And please chuck this: Cloying mementos. You know, the tacky souvenirs from the last 12 sales meetings. The collage of family portraits that makes your office look like the local Fotomat. Those hokey posters that poke fun at being employed (for example, the soaked cat hanging from a bar with the words "Hang in there" above it). Consider removing all but the bare necessities, holding onto a simple picture of your family, just as a reminder for why you're putting in all of those long, hard hours.

Rekindle the Spark of Love

Does your love life have about as much heat as an aging pitcher's fastball? If so, these two things should warm things up and put a smile back on your face.

End the petty fights. It's the little stuff that does it, like using your mate's bath towel to wipe off your excess shaving cream. A small infraction to be sure, but add that to your fondness for stockpiling dirty dishes and belching in church, and these minor things can tally up to something major. If the bickering is getting on your nerves, Dr. Elkin suggests this: In a playful way, ask your mate to make a list of the annoying things you do. Only small stuff: squeezing the toothpaste in the middle, leaving the toilet seat up. "On a scale of 1 to 10, these habits should rate about a 2 or 3," says Dr. Elkin. Make your own list and trade. "This is one step toward eliminating the little stresses that can try a relationship," says Dr. Elkin.

Don't fret over how much sex you get. If you think you aren't burning up the sheets as frequently as your randy neighbors, you may be comparing your sex life to some mythological level that doesn't exist. In fact, one study suggests that on average, most married men have sex a few times per month, and only 7 percent of the population surveyed reported having sex four or more times per week. "Couples tend to find a comfortable sexual level naturally, and they can get into trouble if they wrongly conclude that their natural level isn't good enough," says psychologist Robert Pasick, Ph.D., of Ann Arbor, Michigan, and author of *What Every Man Needs to Know*. "While both people in a relationship start out with different sex drives, they tend to find a happy medium and are able to sustain it over the years."

Invest with Confidence

If you'd rather not end up behind a counter flipping burgers on your 66th birthday, here are two simple ways to make money without needing an M.B.A. in finance.

Use your company's 401(k). If you possibly can, invest the maximum your company will allow. This may be the best no-brainer investment you can make. Here's why. You almost never have to think about it, and the money you invest is tax-deferred. Also, having it taken out of your paycheck reduces your overall tax rate, and most companies match your contribution with one of their own.

Invest in mutual funds through a discount broker. Nowadays, most transactions can be done with a Touch-Tone phone, so you don't have to waste time listening to a broker try to sell you shares in a chain of Kato Kaelin restaurants. Discount brokers also simplify things more by offering monthly reports of a fund's performance and an annual statement for tax purposes. Top brokerages include Charles Schwab (1-800-435-4000), Jack White and Company (1-800-233-3411), Fidelity Investments (1-800-544-7272) and Muriel Siebert and Company (1-800-872-7865). Ask for information on "no-load" mutual funds, ones that have few or no fees attached.

Improve Your Life Online

Imagine booking a flight, buying groceries and talking to the president of the United States, all while lounging in your underwear. That's the beauty of owning a computer. You can do all of this without ever leaving home or even throwing on some pants. Think of the time that you'll save, especially on laundry.

Keep creditors off your back. New software packages can turn your personal computer (PC) into your own personal banker. Checkfree, for example, keeps track of all your transactions, and when a bill needs paying, it deducts the cash from your bank account and adds it to the account of the biller via electronic fund transfer. For information, call 1-800-882-5280. Intuit's Quicken Deluxe (1-800-446-8848) offers added features such as tax preparation and a stock tracker.

Browse the stacks. Avoid smarmy looks from bohemian bookstore clerks by ordering reading material through America Online's Online Bookstore. Choose from lists of new releases, fiction, horror and other subjects.

Hire an assistant. With the software program Lotus Organizer 2.0 (1-800-872-3387), you can enter and scan a month's appointments in a page-turning format and insert and retrieve addresses and phone numbers. And once you punch up a name, your PC can dial the number. The program also has alarms to remind you of scheduled events and anniversaries.

Get rich. Most online systems offer services that allow you to easily check the status of your investments. Prodigy offers news from Dow Jones. On America Online, Morningstar, a fund research company, offers a comparison of more than 5,000 mutual funds, ranking the top performers. You can even read the *Wall Street Journal* on your computer. Its electronic newspaper, *Personal Journal*, gives you the day's top news stories and updated information on your choice of 25 stocks and ten companies or columns. Call 1-800-291-9382, extension 819.

Buy a quart of milk. Or peanut butter. Or, hey, why not both? America Online's Shoppers Express is a convenient service that lets you order groceries and drugstore items from local stores and have them delivered, avoiding such challenging questions as "paper or plastic?" (They have icons for each.) Just punch in your ZIP code and local stores participating in the service will be listed (not available in all locations).

Never get lost again. Automap Road Atlas is a software program that maps trips for you anywhere in the United States, Canada and northern Mexico. You just type in the city you're leaving and the one you're going to, and it will print out a map and written driving instructions. From Microsoft (1-800-564-6277).

Avoid revolutions. Get travel warnings online, courtesy of the State Department, regarding unusual immigration practices, health conditions, minor political disturbances and crime problems in various international hot spots. And if you're still intent on going, jot down the address of the nearest U.S. embassy.

Figure out what that pain means. Check out the various health forums available online. The Better Health and Medical Forum on America Online, for example, offers information on nearly every health disorder as well as listings of more than 23 weekly self-help group meetings. And *Men's Health* magazine is available on the Internet at menshealth@msn.com.

Simplify Your Wardrobe

Stop trying to look stylish. Here's how to create and maintain a great wardrobe, simply, without thinking too hard about it.

Take stock of your inventory. Look in your closet and toss what doesn't fit, what you haven't worn in two years, what's in need of repair and anything considered "retro" (a code word for old). Segment the rest into two groups: career and casual.

Choose gray/blue or brown. Based on what's left, see what "color family" you lean toward and follow suit when expanding your wardrobe. "A color focus narrows the choices you can make," says LaVelle Olexa, senior vice-president with Lord and Taylor department stores.

Don't get fancy. The typical business wardrobe: four suits (for Monday through Thursday), ten white shirts, a pair of dress shoes and plenty of ties and socks. For casual Fridays: a couple of sports jackets, three pairs of trousers (gray flannel, chinos and cords), a casual pair of loafers and a knit or polo shirt or sweater.

Seek out a well-dressed man when shopping. You don't want some poorly dressed sap telling you how to look. Or call ahead for a personal shopper, which most large department stores offer. They'll

---

JUST THE FACTS

Percentage of men who think that they are in better health than their fathers were at the same age: 47

lend you the color sense in case you're a bit lacking.

Peruse the catalogs. Bypass the salesguy altogether and get on the mailing lists of some nifty catalogs.

Trim the Fat from Your Workout

When time is tight, work only your chest, biceps and back muscles. "That's all you really need to give the impression of a good build," says Tom Baechle, Ed.D., certified strength and conditioning specialist and author of *Fitness Weight Training*. Bench presses, biceps curls and dumbbell rows take care of it. Eliminate these.

- Straight leg lifts. Most people do them to build stomach muscles, but these really work your hip flexors. And when was the last time someone said, "Hey, nice hip flexors"?
- Any triceps exercise. If you're doing the bench press for your chest, you're hitting your triceps, too.
- Neck exercises. Unless a skinny neck is making you a target of ridicule, skip it.
- Calf raises. If you're running or doing lower aerobic conditioning, these small muscles are getting enough work.
- Forearm curls. Regular curls take care of your forearms as they work the biceps.

Minor
Maladies

Quick Fixes for Everyday Pains

Childhood is a lot like an old *T. J. Hooker* rerun: not very sophisticated, yet packed with adventure. But unlike *Hooker* star William Shatner, you couldn't call in a stunt double. Whenever you found yourself speeding down the highway of adventure, metaphorically clinging to the hood of life's getaway car, you had to endure the consequences: One minute you were setting land-speed records on your Big Wheel; the next minute you were crying over scraped knees.

As you enter adulthood, life becomes less adventuresome. Your Big Wheel carries an insurance premium. Your speed records are rewarded with fines and tickets. Yet one thing follows you in the transition to manhood: pain. You may not skin your knees as often, but on an average day the average man still faces a raft of petty, but painful, problems around the clock.

Luckily, there's a simple solution to nearly all of life's little nuisances. With this get-well guide—a sort of daily planner of pain relief—you can safeguard yourself from the most irksome irritants morning, noon and night.

7:00 A.M.: Sensitive teeth. Nothing like a good kick in the teeth to get your day started right. For men with sensitive teeth and gums, that's what each morning can feel like. There's a variety of reasons why you might wake up with sore teeth, but the most common cause is breathing through your mouth when you sleep. That dries out your gums, and when you awake, this newly arid environment causes teeth-tingling pain.

Rub it in. Buy one of those over-the-counter toothpastes designed for sensitive teeth, then rub a dab into the offending area. "Let it sit there for a little while, then spit it out. That should keep you pain-free for a few hours," says Charles H. Perle, D.M.D., a private practitioner in Jersey City, New Jersey.

Coat your choppers. To prevent pain in the first place, smear a little petroleum jelly over your gums before bed. That will keep them moist throughout the night, even if your mouth becomes a wind tunnel. And no, it won't taste funny or leave your breath smelling weird.

Go soft on the gums. Overzealous brushing can cause your gums to recede, and that can make your teeth more sensitive than an old John Denver tune. Switch to a soft-bristle brush and use gentle up-and-down strokes, being extra careful near the gum line.

Use caution with hard crusts. Bite carefully into hard-crust breads, such as bagels or pizza crust. "Sometimes when you're having a bagel, you bite into it and jam your gum tissue down, causing a laceration. Then you go for cold orange juice, and the next thing you know you're seeing stars," Dr. Perle says.

7:14 A.M.: Razor burn. No wonder you cut it a little close once in a while: The average man shaves 48 square inches of flesh a day—and that's not including the weird places you shaved while pledging your fraternity. One in four of us gets razor burn on a regular basis.

To prevent it:

Eat breakfast first. Shaving first thing in the morning begs for the razor's wrath. Your face is puffier right after you wake up because body fluids have accumulated under your skin. Thus, you can't cut as close as you'd like. Instead of shaving immediately after waking, move around for a half-hour or so. Iron, run—have sex, maybe.

Act like a barber. You need two to three minutes of warm soaking to sufficiently soften whiskers. Try laying a warm, wet towel over your face for a few minutes. Or take a hot shower before you shave, but keep your face wet, lather up immediately, wait a minute or two for your beard to soften and then shave.

Take the path of least resistance. Shave in the direction of your facial hair. You may get a closer shave by going against it, but you're increasing the chance of irritating your skin.

9:15 A.M.: Coffee gut. You know that breakfast is the most important meal of the day, but that doesn't hold much weight when you have an 8:30 meeting with the vice-president to discuss why your division isn't contributing to the bottom line. So you race out the door with coffee mug in hand and, just as the words "alternative cost-cutting initiatives" hit the table, your old friend Juan Valdez and his mule drop by—in your stomach.

It's coffee gut, that raw bellyaching you feel from drinking joe on an empty stomach. It's actually a form of heartburn, says Swarnjit Singh, M.D., of the gastroenterology division at the University of Alabama at Birmingham. The caffeine in coffee relaxes the sphincter muscle that connects the lower part of your esophagus to your stomach. When this happens, all the acid sitting around in your stomach spews into your esophagus, burning its delicate lining.

To can coffee gut:

Chew gum. According to Dr. Singh, gum chewing increases saliva production, and saliva neutralizes reflux. "Any kind of chewing stimulus will make saliva. If you chew cardboard, it'll probably work," Dr. Singh says. "But that's probably not a good idea."

12:09 P.M.: Neckache. The maintenance guys failed to fix the air-conditioning, so now your office is colder than a meat locker. Thanks to an air vent with good aim, and the fact that you've been staring into your computer screen for three straight hours, your neck feels stiffer than a piece of frozen meat.

Don't settle for this, especially when you can work it out quickly, says Alexander R. Vaccaro, M.D., an orthopedic spine surgeon and assistant professor at Thomas Jefferson University in Philadelphia. Neck pain is a lot like back pain in that it's often just muscle fatigue

JUST THE FACTS

The most popular plastic surgery among men: rhinoplasty, or nose reshaping.

or stiffness at work, Dr. Vaccaro says. You can usually alleviate it with aspirin, exercise or massage.

We trust that you've already mastered the aspirin.

Work those muscles. Dr. Vaccaro suggests the following isometric exercises to warm up the muscles. Take your left hand and place it on the left side of your head. Now, gently turn your head to the left, while lightly applying resistance for six to eight seconds. Relax, then repeat this maneuver on the opposite side, turning your head to the right while gently resisting with your right hand. Do three sets of three, three times a day.

Massage away the pain. A quick self-massage will improve circulation and limber up tight neck muscles. You'll want to target the trapezius muscles, the big ones that run from the base of your skull to the backs of your shoulders. With your left hand, gently begin kneading the left trapezius; start at the base of your skull and slowly work your fingers down the muscle toward your shoulder. As you do this, keep your head turned to the right: This will stretch the left trapezius and make it easier to massage. Once you've worked your way down to your left shoulder, turn your head to the left and begin massaging the right side of your neck.

4:12 P.M.: Eyestrain. Like you, your eyes are overworked. Can you blame them? On any given day, they move some 100,000 times. To give your legs an equivalent workout, you'd have to walk 50 miles a day.

To rest those weary eyes:

Soothe them with heat. Take a tip from massage therapists, who end their sessions with this grand finale to the eyes: Briskly rub your hands together to generate heat, then place them over your closed eyes for several moments. The gentle pressure and warmth will soothe your pooped peepers.

Find a focus. Six muscles control each eye, but when you're doing close-up work, like reading or using a computer, those muscles remain contracted for a long time. Refocusing relaxes them. Stop what you're doing every 15 minutes and focus on something farther away.

(continued on page 66)

The Right Pill for the Job

When you have a toothache or a twisted ankle or sore muscles from a spontaneous game of tackle football, you want relief, not a decision to make. But that's what you're faced with when you visit the drugstore: 50 boxes of different types of painkillers to choose from. Which type is best for your kind of pain? Here's a guide to help you select the right relief.

Acetaminophen (Tylenol)

Best for: Headaches and minor muscle aches and pains. It doesn't have a strong anti-inflammatory action, so it may not be as effective for arthritis or swelling.

Warnings: "Because acetaminophen is considered so safe, it's one of the more common painkillers people accidentally overdose on," says Jutta Joseph, Pharm.D., assistant professor of pharmacology at Washington State University in Pullman. Acetaminophen overdose is insidious. If you start experiencing nausea or dizziness, consult a physician immediately. The recommended dosage is one or two tablets of 325 milligrams every four to six hours, two tablets of 500 milligrams (extra strength) three or four times a day or two tablets of 650 milligrams every eight hours. Don't take more than four grams (4,000 milligrams) in any 24-hour period. Don't take with alcohol or if you have liver disease or are a heavy drinker.

Aspirin (Anacin)

Best for: General aches and pains as well as reducing swelling and inflammation.

Warnings: Aspirin can cause stomach irritation, so take it after meals or with food, or take enteric-coated aspirin, which won't dissolve in your stomach. Don't use aspirin if you have a history of ulcers, since it could cause bleeding problems. Aspirin also thins the blood, so it should not be taken if you are on an anticoagulant drug, such as warfarin. The recommended dosage for adults is 325 to 650 milligrams every four hours, or 325 to 500 milligrams every three hours. Don't exceed four grams (4,000 milligrams) per day. If you develop a ringing in your ears, it could be that you're taking too much. If you experience wheezing or develop a rash, it could be a sign of intolerance. Stop taking it immediately and get to a doctor.

Ibuprofen (Nuprin, Advil)

Best for: Overuse injuries, such as tendinitis; fighting inflammation from sore muscles and arthritis; and relieving pain.

Warnings: Like aspirin, it can upset your stomach, so take it with milk or food. Check with your doctor before using ibuprofen if you have a history of heart failure, hypertension or kidney failure. Don't take with alcohol. Ibuprofen comes in 200-milligram tablets. The recommended dosage is one or two tablets every four to six hours, not to exceed 1,200 milligrams per day.

Naproxen Sodium (Aleve)

Best for: Reducing pain and swelling from toothaches, arthritis and muscle strains. It's long-lasting: 8 to 12 hours.

Warnings: Like ibuprofen, naproxen carries a lower risk of stomach bleeding, though it still may cause stomach upset in some people, so take it with food. Don't take it with alcohol, since the combination can increase the chance of stomach bleeding. This drug can have the same drawbacks for men with high blood pressure or heart or kidney disease as ibuprofen. Over-the-counter naproxen sodium comes in 220-milligram tablets. The recommended dosage is one tablet every 8 to 10 hours, not to exceed 660 milligrams, or three tablets, in 24 hours.

5:20 P.M.: Eye twitches. The workweek's nearly over, and your boss is about to leave for an eight-day salmon-fishing expedition. Ask for that raise now or hold your breath. So you muster up your arguments (hey, you're punctual and seldom, if ever, leave your cubicle looking messy), and you prepare to march in. But just as you're about to knock on the big cheese's door, your eye starts twitching so fast that you think your face is trying to send Morse code.

That's stress, pal, probably combined with too little sleep or too much caffeine—or both, says Linda A. Hershey, M.D., Ph.D., professor of neurology at the State University of New York at Buffalo. If you're in the habit of perking up with some afternoon coffee, your eye may be in the habit of perking up, too, especially in stressful situations. "Often you're tired, so you drink more coffee, which makes you nervous and edgy and stressed. It's a vicious cycle," Dr. Hershey says.

Here's an effective cure.

Breathe in, breathe out. Don't climb a hill, don't manufacture a mantra, don't try to twist your legs into a pretzel knot. Just stop for a moment and stare off into the distance. Now close your eyes and take a few deep breaths, relaxing your whole body with each exhalation as though you're blowing out stress. See your face calm and serene, like the surface of a still pond. Think of this as target meditation, a way of killing the stress that's killing your eye.

7:25 P.M.: Sore feet. Let's say that you gave up your seat on the train to a little old lady. Or let's say that you didn't give up your seat, and she bashed your toes with her cane. Either way, when you get home, your dogs are barking.

To ease them, try a simple foot massage. Lightly knead each foot for ten minutes. Start with the ankle, rub down to the arch, deeply stroke the sole and finish by gently pulling your toes. If the idea of giving yourself a foot massage is kind of creepy, try these tricks.

Fill your slippers with beans. It sounds strange, but it works. Pour a handful of dried beans into each of your slippers. Put the slippers on and walk around the room. The rolling of the beans underfoot will give your soles a massagelike workout. And tomorrow's dinner guests will never guess why you're wearing such a sly smile.

Run hot and cold. Hold your feet under running water in your bathtub for an invigorating soak. Run the water on warm for one minute, then on cold for the next. Alternate for about ten minutes, ending on a cold rinse. Based on a popular European spa treatment, this piggy-picker-upper helps increase circulation while putting the chill on pain.

11:07 P.M.: Back pain. It's finally time for bed, but you won't drift off anytime soon. Your back hurts so badly, it feels like an obese sandman is jumping rope on it.

Nighttime back pain is a common complaint from guys on the go. Called mechanical back pain, it's often activity-related, meaning that your body worked too hard during your waking hours, says Dr. Vaccaro.

To relieve this nighttime nightmare:

Sleep belly up. Proper body positioning goes a long way in soothing your back at night. The proper position for lying in bed, Dr. Vaccaro says, is to lie flat on your back with a pillow under your knees so that they're slightly bent.

"Studies have shown that this position is the best for easing pressure on the lower spine and relieving back pain in bed," he says, adding that you may want to avoid lying on your stomach. "Some people who lie on their stomachs find that it hyperextends their backs, which can make the pain worse."

Get a grip on spasms. Back pain that nags you when you're lying down is often the result of spasms in the large muscles of your back. You're likely to get it from sitting in a jackknife position with your knees higher than your hips (for example, when you're driving for hours at a time). But the pain that those spasms cause can be eased with a simple stretch. Get out of bed and stand with your feet together, toes pointed ahead. Slide your left foot backward and your right one forward until they're about three foot-lengths apart. Now raise your left arm straight overhead, keeping your right arm at your side. Bend your knees slightly and tip your torso back a little. Hold for 15 seconds. Now return to the starting position and repeat on the other side, sliding your right foot backward and raising your right arm.

11:43 P.M.: Stubbed toe. It's been a tough day, but finally sleep arrives. Shortly thereafter, the woman next door comes home, bringing her boyfriend and his band, Rodents with Scurvy, who then decide to have an impromptu jam session in her apartment. Moving across the bedroom to bang on the wall, you instead bang your toe on the nightstand, jolting your toenail from its resting place.

Pack it in ice. The best first move. Apply an ice pack immediately for 15 to 20 minutes, then remove it for 30 minutes and repeat if necessary. Ice reduces swelling and eases pain.

Give a helping toe. Tape your toe to the little piggy next to it with a couple of adhesive bandages. Taping gives the troubled toe extra support, keeping it in place so that it won't scrape against the inside of your shoe.

And finally, say a little prayer. You made it through the working week.

Saturday, 9:08 A.M.: Weekend headaches. We'd be remiss if we didn't discuss weekend headaches, which tend to strike around this time on Saturday. The cause: caffeine withdrawal. Your body's used to a jolt of joe around 7:30. Sleep through your regular coffee break and the result is a drum solo in your brain. To avoid it, limit yourself to two cups or so a day at work. Or wake up earlier on Saturday to get them beans a-brewing.

Do You Measure Up?

Compare Yourself to the Average Guy

One of the central tenets of being a man is wondering how you measure up. Like a noseguard sizing up a center, we find it necessary to compare our state of affairs to the guy idling in the Jag at the stoplight, the well-groomed up-and-comer in the cubicle down the hall or the sinewy personal trainer named Dirk who's dating our ex. Whether it's our paychecks, pectorals or Pontiacs, we can't seem to stop comparing our bag of prizes to everyone else's.

The problem is that we never know exactly how we're doing because we never know exactly which cards the men around us are holding. Worse, we often make ourselves feel inadequate by comparing ourselves to men whose rare, exceptional success makes them oddities—and far from average. So while your card tricks might liven up a dull party, you'd better pray that David Copperfield doesn't show up to put you in your place. And while your golf drive awes your pals, the guy in the pro shop could spank you in a heartbeat. And he's as dumb as a divot.

What you need is an easier way to see where you stand in life's great lineup. A way to check your status without peeking at the pay stubs of your pals, rummaging through your neighbor's garbage cans or peering into his bedroom window to catalog his sexual prowess. So in an effort to cut out all that unnecessary grunt work, we pored over reports, surveys and reams of marketing data and assembled a rich portrait of the average guy. From how much you can bench-press to how many you have kissed, you'll find out where you stand compared with the regular Joe—all without violating any of those confusing stalking laws. If you find that you've come in well above average in many cases, we salute you. But if you find that you're coming up short in some places, don't get your briefs in a bundle. We've also offered a few strategies to help you do much better. You won't get a trailer park named after you, but you'll certainly stand out in a crowd. And isn't that what you really want?

The average guy has 70 to 80 pounds of muscle.

Not bad, unless it's concentrated in one area—say, the neck. Your goal, says Wayne L. Westcott, Ph.D., fitness/research director at the South Shore YMCA in Quincy, Massachusetts, is to shoot for 90 pounds of the hard stuff. Even if you already lift weights, you can do better.

Cut your rest time shorter. A lot of lifters like to rest for two to three minutes between sets to allow their muscles to fully recover. But if you want bigger muscles, shorten rest periods to between 60 and 90 seconds, suggests Tom Baechle, Ed.D., certified strength and conditioning expert and author of *Fitness Weight Training*. "Longer rests can let your muscles off the hook by not stressing them long enough to stimulate growth. Shortening the rest reduces the recovery time for your muscles, so you're more likely to completely fatigue them."

Attempt a "periodization" program. All that this three-dollar word means is varying your workout's intensity. "This helps many power athletes gain strength quickly and without injury," says Dr. Baechle. "It stimulates and challenges the muscular system to adapt to heavier weight, while allowing time to recuperate so that you return with stronger muscles." Here's a typical routine: On Monday, do three sets using your heaviest weights, the kind that fully fatigue your muscles after six to eight repetitions (or about 90 percent of what you'd be able to lift one time). On Wednesday, do the same number of sets and repetitions, but use lighter weights, about 70 percent of what you lifted on Monday. Then on Friday, do medium sets, at 75 to 80 percent of your heavy lifts. "The Monday workout shocks and fatigues your muscles, the light day on Wednesday lets them recover and the medium day on Friday serves as a stepping stone for Monday's intensity," says Dr. Baechle. Keep the number of sets (three per exercise) and repetitions (six to eight) the same. Change only the weight.

The average guy can run a mile in 12 minutes.

This number refers to the typical poster guy for La-Z-Boy—the sloth whose heart rate only elevates when watching stock-car racing and swimsuit competitions. If you compare favorably to him, don't expect a laurel wreath from us, Sluggo. A 7.5-minute mile is a better gauge for an active guy.

Step on it. Simply step up the pace for a minute or two during your regular jogs. "This is called interval training," explains Ray Giannelli, vice-president of engineering for Trotter Treadmills in Midway, Massachusetts, and designer of workout programs for treadmill equipment. "By going slow and then speeding up, your body adapts to the stress, allowing you to gain both strength and endurance." Giannelli suggests following a slow/fast ratio of three to one: For every minute of hard running, do three minutes at a slow pace for recovery.

Raise the grade. Running hills works all your muscles harder, so running on level ground seems like child's play.

Keep those legs pumping. "Bicycling trains muscles that you don't use during running—yet these are muscles that you use to stabilize your body when running," says Giannelli.

The average guy watches 28 hours of television each week.

Watching this much TV might elicit hoots of ridicule from the cultural elite, especially when it doesn't include reruns of *Masterpiece Theatre*. But we aren't going to tell you to watch less, just to watch better.

Avoid:
- Made-for-TV movies. Nearly every plot involves a seemingly successful, upstanding man who turns out to be (1) a rapist, (2) a molester, (3) a wife beater, (4) a Satan worshiper or (5) all of the above. Skip them and use the time to write angry letters to their commercial sponsors.
- Syndicated talk shows. How does a talk-show host sleep at night, anyway? Upside down, from a tree branch?
- MTV, VH1, ESPN2, C-SPAN, The TV Food Network.

- Anything with a Hasselhoff.
- Shows about unsolved mysteries, UFOs, conspiracies, out-of-body experiences, New Age therapies and other wide-eyed claptrap. Why is it that the very same folks who are skeptical of religion openly embrace this kind of malarkey?
- Shows featuring precocious children, cranky old people or, worse, a combination of both.
- The Playboy TV channel, scrambled. You'll go blind.
- ABC's *Wide World of Sports*. What? More figure skating?
- And any show featuring the likes of Bea Arthur, Blythe Danner, Tony Danza, Sharon Gless or members of the Lamas or Spelling family.

Watch:
- Any Clint Eastwood film made between 1967 and 1973.
- Infomercials. Where else can you gain satisfaction knowing that former *Miami Vice* star Philip Michael Thomas's career has sunk so low that he has to shill for psychics?
- And, of course, The Weather Channel. It's 24-hour Valium.

The average guy spends 44 minutes each day arranging his hair and clothes.

Leave the primping to the Baldwin brothers. There are ways to cut your grooming time in half. You can do better.

Trim your locks. Very short. Get a haircut that requires little or no maintenance. No parts, cowlicks, sideburns or team logos shaved on the side. "Get a cut you don't have to fuss with—just towel it dry and go," says *Men's Health* magazine's clothing and grooming editor Warren Christopher.

Organize your tasks. Hey, you don't take out the trash one milk carton at a time, do you? So shine four pairs of shoes at a time. Take three suits instead of one to the dry cleaner to be pressed. And while you're at it, take all your dress shirts, too. "You'll save extra trips and countless minutes foraging through your closet for a clean button-down," says Christopher.

Plan ahead. Use a Sunday afternoon to match your shirts, ties and suits into groups so you aren't a groggy ball of confusion mixing and matching before work. "Now you just look in the closet and grab a set," says Christopher.

Stow an emergency grooming kit. Keep a drawer in your office full of the stuff you need to stay as dapper as a show poodle: a hand mirror, hair gel, a comb, an extra tie, some breath mints. And for when you're in desperate shape, a "Do Not Disturb" sign.

The average guy saves less than $3,000 for retirement each year.

"Guys say they can't save, but I can find somebody with the same income, mouths to feed, rent or mortgage as you who's saving quite well," says Jonathan Pond, personal finance commentator in Watertown, Massachusetts, and author of *The New Century Family Money Book*. The difference: The other guy can live within his means; you can't.

Stash the dough. Call it living better through automation. Have the money taken out of your paycheck or bank account and put into a retirement account, such as a 401(k); mutual fund; credit union or savings account before you can get your grubby hands on it. That way, you won't be spending your 65th birthday stealing pizza coupons from mailboxes.

Fight the temptation. Even if you're reining in the cash flow, you still may be spending money on things that, days later, make you wonder what medications you were on when you bought the junk. Examples are coffee-table books, T-shirts with humorous sayings, LeRoy Neiman prints. Try this trick: Take a $100 traveler's check, wrap it up and hide it in your wallet. "With that as a backup, you can carry less cash, forcing you to spend less," says Pond. Turn it into a game. See how long you can go without cashing that check.

The average guy has sex about seven times a month.

Mind you, we're not counting practice. But there are things that you can do to increase your chances of having sex more often.

Stay true to one. Contrary to what you've been told by your single pal with the waterbed and a medicine cabinet full of antibiotics, if you want to have as much sex as possible before you die, one warm body will do. "A man who sticks to one partner has more sex than a man with two, three, even four partners during the course of a year," says Edward O. Laumann, Ph.D., professor of sociology at the University of Chicago. The reason is that a man with many partners spends less time having sex and more time planning on it. And get this: Men with more than one sex partner report being less healthy than monogamous men. Could it be all the juggling? Or all the Chinese takeout?

Keep yourself fit. By putting more focus on your physical and emotional health, you'll become a better, all-around congenial guy who gets along easily with people—notably women. "And that type of man is better able to maintain a relationship, which makes consistent sex easier to obtain," says Dr. Laumann.

Reminisce about the good old days. If your sex life is as stale as Peter Frampton's career, it's your own fault. "If sex is dull and infrequent, you may be too busy or lazy to make it exciting," says Howard Rupple, Jr., Ed.D., Ph.D., executive director of the Society for the Scientific Study of Sexuality in Mount Vernon, Iowa. So hark back to the early courtship—before the kids, the job stress and the mortgage—when sex was so good that the neighbors complained . . . and they were bikers.

"Make each encounter rich in detail and preparation, with extended foreplay, all the while thinking about what you used to do way back when," says Dr. Rupple. If those memories happen to involve someone else, though, keep it to yourself.

The average guy will live for 72.8 years.

Experts are unanimous: To ensure a longer life span, avoid gunfire and modern dance. Now that we have that settled, here are some ways to increase your chance of living past 72.8.

See the glass as half-full. One study found that people who believed that they were destined to suffer from certain diseases died up to four years earlier than those who did not hold such pessimistic beliefs. Other research suggests that a positive attitude can keep you from getting buried. A study of male Harvard graduates found that pessimistic subjects came down with diseases earlier and more severely than did more optimistic subjects.

Go fish. Another study found that eating one fish dinner per week can cut the risk of cardiac arrest by up to 50 percent. Researchers believe that the polyunsaturated fatty acids found in fatty fish may reduce the clumping of blood platelets that leads to coronary spasms. Four three-ounce servings of salmon during a month would provide nearly six grams of these acids—enough to protect your heart.

The average guy makes $29,533 annually.

Look, if you want to make more, you have three obvious choices: Ask for a raise, wait for one or leave. Or if you're an industrious type, you could pilfer office supplies and sell them on the black market. Frankly, we'd all like to make more money, and we could. But we know that with every promotion comes a trade-off—in the ugly form of more responsibility, longer hours, a pricier wardrobe and an accelerated loss of hair. So if you want to make more dough, fine. But you can do better.

Move to the big city. To the Big Apple, to be precise. The per capita income is the highest in the United States: $52,277. Just enough for dinner at Le Cirque.

Teach the three Rs. The average salary for a schoolteacher is $36,874.

Be a bookworm. Senior librarians in major cities can pull in more than $80,000 annually.

Work for the people. The average salary for a government worker is $31,533.

The average guy sleeps 7.5 hours a night.

You already know what keeps you up at night—caffeine, car alarms and crank phone calls from old girlfriends—so we won't bore you. There are ways to get a good night's sleep, though.

Try not to sleep. Think about it. How many times have you sat in a budget meeting, trying to keep your eyelids from folding shut like cheap beach chairs, and it just makes matters worse? Use the same strategy to get to sleep at night. Try to stay awake. "Trying to sleep only leads to sleepless frustration," says Peter Hauri, Ph.D., director of Insomnia Research and Treatment at the Mayo Clinic in Rochester, Minnesota. So try using "paradoxical intention"—resist slumber. Read something, watch something and fight the urge to doze. "If you stop caring about falling asleep while lying in bed, sleep comes more naturally," says Dr. Hauri.

Think lavender. We're not talking pajama colors; we're talking about oil. One study found that sniffing lavender oil before bedtime was just as effective as sleep medication for some insomniacs. "The oil may reduce the time it takes to fall asleep as well as the need for sleeping pills," says Alan Hirsch, M.D., neurological director of the Smell and Taste Treatment and Research Foundation in Chicago. The odor, he says, may lead us to sleep because of a direct link between the nose's olfactory bulb and the brain's wakefulness center. "The odor may also cause you to recall a pleasant childhood memory that makes it easier to sleep," says Dr. Hirsch. Or it may just smell good.

The average guy can do 33.5 sit-ups in a minute.

We would never tell you to perform sit-ups as fast as possible. They'd be sloppy, and you'd only wear out the carpeting. But fitness clinics use sit-up tests to gauge muscular fitness. "It measures the endurance of your trunk muscles," says Johann Coetzee, M.D., from the Cooper Institute for Aerobics Research in Dallas. Sure, 33.5 sit-ups sounds like a lot. But fall below average and you may be more vulnerable to lower-back problems.

Do a front crunch. It's safer than a full sit-up. Lie on your back, with your hips flexed at 90 degrees, so your thighs are perpendicular to the floor. Keep the knees at 90 degrees with your lower legs parallel to the floor. Place them lightly against a wall, just for balance. With your hands between your legs, come forward, reaching with your hands, just lifting your head off the floor. Return. Do 15.

Do a reverse. Lying on the floor, extend your legs in the air with one leg over the shin of the other. Bend the legs slightly, still pointing them toward the ceiling. Then simply flex at the hips, pushing your pelvis toward the ceiling. Do 15.

PART 3

Muscle
Mastery

TOP TEN

1996 Olympic Records

The 1996 Olympics held in Atlanta had no shortage of record-setting performances. Eighteen Olympic records altogether were broken in the men's events. Following are some of the more memorable athletic feats that were witnessed. Unless otherwise noted, times are listed in minutes, seconds and hundredths of seconds.

1. Swimming, 4 × 100-meter freestyle relay — USA — 3:15.41

2. Swimming, 4 × 100-meter medley relay — USA — 3:34.84

3. Swimming, 100-meter butterfly — Russia — 52.27
   Denis Pankratov

4. Track, 100 meters — Canada — 9.84
   Donovan Bailey

5. Track, 400 meters — USA — 43.49
   Michael Johnson

6. 110-meter hurdles — USA — 12.95
   Allen Johnson

7. Triple jump — USA — 59' 4¼"
   Kenny Harrison

8. Pole vault
   Jean Galfione — France — 19' 5"
   Igor Trandenkov — Russia — 19' 5"
   Andrei Tivontchik — Germany — 19' 5"

9. Track cycling, team pursuit — France — 4:05.93

10. Weight lifting (snatch, clean and jerk, over 238 lb.) — Russia — 1,008 lb. over two lifts
    Andrey Chemerkin

No More Excuses

Overcoming Obstacles to Workouts

You exercise. Most of the time. When you can get to the gym. When the job isn't keeping you nailed to the desk. When the sky isn't pouring rain or snow down on your favorite jogging trail. When the lower back or the crick in your shoulder isn't acting up. Sure, you'd like to exercise more often, really get in shape, but there are plenty of reasons why you can't. Plenty of explanations. Rationalizations. Complications.

Excuses.

If you're anything like us, you have an arsenal of them. And chances are that, deep in your heart, you know that most of your excuses are bogus.

Sure, there are legitimate outs, serious problems such as "I have a work deadline" or "I have a bad headache" or "Flesh-eating bacteria have rendered the entire right side of my body worthless." In instances like this, okay, we'll cut you some slack. But you probably have a few other excuses in your bag of tricks, some so rational-sounding that they make skipping workouts seem like the only sane, responsible thing to do. A clever procrastinator can call on them time and time again.

Until now.

We have compiled a thorough list of the most overused excuses and found ways to get around them. If you have the excuse, then we have the solution. Here's what to do the next time you hear yourself say:

"I'm too tired to exercise."

Get off to a good start. Your blood sugar levels may be low in the morning, and running out of the house without an adequate breakfast sets you up for an energy crash later. Fuel up with a balanced meal at the start of the day. One good combination is a bowl of cereal, a piece of fruit and a glass of skim milk. Then, to keep energy levels high, eat every four hours. As a rule, eat until you feel just somewhat satisfied, then stop.

Eat some chicken. Some athletes make the mistake of eating too many carbohydrates. A diet high in carbohydrates (75 percent or more) and lacking in protein may keep you in low gear all day long. During lunch and dinner, try to get between 10 and 15 percent of your calories from protein sources (chicken, eggs, lean meat) and keep carbohydrates like breads and pastas between 60 and 70 percent.

Wait until after work. Getting exercise over with in the morning before you're tired from a long day seems logical. But studies have shown that aerobic training is most effective in the afternoon. Subjects experienced faster recovery times and took in more oxygen. This can help you exercise longer and with more intensity than an early-morning workout, giving you more workout energy than you'd expect.

Go easy on the sugar. Simple carbohydrates (those found in sweets, candy bars and baked goods made from white flour) are rapidly absorbed into the bloodstream. Your body responds by releasing a large dose of insulin, a hormone that clears the blood of sugar. The problem is that insulin tends to do its job too well; it can bring blood sugar levels too low, causing your body to crave even more sugar. This roller-coaster ride of high-to-low blood sugar can put your body through a wringer and deplete your energy. Stick to complex carbohydrates like fruit for energy and keep simple carbohydrates to a minimum.

Get your C's worth. Vitamin C may help you work out longer and with less muscle fatigue. Doing high repetitions when you exercise causes lactic acid to pour into your muscles. This triggers a burning sensation in your muscles, which may prompt you to run out of steam before you should. Vitamin C can help slow lactic-acid buildup, thereby minimizing muscle fatigue.

"I have a bum
shoulder/knee/wrist/ankle."

Do more with less. Switch to lighter weights and do more repetitions. If you're concerned about getting weaker on this kind of routine, try using the superslow method. Instead of lifting a weight for two seconds and lowering it in four, try lifting the weight in four seconds. Research from the YMCA has shown that men using this technique can increase their strength as much as those using the conventional method. Plus, slow lifting with light weights is less taxing on an injury.

Rotate the training. Training your upper body two days in a row keeps your elbows and shoulders constantly stressed. Train your legs or rest the day after upper-body training.

Avoid the tender areas. Here's a list of typical injuries and exercises you can do to work around them.

Rotator-cuff strain: Try stationary cycling and rowing. Avoid overhead exercises.

Tennis elbow: Try swimming, running, stationary cycling and water exercises. Avoid pressing movements and perform exercises for your wrists and forearms.

Sprained ankle: Try cycling and swimming. Wear cross-trainers with adequate ankle support.

Knee pain: Try upper-body exercises (circuit-train for more fat loss) or swimming without kicking. Avoid stair-climbers, squats and exercises that put weight on the knee.

Low-back pain: Try water exercises. Avoid diving and overhead presses.

Form some ice to fit. Pain, soreness, inflammation or swelling should tell you to back off for a couple of days and ice the area that hurts. Thera-Med (1-800-327-7845) makes specially designed ice packs that fit every part of the body. If pain continues, stop and see a doctor. Bearing through the pain can only lead to more serious problems later.

Prepare the muscles. Warming up and stretching your muscles before you tax them is crucial. Aerobic activity done for 12 to 15 minutes before a workout increases tissue temperature, lubrication and elasticity in the muscles. What this means for you is less tendency toward reactivating an old injury or starting a new one. Do two or three sets with very light weight (20 percent of your maximum) before you lift. Light aerobics will do the same thing.

"I can't stick to a routine."

Take it bit by bit. Long-term goals, such as a 300-pound bench press or running the Boston Marathon, are fine as long as you set short-term goals, such as adding a half-mile a week to your running schedule.

Consult a physician. Many people blow off having a checkup before starting an exercise program because they feel fine. But look at a visit to the doctor as an investment in staying motivated. A study from the University of Colorado Health Sciences Center has shown that a strong medical recommendation is more effective than you think. Patients who were given advice by their doctors tended to exercise for longer amounts of time and more often throughout the week.

Limit the fattening foods. Look at exercise as a way for you to indulge once in a while. As you age, your resting metabolic rate (RMR), which dictates how many calories you burn when you're not exercising, slows. That's why your 14-year-old nephew can down an entire cake and stay slim, while you just look at the icing and gain ten pounds. But researchers from Tufts University in Medford, Massachusetts, have concluded that regular exercise could make all the difference. Subjects who were asked to train three times a week for 12 weeks increased their RMRs by 7.7 percent, just what you need to help keep off the pounds. In some cases, subjects were able to consume 15 percent more calories and still keep their weight steady.

Make an appearance. Make it a point to leave something in your locker or with your gym partner that you can't be without the next day. This forces you to go to the gym whether you feel like exercising or not. Once there, you'll be more inclined to exercise. If you exercise at home, put your exercise clothes on as soon as you get home from work.

Spread the word. Tell your friends, co-workers and spouse about your workout plan, and let them know that you need some encouragement. Tell them your exact goals, then urge them to check on your progress from time to time.

Treat yourself. Promise yourself something at the end of the week if you've met all your goals. It can be an afternoon of golf, a night out with the guys and so on. If you want a better incentive, ask your partner for some kind of reward for a job well done, like a massage or a romantic evening. (Use guilt: "Hey, honey, I'm doing this for you.")

Write it down. Get out your calendar and pencil in three exercise sessions a week. Treat them like business meetings. Now you can schedule the rest of your week around them. Make a habit of considering exercise as much of a priority as a work or family obligation.

"I don't have enough time."

Prioritize your exercises. If time is of the essence, don't waste it doing isolation exercises, such as chest flies, that work only one muscle group. Compound exercises, such as bench presses, squats, pull-ups, dead lifts and dips, that work several muscle groups will let you hit more of your body in half the time.

Chop up the workouts. Split your routine in half or in three 20-minute workouts. You'll feel less stressed and have more energy for each session. One way to divide it up is to do weight training in the morning and aerobic exercise at night. "Hit the weights early when you have the energy," says Rick Valente, champion bodybuilder and co-host of ESPN's *Bodyshaping*. An added benefit is that you'll burn more overall calories. Your body stays revved

Try Topping These Excuses

We asked America's top personal trainers for the all-time worst excuses they have heard from clients trying to weasel out of a workout. The clients' names have been withheld to protect the slackers.

"I'd rather devote my energy to my sex life."
—*Laure Redmond, star of* The Workout Warehouse *infomercials*

"I'm allergic to exercise." (It turns out that the client was, indeed, allergic to her own sweat.)
—*Richard Simmons, famous fitness trainer*

"I did it in college."
—*Radu, Cindy Crawford's trainer*

"Why do you Americans exercise? This is so silly. If we Frenchmen want to exercise, we make love all day or we ski."
—*Gin Miller, inventor of step training*

up after each workout; by doing two or three instead of just one, your heart rate stays higher for a longer time.

Work out by the clock. If you can't get a good workout in less than 45 minutes, you're wasting time somewhere. Try shortening the time between sets to 30 to 45 seconds. Bring a watch with a second hand to keep yourself on schedule. Working at this pace will allow you to do at least 20 sets within a 45-minute period.

Do two things at once. You can purchase a reading rack that can attach to any stationary machine and take some of the mundane, time-eating tasks you do in the office to the gym. Go through your mail or write in your daily planner as you stationary-cycle, or dictate memos in between sets.

"I need to lose 20 pounds before I start exercising."
—*Dr. Pete Gratale, cast member of ESPN's* **Bodyshaping**

"I'm too busy making money."
—*Rick Valente, champion bodybuilder and co-host of ESPN's* **Bodyshaping**

"I can't find any tasteful pants in a 29, so I'm going to take it easy for a while until I get back up to a 31."
—*Scott Cole, Man of Steel and Nike Fitness Athlete*

"I'm afraid of getting smelly."
—*Donna Richardson, star of ESPN's* **Fitness Pros**

"I'm so thin now I would be afraid to lose any more."
—*Jack LaLanne, the godfather of fitness*

"The Rolls is in the shop, and the Ferrari is a stick. And I can't drive stick."
—*Tony Little, "America's Personal Trainer"*

"I get bored easily."

Play with the numbers. Even the simplest changes can keep you interested in your workout. Adjusting the number of repetitions or sets in your exercises can be enough. If you normally do 12 repetitions for three sets of an exercise, try doing 18 for two sets.

Vary the courses. If you have a favorite trail that you run or cycle, reverse the route. Or make it a point to find a new route every week. You could even challenge yourself to ride or run every street in town.

Break out of patterns. Make it a point to learn 2 new exercises a month. Try them, then write them down on a master list. Your goal could be to try 25 different exercises in one year or to find 10 exercises that you can do strictly for your chest.

Get around. Make a point of trying out every gym in your area. If your membership is at Dave's Dumbbells, shell out the visitor's fee and drop by Bob's Barbells once in a while. Not only will it give you a change of atmosphere, but also the equipment will be somewhat different, giving you some variety.

Try less traditional activities. Exercise isn't limited to weight training, running and cycling. There are alternatives for those looking for something different, such as boxaerobics (a combination of boxing and aerobics), karate aerobics and swimming-pool exercising. A unique exercise class may hold your interest better and also introduce you to a new sport or way of life.

"I need more family time."

Bring along your wife. A study conducted at Indiana University in Bloomington showed that married couples who exercised together worked out more often and were less likely to quit than married couples who worked out separately. Their dropout rate was a mere 6.3 percent, compared with 43 percent for those who chose to fly solo.

Combine dates and workouts. Your better half is complaining that you don't do anything special together anymore. You can get in a workout, and shore up the home front, by making a date out of an active event. Here are some ideas.

- A walking tour of a large museum. Take the stairs between floors and keep moving; don't linger in front of the nudes.
- A bike ride/picnic. Find a romantic spot, then bike to it and back.
- A row around the local pond.
- Ask her to move in. Carry all her stuff to your house. Then, next weekend, break up, and carry it all back. For some guys we know, this is a regular exercise program.

Take your kid for a ride. Look for specially designed jogging strollers that resemble miniature 4 X 4 monster trucks. They absorb shock and let you get in a great run while taking your child for the ride of her life. If you like to cycle, hook up a child bicycling seat to your two-wheeler.

Experience a second childhood. If your children are too big to fit in a stroller but not old enough to be embarrassed to be seen with you, then get involved with the activities they like. Shoot hoops, play football, try in-line skating. Sometimes kids make the best personal trainers because they never seem to run out of steam. Keeping up with them can turn into a terrific aerobic workout. Here's the breakdown of some activities that you can do together.

Activity	Calories burned in 20 min.*	Equivalent to:
Badminton	156	14 min. running
Baseball (pitcher)	144	18 min. cycling
Basketball	236	23 min. stair climbing
Bicycling	160	16 min. rowing
Frisbee	160	15 min. running
In-line skating	186	18 min. stair climbing
Jumping rope	260	32 min. cycling
Soccer	218	22 min. rowing

*Based on 176-lb. man

"I don't see results."

Track your training. By comparing each week, you will be able to see the results that you had previously missed. You can use any old notebook, but if you need more organization to stay on track, the Pocket Personal Trainer (about $30) not only helps you keep records but also offers meal planners, goal-setting sheets and fitness tips. To order it, call 1-800-482-3348.

Take your stats. Measure yourself around the neck, shoulders, chest, arms, waist, thighs and calves, taking new measurements each month. You'll be able to see the results with tangible numbers.

Alter your routine. Shuffling the order of your exercises or alternating the exercises you do for a body part is an excellent way to shock your muscles into showing results. If your shoulder routine starts with presses and ends with side raises, reverse the order. If you always work your triceps after your chest, work your shoulders instead.

"It's just too hot to exercise."

Ease off for a fortnight. Acclimating yourself to hot weather takes about 10 to 14 days of heat exposure combined with moderate exercise.

Cut back on your usual regimen and gradually build back to the level at which you were working. Once you've become acclimated, you'll sweat more, sweat faster and have a lower body temperature and heart rate when you exercise.

Sport a loose and light look. Wearing loose-fitting clothing lets sweat evaporate faster to keep you cool. Don't go shirtless, though; the increased sun exposure will prevent you from cooling down. Also, wear light-colored clothing, which reflects heat from the sun's rays. (Dark colors absorb it.)

Use sunscreen for double protection. Not only will it protect you from the sun's harmful rays, but it can also help keep you cooler. In addition, researchers have found that wearing sunscreen can lower your core and skin temperatures, helping to prevent heat illness.

JUST THE FACTS

Time of day when a man's hand-eye coordination and reaction time are at their peak: between 2:30 P.M. and 4:00 P.M.

"It's just too cold to exercise."

Heat up for starters. Joints are stiffer, and muscles and tendons are more susceptible to injury, in cold weather. Before heading outdoors, warm up until your limbs feel "glowing warm" and you experience a slight feeling of breathlessness. Try this full-body combo: Jog in place for a minute followed by 30 seconds of push-ups. Repeat eight to ten times to warm up your upper and lower body.

Clothe completely but not tightly. If you're afraid of frostbite, cover the areas most susceptible—hands, feet, ears, nose and cheeks. Avoid tight clothing and tight training shoes. They restrict blood circulation and increase your risk of injury from the cold.

"My gym burned down/was condemned/just plain stinks."

Thought you had us there, didn't you? Sorry.

Use calisthenics. The gym isn't the only place you can get a quick workout. You can hit nearly every muscle in your body by just doing push-ups, pull-ups, crunches and lunges, all of which cost nothing. Try this full-body circuit routine: 20 push-ups, 10 pull-ups, 20 crunches and 20 lunges. After each exercise, immediately move to the next one. Rest for 30 seconds and repeat the circuit twice.

Go back to nature. Treadmills and stair-climbers are, in reality, expensive pieces of equipment that allow you to perform exercises that cost nothing at all to do. Take it outside.

Precise
Moves

How to Correctly Use Exercise Machines

That burly guy at the gym slamming the weights in a fast and furious manner looks pretty impressive. All that weight. All that noise. All that badly bleached hair. When he's through, you half expect him to pick his teeth with a barbell. Sure, he's not the kind of guy who's up on foreign policy, but be honest; you wouldn't mind tossing around so much metal with such brute force.

But, really, all that sound and fury signifies little when it comes to building muscle. "Demonstrating strength isn't the same as building it," says Ellington Darden, Ph.D., strength-training researcher and author of *Living Longer Stronger*. In an effort to lift a lot of weight in a fast, sloppy manner, you call into action muscles that you shouldn't be using. "It's far better to isolate and build the targeted muscle slowly and carefully and, at the same time, relax the rest of your muscles. That encourages better muscle growth," says Dr. Darden.

Because men tend to sacrifice form on the weight machines, especially when they're racing through their lunch-hour workout and bouncing from one station to another, we offer a blueprint for doing it right—down to the finest detail. Step by painstaking step, we take you through each exercise, showing you where the most common mistakes are made and how you can get the most out of your moves.

Arm Curl Machine

This machine targets the biceps muscles of the upper arm. When seated, grab the handle loosely and curl it up until your thumbs nearly touch your shoulders. Let the handle return, and repeat the movement.

Keep your shoulders low. Without thinking, most of us slowly lift ourselves off the seat during a set, allowing the shoulders to move toward the weight stack until, by the last repetition, we're practically vaulting over the bench. With our shoulders meeting our hands as the weight comes up, we've shortened the distance the arms must travel, letting the biceps off the hook. Instead, adjust the seat low enough to keep your shoulders from creeping over the bench. Keeping your butt planted firmly in the seat also prevents you from lifting your torso.

Keep your head still. By moving your head forward, backward or sideways, your neck muscles are muscling in on the exercise, again letting your biceps off easy. If you find that you can't keep from moving your head, then lighten the weight until you can comfortably keep your head still for 10 to 12 repetitions.

Machine Chest Press

This machine is excellent for developing the chest, shoulders and triceps. Sit in the seat and stabilize your body by placing your feet flat on the floor. Press the handles up and out slowly, and then let them return slowly.

Situate your body between the handlebars. Sounds pretty basic, doesn't it? But most guys get a little sloppy here. If you're not perfectly centered, your chest ends up at an awkward angle and one arm may overcompensate, leading to uneven stress placed on your muscles. Do this over the course of a few months, and you'll be a walking fun-house mirror.

Use a grip an inch or two wider than shoulder width. Go any wider and you won't push the bar as far out as you'd like, shortening the path of motion and not working the muscles as fully. Don't take a grip that's narrower than shoulder width, however. You'll cheat your chest muscles this way, too, relying more on your triceps.

Don't lock your elbows. Locking the elbow joint at the top of the movement transfers weight resistance off the muscles and onto your joint structure. That allows your muscles a few seconds of rest, destroying that continual stress needed to stimulate muscle growth.

Keep your hips and legs still. Moving your hips and legs up or out allows more leverage and momentum, introducing other muscles into the exercise. Either place your feet firmly on the ground or lift your legs and cross your ankles. This forces you to flatten your back, removing any extra leverage and putting all the emphasis on your chest to push the weight up and out.

Bent-Arm Fly Machine

The chest and front shoulder muscles are targeted with this machine. Sit erect, look straight ahead and place your forearms on the arm pads with your elbows raised and level with your shoulders. Grip the handles between your thumb and index finger, then push with your forearms until the pads touch in front of your chest. When your elbows come together, pause for a moment and slowly return to the starting position.

Align your shoulders correctly with the movement arms of the machine. If your forearms are resting too far below the pads, you'll put a lot of undue stress on those muscles and compensate by arching your back—which ruins the exercise and looks plain silly. Reposition the seat or use a seat pad so that your forearms are resting fully against the movement pads of the machine.

Press with your elbows, not with your hands. Many people use their hands to push the arm pads together. Instead, think "press elbows together." This helps isolate more of the chest muscles instead of the arms.

Keep your head and shoulders against the back pad. If your head and torso are leaning forward, the weight is too heavy. And straining like that cheats your chest muscles out of most of the work. Lighten the weight and concentrate on using only your chest and shoulder muscles. To help yourself keep your head and shoulders straight, look in a mirror or focus on an object in front of you.

Triceps Pressdown Machine

This machine targets the triceps of the upper arm. Starting with the bar at chin level, slowly bring it down to crotch level, about a foot from your body. Then return the bar to the original position and repeat the movement.

Keep your elbows still. You may have seen a lot of lifters work the bar like they're feverishly pumping a bicycle tire. Big mistake. They're using their body weight to do a job intended only for the triceps. Instead, keep your elbows tucked in, close to the sides of your belly. Once your elbows spread out, you're more likely to start pumping.

Keep your feet a few inches behind you and the bar. Most of us tend to stand perfectly straight and push the bar straight down. But if you move slightly backward, you'll get a fuller extension of the triceps because your thighs won't be blocking the downstroke. At the low point of the movement, your arms should be fully extended but angled away from your body, with your thumbs out in front and your elbows in perfect alignment behind them.

Use the back pad. By pressing the small of your back against it, you'll keep your body weight from helping your triceps.

Leg Press Machine

This machine is for developing the muscles in the thighs and the calves. Push out with your feet and straighten both legs in a smooth, continuous movement. Keep your knees slightly bent without locking them. Then return to the original position and repeat the movement.

Start the exercise with your knees near your chest. A common error is to begin this exercise with your body far enough from the movement arm (the bar with the weight attached) so that your legs are only slightly bent. When you extend your legs, you end up working only part of the quadriceps and little else. Instead, allow the movement arm to drop lower so that you feel a little cramped— that's okay. The closer your torso is to the movement arm, the more of your thigh and hip muscles you'll hit. Also, make sure that your feet are placed evenly on the foot pads, about six to eight inches apart.

Relax. In this exercise, many of us will gulp for air, grit our teeth or shift and move our hips from side to side. All of these slight movements take the focus off the legs. If you find that your legs do need help, lighten the weight instead and concentrate solely on using your leg muscles.

Leg Curl Machine

The hamstring muscles on the back of the upper thigh are targeted with this machine. Lie facedown on the machine and place your feet under the roller pads. Hold the handles to keep your body from moving. Curl your legs up slowly, and try to touch your heels to your buttocks. Pause, and then lower the weight.

Relax your quadriceps by lifting your hips slightly and arching your back. With most exercises, arching might draw frowns from the peanut gallery. But here it actually helps. It extends the path of movement involved in the exercise, allowing you to use more of the hamstrings. If you don't lift your hips and arch your back, the distance your leg travels bringing the weight up becomes considerably shorter, and you end up working less muscle. Many machines now have a built-in arch that keeps your hips elevated and arches your back for you.

Flex your ankle with your heel down and your toes pulling toward your shin. By stretching your calf muscles fully (the opposite of flexing your calves), you'll make it impossible for yourself to cheat by enlisting those muscles to help the hamstrings. You'll notice that the weight you used to lift ten times is now difficult to lift in only four or five reps. So lighten the weight; you'll still get more benefit than if you cheat and use a heavier setting.

Leg Extension Machine

This machine targets the quadriceps muscles on the front of the thighs. Sit in the machine and place your feet behind the rollers. Smoothly straighten your legs out. Pause a moment and then return.

Lie back as far as the machine will let you. By sitting up straight, you're less likely to straighten your knee fully, which you need to do to really nail the quadriceps. Most machines allow you to recline, so take advantage of it and gently rest your back against the back support. You can now bring your leg up to a full extension and feel your quadriceps fully contract. Plus, you're also able to relax your hamstrings completely, effectively preventing you from using them at all in the exercise.

Okay, you've mastered a few important individual exercises. But let's face it, bizarre new workout machines are being invented every day. So the next time you stroll into your local gym and spot yet another medieval torture rack–cum–resistance machine, approach it with a few key principles in mind. They'll help you get in a great workout on just about any exercise gizmo.

Set the seat. It's like driving your buddy's car. If he's a foot taller than you, you'll be staring at the odometer instead of the road unless you adjust the seat to your height first. Do the same at the gym. You might even grab the seat pad usually floating around the gym and place it on the machine seat if you're shorter than the average Joe.

Relax your grip. A hard grip may give you the forearms of Popeye, but you'll end up with the body of Olive Oyl, since intense gripping cheats the rest of your more noticeable muscles.

Go slow. Stop taking the runaway-freight-train approach to lifting. To eliminate momentum and push your muscles to the limit, take four seconds lifting the bar up and the same amount of time on the way down.

Don't slam the weights. Besides annoying the rest of us who are trying to work out in peace, slamming the weights down gives your muscles an unnecessary break. "Every time you pause for that brief second or two, you remove resistance from the muscles instead of working them harder," says Dr. Darden. Instead, once the weight stack touches down, immediately, but slowly, bring it back up.

Cross your ankles. Here's a simple maneuver that most guys don't know about that can really up the intensity of an exercise. By crossing your ankles at the seated stations, you prevent your legs and hip muscles from helping you push the weight up—a mistake that most lifters make. When your legs are free, it's far easier to push off the floor to help squeeze out that extra repetition.

If the machine has a belt, use it. It's not for safety purposes, so you're not proving your manhood by sitting on it instead of using it. By strapping yourself in, you keep from squirming your torso forward or sideways, which prevents your midsection muscles from helping out.

Cogs in the Machine

Take Care of These Small but Important Muscles

The 1964 Mustang was an amazing car. If it was properly cared for, it could go from 0 to 60 in a millisecond and would purr like a kitten.

But for it to perform at its best, you had to take great care of it. You had to take the time to oil tiny gears and replace miniature springs that most people never knew existed. Because without these seemingly insignificant parts, the car wouldn't last as long, wouldn't run as smoothly and wouldn't peel tar off the road when it was thrown into third.

Your body is like the Mustang. Okay, maybe it's an older model, and maybe it could use some front-end work. But it's a muscle car, too, and it's made up of a lot of little muscles that you never notice until they go awry. Some of them tie in with larger muscles, helping them do their jobs better. Others have their distinct functions that you wouldn't want to do without. They're the tiny gears that make your whole machine perform at its highest possible level.

These miniature muscles need exercise just as every other part of you does. And although it's hard to impress people in the gym by working muscles that you can't even see, let alone flex, look at it as health insurance. "Choose to ignore these muscles and they can easily stop you dead in your tracks," says Lyle Micheli, M.D., former president of the American College of Sports Medicine and author of the *Sports Medicine Bible*.

In other words, learn about these muscles now, or the next time you see them may be on an anatomy chart in your doctor's office. Here's what they can do for you and what you can do for them.

Neck Extensors

Located in the back of the neck, these muscles are responsible for lifting your head up and back. Without them, you'd constantly be caught looking down women's blouses, so they're kind of important. They can also hurt, if you don't exercise them once in a while. "During most of the day, your head is dipped downward whether you're eating, typing or even watching TV," says Judith Lasater, Ph.D., author of *Relax and Renew*. In fact, you're probably stretching them right now as you're reading. But if you continually stretch a muscle and never take time to strengthen it, the result can be a muscle imbalance that makes itself known through soreness—in this case, neck soreness. The pain is your extensors being overstretched and weakened and finally tiring out. Try this exercise to strengthen them.

Bed raise. Lie on your bed on your stomach with your head hanging over the edge. Slowly lower your head as far as is comfortable, then, bending only at the neck, raise your head straight up and back as far as is comfortable. Hold for a moment, then slowly lower your head again. Do two or three sets of 10 to 12 repetitions every other day.

Rotator Cuff Muscles

The muscles known collectively as the rotator cuff are the supraspinatus, infraspinatus, teres minor and subscapularis. These four tiny muscles work closely with other, larger muscles to lift, lower and rotate your arms. But when you exercise, you're primarily strengthening the larger muscles, leaving the rotator muscles unchallenged. You'll never get as strong or as big as you could be unless you also concentrate on the smaller muscles. Since there isn't one exercise that works all four muscles, you'll need to do several.

The open-can raise. For the supraspinatus, stand straight with your arms at your sides. Hold a very light dumbbell in your right hand, palm facing in. Keep your arm straight and lift it out from your side about 45 degrees so that your right hand is about two feet from your right hip. Rotate your hand forward until your thumb is pointing toward the floor. This is the starting hand position. Slowly lower the weight to your side and raise it again. Do 15 to 20 repetitions with your right arm, then switch the weight to your left hand to work the other side.

Arm twist. Attach an elastic cord to a doorknob. Stand alongside the door so that your right shoulder is facing the doorknob and grab the loose end of the cord with your right hand. Stand with your arms straight at your sides, palms facing away from your body. To work the subscapularis, rotate your body a quarter-turn to the left until you're facing away from the doorknob; you'll feel a pull from the elastic band behind you. Keeping your right arm at your side, slowly rotate it inward toward your body until the back of your hand is touching your right thigh. Hold this position for a moment, then rotate your hand back to the starting position. Do 12 to 15 repetitions, then switch to work your left arm.

Reverse arm twist. To work the last two muscles (the infraspinatus and teres minor), attach the cord and hold it in your right hand the same way you did for the arm twist. But this time, instead of rotating your body to the left, you'll need to rotate to the right so that your left side is facing the doorknob. Turn your right hand inward so that your right palm is facing your leg. The cord should be stretched across your body, down below your waist. Keeping your right arm by your side, this time rotate it outward from your body until the back of your hand is against your right thigh. Do 12 to 15 repetitions for each arm.

Brachialis Anticus

Few people pay attention to the broad, flat muscle that lies beneath the biceps and the humerus (the upper arm bone).

That's a big mistake. When this muscle grows, it has no choice but to press upward, adding size to your biceps and making it larger than it could get on its own. Here's an exercise to make your biceps look like Popeye's.

Incline hammer curl. Sit on an incline bench with a light dumbbell in each hand. Your arms should hang straight down with your palms facing each other. With your head and back flat against the bench, slowly curl both weights up toward your shoulders, keeping your palms facing each other during the movement. Squeeze your biceps muscles, then slowly lower the weights until your arms are straight. Do 10 to 12 repetitions for three sets.

Forearm Extensors

These thin muscles, which run from the back of your wrists to your elbows, control your fingers and wrists. When you repeatedly put stress on them, say by swatting a fuzzy green ball around a red clay court, pain can start to develop at the point where the muscles insert into the outside of your elbow. By strengthening them, you'll prevent that pain from setting in.

Hammer twists. With your left hand, grab a hammer at the end of its handle and sit with your elbow propped on the end of a table. Keeping your wrist straight, allow your forearm to hang off the edge of the table. Slowly rotate your hand from side to side as if pouring a glass of water. Work up to three sets of 16 to 20 repetitions.

Intrinsic Muscles in the Hands

The muscles in your hands are too numerous to mention, but the fact that you can't name them all doesn't mean that you shouldn't exercise them. Disuse can cause these vital muscles to lose a certain percentage of their function. That means that you'll be a little slower and weaker whenever you write, build something, drive, shake hands, fondle delicate flesh or try to haul in a Hail Mary pass. They can even interfere with your regular workout, since your grip strength can often dictate how much weight you can lift. This exercise will keep those muscles strong.

Silly Putty squeeze. Hand grippers will work, but what fun are they? Instead, buy some Silly Putty, recommends Dr. Micheli.

Squeezing it in your palm throughout the day will give your hands a workout without calling attention to you. Try squeezing an "eggful" worth of putty for three minutes, five times a day. And no making putty copies of the boss's memos.

Quadratus Lumborum

This muscle is found deep within the lower back and is largely responsible for holding your back vertical. A big job for such a small muscle, which makes it very susceptible to injury when stressed. Just picking up a heavy suitcase is more than enough to cause strain if it's weak. Because of this, it's usually the root of many back problems. Keeping it strong can help prevent slouching and keep you standing straight and tall. It may also save you a trip to the drugstore for some back pills. Here's how to work it.

Side bends. This exercise will hit the small muscles deep in the back as well as tone your oblique abdominals, which can help hide those love handles. Stand straight with your arms at your sides and a light dumbbell in your left hand, palms facing in. Looking straight ahead, slowly bend toward your left side, keeping the dumbbell close to your left leg, until you feel a stretch on the right side of your torso. Raise back into the starting position and follow through by bending over to your right side as far as you can. Do this for 10 to 15 repetitions, then switch the weight into your right hand and repeat the exercise.

Pyriformis

This muscle stabilizes the hip joint and rotates the thigh outward. Any activity that involves twisting at the hip, such as swinging a golf club, impersonating Elvis or spending a vigorous night under the sheets, uses this muscle to some degree. By strengthening it, you can give yourself more control over the muscle and enhance your ability to perform whatever it is you're performing. The best part is that you need your partner to help you. (This is what we call very personal training.)

Leg twist. Lie flat on your back with your legs straight. Your partner should be sitting by your feet. Raise your left leg about a foot above the ground and have your partner gently grab your left foot with both hands. Starting with your leg straight and rotated inward, slowly rotate it outward as if you're trying to point your left knee away from your body. Your partner's job is to resist your movement by gently twisting your foot in the opposite direction. Twist as far as possible, keeping constant tension on the muscles for about 10 to 15 seconds, then repeat with the other leg. Do this exercise four or five times for each leg every other day.

Gluteus Medius

This poor muscle never gets the recognition it rightfully deserves. Its big brother, gluteus maximus (otherwise known as your backside) takes all the glory for giving you a seat to sit on. But without the gluteus medius, you'd be sitting on your butt 24 hours a day. Whenever you stand on one leg, this fan-shaped muscle located on the side of your hip keeps you from falling over by making sure that your pelvis stays level. "If that doesn't sound important," says Dr. Lasater, "just remember that whenever you walk or run, you're standing on one foot or the other." If you're involved in any type of sport, this muscle could make all the difference in keeping you on your feet during tricky situations, such as skiing a difficult ski run or taking a hip check on the ice while playing hockey. This exercise will keep you off your can.

Couch hangs. This exercise will help stretch the gluteus medius, keeping it limber. It will also stretch your credibility as you attempt to explain to your mate that you need to lie on the couch every night. Lie on your left side on the couch, facing its back. Keeping your right leg straight, raise it an inch, then move it about three inches behind your left leg. Relax your hip and let your right leg angle down toward the floor. It's important to concentrate on keeping your pelvis facing the back of the couch to get a full stretch. Hold this position for 20 seconds, then reverse position and work the left side.

Soleus

This broad, flat muscle lies just below your calves, where it runs from your knee all the way to your ankles. Its job is to help propel you when you walk, run or jump. Keeping this muscle well-stretched on a regular basis can add inches to your leap and prevent tendinitis and Achilles tendon injuries.

The problem is that doing a regular calf stretch doesn't loosen up this muscle very well. You need a special stretch to isolate it and help it stay limber.

Soleus stretch. Stand two feet from a wall and step forward with your left foot. Place your hands on the wall and rotate your right foot inward so that your toes point toward your left foot. Slowly bend your left leg, keeping the heel of your right foot firmly on the ground. Hold for five seconds to get a full stretch, take a rest, repeat, then switch your position to work the left foot.

Peroneals

These stabilizing muscles located on the sides of your ankles help you move laterally (from side to side). Activities that require a lot of lateral motion, such as basketball, tennis or doing the polka, call on these muscles a great deal. They can also aid your manuevering abilities on the slopes. And strengthening them is the best insurance against a sprained ankle. Try this exercise to keep them strong.

Side ankle lifts. Lie on your left side with your right leg straight and your left leg bent. Your knees should be together with your left foot behind you. Have a partner place a three- to five-pound ankle weight across the edge of your right foot. Your partner should keep a loose hand on the weight to make sure that it doesn't slide off. Slowly rotate your right foot to the right so the little toe moves toward the ceiling. Pause for a moment, then lower your foot. Do 30 to 50 repetitions, then switch sides to work your left ankle.

Intrinsic Muscles in the Feet

There are 19 muscles in the foot that support the toes and arch. The arch acts as a cushion or spring. As you walk or run, it minimizes the impact of each step. But when these muscles are not used, the arch starts to flatten out, causing more stress to be transmitted up the body to your knees, hips and back. To keep your arches from falling, try this exercise.

Toe walking. First, go someplace where no one can see you. Take off your shoes and stand straight. Lift up onto your toes and walk around the room, as if you're a ballerina. Walk for a minute, rest for a minute, then get back up on your toes for another minute. Do this four or five times every other day and you'll find that your feet aren't as tired by the time the ten o'clock news comes on.

Visible Results

Have Something to Show from Your Workouts

Every morning after a shower, you look in the mirror. Like a teenager searching for facial hair, you hunt for an ab—one of those ravioli-like muscles that are supposed to spring from the stomach if you do enough sit-ups. But the only thing that you detect is a possible hernia from helping Aunt Hefty away from the table last Thanksgiving. So you turn sideways and slowly make a muscle, willing your biceps into the grapefruit that dumbbell curls are supposed to produce. But only a kiwifruit emerges.

Like thousands of men emerging from showers across the nation each morning, you yearn to see results in that bathroom mirror. You want abdominals worthy of a Janet Jackson video, biceps that you can tattoo with "Mother" instead of just "Ma." So why isn't it happening? What are you doing wrong?

There are a lot of frustrated body warriors out there—guys who realize the benefit of exercise and fight to fit it into their lives but are puzzled by their lack of performance and disappointed by their fitness gains. Some are runners struggling to build 10-K endurance, others are mountain bikers trying to keep their wheels under them, a few are golfers and tennis players chasing that elusive mental edge and many are average Joes who can't get a grip on losing their love handles.

We gathered the most common of these fitness dilemmas and went to the experts for help. Whether it's endurance that won't endure or abs indistinguishable from flab, we'll help you pinpoint your training mistakes and finally get the results you want.

Dilemma: "I do sit-ups every day, but nobody would confuse my abdominals for a scrubbing surface."

Solution: Look at it this way. If you want to earn a degree in law, you don't just study legal history for four years. You dabble in psychology, public speaking, maybe even a little basic BMW repair. The same holds true if you want your abs to graduate to the next level.

Kurt Brungardt, author of *The Complete Book of Abs*, explains that you'll never reach your goal by doing just one thing. Instead, you need "a more holistic approach," combining a variety of abdominal exercises with aerobic work and a low-fat diet. Above all, think of your abdomen as being three distinct muscle groups: the lower abs, upper abs and obliques (where your love handles lie). Each one needs to be exercised separately.

Here's his strategy—one that's so effective that he promises results in six weeks.

Do traditional crunches for your lower abs. Lie on your back with knees bent, feet flat on the floor and hands lightly touching your ears. Repeatedly raise your shoulder blades off the ground in a forward-curling motion, then lower them. Don't do sit-ups—they can hurt your back.

Do reverse crunches for your upper abs. These are done from the same prone position but with both legs lifted so that your thighs are perpendicular to your torso (knees bent). Repeatedly roll your hips off the ground toward your rib cage, then lower them.

Do crossovers for the obliques. Lie on your back with your right foot flat on the floor and knee bent. Rest your left ankle on your right knee, place your right hand behind your head and put your left hand on your right side. Raise and twist your right shoulder toward your left knee. Do as many of these as you can, then switch sides.

Beginners should do these exercises twice a week at first, then gradually build through three or four times. On interim days, Brungardt recommends aerobic exercise lasting 30 minutes or more. Along with a low-fat diet, this will help shed pounds and unveil those abs.

"Even if you don't see results quickly," he says, "you'll be able to feel the musculature developing, and that'll inspire you to continue."

Dilemma: "Every January I resolve to exercise, but usually by April I've broken my vow."

Solution: Think back to when you were a kid, when you biked, ran around and played ball all day. You never trained or consciously tried to get into shape; it just happened naturally. And you and your buddies called it play. Now flash ahead 20 to 30 years to the present. You still have a lot of kid left in you, but to bike, run or even hit a few balls takes a humbling amount of energy. So you vow to start an exercise routine, discipline yourself and make a serious effort at getting fit. And you call it working out.

See the problem? According to Jonathan Robison, Ph.D., executive co-director of the Michigan Center for Preventive Medicine in Lansing, many men abandon exercise programs because the regimens become stressful and boring. The solution is twofold.

Make exercise as social an activity as possible. Join a softball team, buy a tandem bicycle, gather some guys for a regular Sunday-morning run or just walk the dog. Not only will conversation and camaraderie make the time pass faster and the effort seem less, but it's also tougher to skip a workout when a neighbor (or Rover) is waiting on the doorstep.

Stop trying so hard to exercise. Instead, make an attempt to be more physically active in your daily life by taking the stairs, using your bike for around-town errands or buying a push mower. This subtle shift in mind-set is very important, and it represents the new view of fitness.

"All exercise is physical activity, but not all physical activity is exercise," explains Dr. Robison. "Still, it's just as good for you, and in some ways it's even better.

"The way to develop consistency is to have a broader perspective on health," he continues. "Don't get hung up on just exercise or nutrition. Remember that there are emotional, spiritual and psychological—as well as physical—components of health. Many men subscribe to the notion that 'I exercise, therefore I am healthy.' But that's not always true. Health involves striving for a balance in all these areas."

Dilemma: "I run regularly, but I can't seem to build much endurance."

Solution: Suppose we promised you that in six months or less, regardless of how pathetic you now look in running shorts, you could finish a marathon. Preposterous? Not at all. Jeff Galloway, a former Olympic distance runner from Atlanta who conducts marathon-training clinics, says that he has a 99 percent success rate with joggers just like you.

"The key to building endurance or speed is to treat each one as a separate component," he explains. "When you're working on endurance, forget about speed."

For example, once every week do a long workout, running one mile more than you're accustomed to during the week. But instead of maintaining your usual pace, go slower and alternate five minutes of running with one minute of walking.

"Ultradistance runners have been doing this for years, except they run for 25 minutes and walk for 5," explains Galloway. "But it's a relatively new concept for recreational runners. The thing is, you get the same endurance benefits as if you were constantly running."

In each successive week, extend your long workout by another mile, remembering to alternate slow running with walking. After you work up to ten miles, do your long run every other week, increasing the distance by two miles each time. Forget about speed, heart rate and feeling guilty about strolling. Focus on just staying upright.

To further minimize fatigue, avoid large quantities of caffeine and alcohol for 24 hours before each long run, while drinking plenty of water. To ensure that your muscles are packed with fuel, eat five to six grams of carbohydrate per kilogram of body weight each day. (Convert your body weight to kilograms by dividing by 2.2.) Also, have an energy bar with an eight-ounce glass of water one hour before each long run and, if you'll be on the road for more than ten miles, pack another bar and some liquid as a snack.

"Doing all this will allow you to increase the distance you run without dramatically increasing the fatigue," says Galloway.

Dilemma: "I recently bought a mountain bike, but I can't keep up with the guys (or even the kids!) on my local trails."

Solution: Off-road riding is one of the toughest sports going. Think about it. Not only do you have to keep the bike upright, but you must also look for rocks, duck under branches, shift gears, brake, pedal and steer—all while barely being able to breathe.

"It takes a lot of athleticism to ride a mountain bike on technical terrain," says Fred Matheny, an off-road riding coach and the training and fitness editor for *Bicycling* magazine. "The reason is that you're getting a lot of stimulus at the same time. But tremendous improvements can be made. You just have to know the tricks."

Keep an eye on where you're going. In other words, don't stare at that rock in the middle of the trail or that 1,000-foot drop-off a yard to your right. Instead, trace a clear line well up the path. Trust us: It's no coincidence that traction is a part of distraction.

Become laid-back. Most mountain bikers get into trouble by leaning too far forward. This can cause the front wheel to jolt to a stop on obstacles and launch the rider over the handlebar. For optimum balance and maneuverability, keep your weight back.

Act like a feline. The more rigid and tense your body is, the more likely a rock or limb will throw you off balance and cause a crash. "Be like a cat on the bike," says Matheny. "I always show riders the basketball defensive stance or the wrestling ready position— on the balls of your feet, knees and elbows bent, ready to move. That's the exact position you want on the bike."

Make speed your ally. Despite what that surly police officer said, speed is your friend—at least in the outback. It allows you to ride over rough stuff that would otherwise stop you. In fact, if you can push back your fear and flirt with the outer edge of control, you'll find that mountain biking becomes a lot easier.

Dilemma: "I'm lifting weights, but my muscles don't seem much bigger."

Solution: The secret to building an impressive body, a veritable bikini magnet at the beach, is what is known as the muscle confusion principle. As nationally ranked powerlifter Barney Groves, Ph.D., a professor of physical education at Virginia Commonwealth University in Richmond and co-author of *Weight Training*, explains, by varying the intensity and the amount of weight being lifted, "you keep the muscles a little confused, a little sore, so they're always adapting and growing." Here's the program.

First phase: Do 12 to 15 repetitions of each exercise in your workout regimen, using 65 to 70 percent of your maximum liftable weight for each. You should just be able to get that last rep up. Do this three to four weeks, increasing the weight slightly as you get stronger.

Second phase: Do eight to ten repetitions of each exercise with 80 to 85 percent of your maximum weight. Do this three to four more weeks, again adding an additional plate if you still have some strength remaining after the last rep.

Third phase: Do three to five repetitions with 85 to 95 percent of your maximum weight. This is the real strength-building part of the program. After three to four weeks, cycle back to the first phase, slightly increasing the weight that you originally used.

"I guarantee that you'll see improvement," says Dr. Groves. "But you also have to eat properly and get enough rest."

The biggest myth about nutrition and weight lifting, he says, is that you need lots of extra protein. "Protein is the building block of muscle," he explains. "But you get energy from carbohydrate. Without energy, you're not going to be able to take those blocks and build a skyscraper." Therefore, he recommends following the standard diet prescription of 60 percent carbohydrate, 25 percent fat, 15 percent protein.

Rest is also vital. Ideally, Dr. Groves says that you should work your upper body on Monday and Thursday and your lower body on Tuesday and Friday. "Exercise tears muscles down," he explains. "Proper rest, both in between workouts and at night, helps them recuperate and rebuild to a stronger level."

Dilemma: *"I'm exercising and losing weight, but my gut isn't getting any smaller."*

Solution: The first commandment of weight loss is this: "The first place thou hast gained weight is the last place thou shalt lose it."

Men start depositing fat around the abdomen as our metabolisms slow in our mid-twenties. Then it takes another decade for us to notice the belly roll and vow to do something about it. By this time, a few weeks on the "dreadmill" isn't going to evict the accumulated fat. According to Jerome Brandon, Ph.D., an exercise physiologist at Georgia State University in Atlanta, only these things will work.

Watch your fat intake. This advice isn't new, but a study at Vanderbilt University in Nashville has put an interesting twist on it. After overfeeding one group of men on fat and another on carbohydrate, researchers found that excess dietary fat is far more likely to be stored as stubborn body flab than excess carbohydrate, which ends up as energy-producing glycogen. This means that you don't have to be as uptight about watching your carbohydrate intake if you're exercising and trying to lose weight. In fact, if you're moderately active and limit your fat intake to 1 gram per kilogram of body weight each day (that's about 73 grams for a 160-pound guy), there's no evidence that you can voluntarily eat too many carbohydrate calories.

Strive for the zone. Maintaining at least 60 to 70 percent of maximum heart rate during aerobic exercise is best for burning fat. To approximate this pace without buying a heart rate monitor, make sure that you're running, cycling or stair climbing at a level that's strenuous, but not so tough that you can't carry on a conversation. Once in this zone, you'll be able to exercise longer and therefore burn more fat.

Strengthen your stomach. Part of the reason your middle is sagging is because the muscles there are weary of carrying so much luggage. You can make yourself look leaner by doing two simple exercises—the crunches and crossovers described earlier—to tone and strengthen your midsection. "Unfortunately, getting rid of a gut is a time-consuming thing," says Dr. Brandon. "You can't do it for a

JUST THE FACTS

Number of Americans who belong to health clubs: 20 million

few weeks or months and be done with it. It's a process, not a state."

Dilemma: "I've been in-line skating, but it never feels like I'm getting a good workout."

Solution: Because you're gliding, and therefore resting, between strokes, it takes about three times longer to derive the same benefit from skating that you would from other aerobic sports, says Joel Rappelfeld, author of *The Complete Blader*. For instance, if you're used to running for 20 minutes, then it'll take approximately an hour of skating to feel similarly spent.

But don't pitch your elbow pads just yet. Hills, of course, can dramatically raise your energy expenditure, but if there are none in your area or if you just aren't daring enough for high-speed descents, there are other ways to make your heart pump.

Simulate the gears on a bike. There are three basic skating styles: an upright figure-skating stance, a lower ice-hockey crouch and a very low speed-skating position. The farther you bend over, the better workout you'll get, since you create more resistance with longer strokes and use additional leg muscles to overcome it. "It's just like working the gears on a bicycle," says Rappelfeld. "Shift down for a better workout."

Mix in other exercises. For an innovative full-body workout, Rappelfeld suggests combining skating with other simple exercises. For instance, skate for ten minutes, then stop and do some crunches. Skate for ten minutes more, then try some push-ups. And since each skate weighs three to five pounds, you can even use them for leg lifts.

Dilemma: "No matter how much I work out, I never feel fit enough."

Solution: It used to be that this complaint was chiefly voiced by women, who were frustrated by the narrow-waisted ideal of their sex portrayed in *Cosmopolitan* and other media. But psychologists are now hearing the same concerns from men, who are feeling increasingly inferior to the lean, muscular model-boys in ads and movies.

"Fitness is a part of life," says Andrew Meyers, Ph.D., a clinical psychologist who has worked with Olympic athletes. To avoid frustration and dissatisfaction, you need to decide how important exercise or appearance really is. "You have to place it in context with the rest of the issues in your life, like family, job, friends and faith," says Dr. Meyers. "Then you can devise a pyramid of goals in any of these areas."

This is a strategy that he has used successfully with elite amateur weight lifters. For example, at the top of their pyramid was the dream goal of making the Olympics. Below it was the slightly more realistic goal of qualifying for the Olympic trials. Beneath this was a list of specific things they had to do during the next few months to make the trials. And at the base of the pyramid was the exact type of training, nutrition or rest they needed each day.

"I don't think you can be good at anything, whether it's sports, health or work, unless you have a goal structure," says Dr. Meyers. "Most men have dream goals, but they don't get around to building the supporting parts of the pyramid."

Fitness
Challenges

*Can You Handle
These Feats of Athleticism?*

Isaac Newton must have been a cross-trainer. Sure, it's easy to see how he got the gravity idea from a falling apple. But how about all those other scientific laws governing motion?

We think that he must have been out jogging after a couple of hours of calculus when he developed that basic principle of motion, which led to our understanding of momentum—you know, from 11th-grade physics: "A body in motion stays in motion . . . a body at rest, well, it forms indentations in the sofa cushions."

As you face the continuous struggle to find the time and momentum to stay in shape, we thought we'd help keep your body in motion with a little challenge. Actually, several little challenges. Each challenge is a new physical test, a dare, if you will. Something like "swim a mile." Then we offer a workout that will help you reach that goal within 30 days.

"Without a doubt, the best way to maintain interest in a fitness program over an extended length of time is to diversify your workout," says Herman Falsetti, M.D., a cardiologist from Irvine, California, who has worked as a training consultant to cyclists on the 1984, 1988 and 1992 U.S. Olympic teams.

And that's the terrific thing about the following program. You'll never get bored. Each goal builds on the last, so by the end of the program, you'll probably be in better shape than ever.

Start a Cross-Training Program

For the benefit of those who haven't broken a sweat in months, we'll begin slowly. Starting now and moving through the next challenge, you're going to create a foundation of fitness upon which to build. (But first, be sure to get your doctor's okay to start this or any conditioning program.)

Aerobic conditioning. The best way to get fit fast is to mix walking into an easy jogging workout, according to Budd Coates, a four-time Olympic marathon trials qualifier, who instructs a beginning running program at Rodale Press publishing company in Emmaus, Pennsylvania. "Novice runners make two mistakes," he explains. "First, they tend to think in mile increments instead of in minutes of running and, second, they try to run too fast."

Coates has designed a program that avoids these pitfalls. Don't worry about overlapping with the next few challenges. This plan fits nicely into the workouts designed for them.

Each week, do your run/walk workouts on Monday, Wednesday, Friday and Saturday, taking the other days off. The idea is to gradually build the number of minutes you run: For example, you start out by running two minutes and walking four, and doing that four more times. A chart of the whole plan is shown on page 114.

Strength conditioning. The goal here is to build some muscle mass and increase strength without spending a lot of time in the gym. You'll lift three days a week for only 30 minutes a session. How? By doing just one set of each lift.

"The research sug-

Run/Walk Workouts

Week	Minutes Run	Minutes Walked	Repetitions
1	2	4	5
2	3	3	5
3	5	2.5	4
4	7	3	3
5	8	2	3
6	9	2	2*
7	9	1	3
8	13	2	2
9	14	1	2
10	30	0	1

*Finish by running another 8 minutes.

gests that one good set of resistance exercise is as effective as two or three sets for producing significant strength gains," says Wayne L. Westcott, Ph.D., fitness/research director at the South Shore YMCA in Quincy, Massachusetts.

Do one set of 8 to 12 repetitions of each exercise, using 75 percent of your maximum resistance. In other words, if you can bench-press 100 pounds once, do your set with just 75 pounds on the bar. See the exercises described in "Strength Workout" on page 116.

Jump Rope for 15 Minutes

If you've never jumped rope before, you may think it's easy—schoolyard stuff. But it's one of the true tests of aerobic endurance. The first thing to do is get a jump rope that fits. According to champion rope-jumper Ken Solis, M.D., author of *Ropics*, you test a rope for fit by standing on its middle and checking to see that the handles reach almost to your armpits.

To jump properly, stand on a mat or wooden floor with your feet together in front of the rope. Your hands should be just below your waist, your elbows close to your sides. The trick is to use only your wrists and forearms to swing the rope over your head and down in front of you. Try it. As the rope falls in front of you, jump an inch off the floor so it can pass under. Land on the balls of your feet.

Once you have the rhythm, practice endurance, but start slowly. Jumping rope brings your heart rate up very quickly. If you haven't already gotten an okay from your doctor to embark on a vigorous plan of exercise, do so before continuing.

For the first week, try to jump rope for about 2 minutes without missing. Focus on technique: Stay on the balls of your feet so the impact is absorbed by your calves, rather than your shins and knees. Work in about 10 minutes of rope jumping a couple of times a week. Once you can jump 2 minutes without stopping, build to 5, then 10, then 15. And keep up with your lifting and running.

Bench-Press 20 Pounds More

It's fair to say that there are three measurements that every American male knows about himself—his shoe size, the length of his penis and his "max" in the bench press. Your goal this month is to increase your maximum bench press by 20 pounds.

"People think that you have to lift for hours four or five days a week to increase strength," says Greg O'Bryan, a Los Angeles–based trainer who works with Robin Williams and Victoria Jackson. "Actually, the muscle gets stronger during the rest process rather than the weight-lifting process, so you don't have to overdo it."

To give your chest muscles a boost without adding extra sets, do your bench presses in slow motion. Instead of lowering and raising the weight to four counts, take four seconds to lower the weight and ten seconds to press it up. You use more muscle fibers more intensely by going slowly, according to Ken Hutchins, author of *Super Slow: The Ultimate Exercise Protocol*. Studies done by the

Strength Workout

Bench press. Lie on your back on a bench with your feet flat on the floor. Hold the barbell at arm's length above you with your hands a few inches wider than your shoulders. Lower the bar to your chest, then push it up to arm's length.

Military press. Stand facing a squat rack with a barbell resting on it at shoulder height. With feet shoulder-width apart and hands a little wider than that, lift the bar and rest it at the top of your chest, just below shoulder height. Slowly press it overhead.

Front squat. Stand facing a barbell on the squat rack, legs shoulder-width apart and feet pointing straight ahead. Cross your arms in front of you, palms facing in. With your hands about ten inches apart, step in and lift the bar so that it rests across your chest. Keeping your back straight and head up, squat until your upper thighs are almost parallel to the floor. Pause and straighten up.

Triceps extension. Lie on your back on a bench, with your head resting on it. Hold a barbell with a narrow grip (about six inches wide), palms facing up. Extend your arms so that the bar is above you. This is the starting position. Slowly bend your

YMCA have shown that men who lifted less weight, but took longer to lift, increased strength faster than men using normal lifting technique.

To try the slow method, trim about 30 percent off the weight you normally lift. Do four to eight repetitions. This is tough to master at first, so be sure to use a spotter. At the end of each week, test your maximum. By following this program, you should be able to add five to seven more pounds to the bar each week.

Play Basketball Each Week

Thanks to the jogging and rope-jumping that you've been doing, you should be able to make it through a full-court game without

elbows, bringing the bar toward your forehead. Press it up, following the same path.

Calf raise. Grasp a bar and rest it on the back of your shoulders. Your feet should be about 12 inches apart, toes pointing straight ahead. Slowly push up on your toes, raising your heels as far as you can. At the top, pause a second, then slowly lower your heels.

Biceps curl. Hold a barbell with palms up, hands about 18 inches apart. Keeping your elbows at your sides, curl the bar until your forearms touch your biceps. Then slowly lower the bar.

Upright row. Stand and hold the barbell with your hands three to four inches apart, palms down. Allow the bar to rest against your thighs. Pull it straight up until it nearly touches your chin. Keeping the bar close to your body, pause, then lower it to your thighs.

Crunches. Lie on your back with your legs bent at a 90-degree angle, feet flat on the floor. Touching your ears lightly with your fingertips, curl up until your shoulders rise four to six inches off the floor.

sucking wind. If you can't rustle up enough friends for a weekly game, go to the health club, the local YMCA or playground to find a game.

To improve your quickness, lateral movement and jumping ability, we suggest a couple of exercises.

The obstacle jump: Place a shoebox on the ground and stand with your feet together next to it. Now jump sideways across the box. As soon as you touch down, jump back. Jump as high as you can. Do two sets of five, resting between sets. Each week this month, add five repetitions. This is one of the best drills for building leg power.

The second exercise is the classic box drill: Mark off a 15- by 15-foot box on a blacktop. Starting in the bottom-left corner of the box, sprint to the top-left corner and tap the corner with your left hand. Sidestep to the right corner, keeping your feet spread. Touch down with your right hand, then backpedal to the bottom-right corner and touch it with your right hand. Finally, shuffle laterally to the bottom-left corner and touch down with your left hand. Repeat in the opposite direction.

The best thing to do to improve your technique is to play a lot, says Tom Danley, who has run basketball camps in southern California for more than 20 years. "Keep your game as simple as possible," he says. "Execution breaks down when you try to get too fancy."

Run a 10-K

Thirty days isn't enough time for the average Joe to prepare for this 6.2-mile race, especially if the course has hills. But if you followed the running program and played basketball once a week, you're ready. Increase your running to five days a week, following this four-week schedule.

Week 1

Sunday: Run for 30 to 45 minutes at an easy pace that's slow enough so you can carry on a conversation with a partner.

Monday: Rest.

Tuesday: Run easily for ten minutes to warm up. Next, quicken your pace for five minutes, then jog for five minutes, speed up for another five, then slow down a bit for five minutes. Finally, cool down with ten minutes of easy jogging.

Wednesday and Thursday: Run easily for 15 to 30 minutes.

Friday: Take a ten-minute warm-up jog. Then run up a 100- to 200-yard hill at a modest pace five times, and at your race pace five times, recovering with a slow jog on the way down. Finish with a ten-minute cooldown.

Saturday: Rest.

JUST THE FACTS

Number of sweat glands that are found on your feet: 250,000

Weeks 2 and 3

Repeat the week 1 workout, but increase your Sunday runs by 15 minutes each week, picking up your pace slightly.

Week 4

Sunday: Run for 45 to 60 minutes at an easy pace.
Monday: Rest.
Tuesday: Warm up for ten minutes. Alternate two minutes of race-pace running with three minutes of easy jogging for three cycles. Cool down for ten minutes.
Wednesday: Rest.
Thursday and Friday: 15 to 30 minutes of easy running.
Saturday: Rest or jog easily for ten minutes to keep your legs loose.
Sunday: Race day.
Some tips on racing smart: Above all, don't start out too fast. The idea is to cover the distance, not finish in the top ten. If you're gasping for breath, it's okay to walk awhile; many runners do in a race this long. You can always pick up your pace as you approach the finish. Okay, you only have 200 yards to go and you're feeling strong. Start your kick. To eke more speed out of your body, try this trick: Pick a runner 20 yards in front of you and hunt him down like a greyhound after a rabbit. Blow past him to the finish line. Once you cross the line, grab a victory water and walk for five to ten minutes.

Improve Your Golf Game

If you're lucky, you get in one or two games of golf each week. Most of us don't, and yet we expect to play skillfully at the company tournament. It doesn't work that way, unless you're an undiscovered John Daly.

But there are simple exercises and drills that you can do at home, at the driving range and on the course that can help you knock strokes off your game, says golf instructor Jim McLean, author of *The Putter's Pocket Companion.*

At home: Putt in your living room a couple of nights a week. You don't need a green and a cup; just practice keeping your clubface aimed correctly. To do this, stick a length of masking tape to the rug and putt balls along the line. If the ball follows the line, you know your clubface is steady. Next, hit 25 putts into a bedpost that is about three feet away. Concentrate on keeping your knees still and accelerating the putter toward the target.

On the driving range: Pretend that you're on the golf course. This means mimicking everything you do when you swing on the course. After every ball you hit, change clubs and aim at a different target.

"Some players have a range game, and they can't take anything to the course," says McLean. This drill helps you simulate course play in practice.

Before you play: Practice putting and chipping before you go to the driving range. "Most people warm up in the opposite order," says McLean. "They go from the practice green straight to tee-off, and they're cold and tight—it's been 20 minutes since they've driven a ball." Instead, start at the practice green, using 25 percent of your preplay time to work on long and short putts and chipping. Then go to the driving range just before teeing off.

During play: "Tension kills the golf swing," says McLean. "You have to relax your shoulders and arms." To loosen up, twist your trunk a few times with the club resting across your shoulders, lift the club far over your head to stretch your shoulders and arms, and take practice swings, working from small ones to full swings.

Swim a Mile

Assuming that you haven't forgotten how to swim, this program will turn you into a tuna in 30 days.

Find a 25-yard lap pool; swim one length and count your strokes. "If you take more than 20 armstrokes, you should improve your stroke efficiency first," says Terry Laughlin, director of Total Immersion national swimming camps for adults, based in Goshen, New York. "For novices, swimming is at least 80 percent proper mechanics. It's not swimming faster; it's swimming easier."

The keys are keeping your hips and legs from dragging, and

lengthening your stroke. "Try leaning on your chest more so that it feels as if you're swimming downhill," Laughlin says. "That'll keep your hips and legs near the surface so that you'll be more streamlined."

Two tricks for lengthening your stroke: (1) As each arm enters the water, reach—just as you would for something on a high shelf—before starting your pull. (2) Roll your hips from side to side with each stroke. "Your hips, not shoulders, are your engine," Laughlin says.

To do the workout, swim one or two lengths practicing the moves mentioned above, then rest. Repeat this routine for 30 to 40 minutes three times a week. When you can swim 100 yards in 80 strokes or less, you can start building sets of 100-yard repeats, resting for 15 to 30 seconds between 100-yard swims. Once you can swim about 18 of these, you're ready to attempt a mile swim. That's 1,760 yards or 71 laps in a 25-yard pool. To beat the boredom of lap swimming, swim your mile in a lake, with a buddy rowing a boat ahead of you for safety. For more information on Total Immersion workshops or a video on proper stroke technique, call 1-800-609-7946.

Learn to Juggle

Every man should be able to juggle, if only to impress women and amuse children at family reunions. So give your body a break after months of these hard challenges. Relax and exercise your hand-eye coordination. As a side benefit, juggling is a superb stress reducer.

First, get three weighted juggling balls or beanbags (nothing that will bounce). Now find a spot to practice. Standing in front of a bed is a smart idea; you won't have to stoop to pick up dropped balls.

JUST THE FACTS

You are almost twice as likely to be killed while walking with your back to traffic as you are when facing traffic, according to the National Safety Council.

Imagine an X that crosses the upper half of your body, with the intersection just above chin level. You'll want to follow this X pattern as you throw the balls. Aim for a point above your opposite shoulder and throw strongly enough to reach above forehead height.

For starters, practice with only one ball. Toss it back and forth between your hands. Try to make the ball follow the same path each time, a gentle curve. Keep your hands about waist level. Don't reach to catch the ball; let it fall into your hand. Keep your hands relaxed. Let your wrists do the work.

Next, try the two-ball pattern. Put a ball in each palm. Toss one from the left hand. Just as it reaches its peak and begins to drop, toss the other from the right. Catch ball 1 with the right hand; catch ball 2 with your left. Freeze. Check your position. Do it again. Once you feel comfortable with this toss, try to keep it going for a few minutes.

The three-ball cascade adds one more step. Start with two balls in one hand and toss one of those to start. As that ball reaches your opposite shoulder point, toss ball 2 from your other hand, leaving that hand free to catch the first ball.

Remember, the next ball you toss is always the one underneath the ball in the air. As ball 2 descends, toss the third ball and catch ball 2. Freeze and check your position after each three-toss cycle. After you get the hang of it, try adding more tosses until you can keep the juggling going. To find expert help, call the International Jugglers Association at (413) 367-2401 for a juggling club in your area.

PART 4

Disease-Free

Hot Health Facts

We've searched through hundreds of documents for the latest medical research. Here are the most important findings.

1. Ulcers. A simple breath test—blowing air into a bag— shows doctors if a patient's ulcer is caused by the bacterium *Helicobacter pylori*. The treatment is antibiotics.

2. Sex. A Swedish survey of 85-year-old married men found that 22 percent of them reported still having sex.

3. Accidents. Just 50 minutes a month on a car phone can increase the likelihood of an accident fivefold.

4. Stroke. Men who drink more than 4.7 cups of black tea a day may reduce their risk of stroke by 69 percent, compared with those who drink less than 2.6 cups.

5. Aging. A British study found that as men age, their ears grow an average of 0.008 inch each year. Over a 50-year span, that's more than one-third of an inch.

6. Impotence. A pill that restores full function to impotent men could be offered for sale by 1997. The drug, called sildenfil, is taken an hour or so before it is needed. Side effects are minor: headache, muscle soreness and stomach upset.

7. Alzheimer's disease. Preliminary reports suggest Advil, Motrin and Nuprin—which contain ibuprofen—may reduce the risk of developing this disease by 30 to 60 percent.

8. Alcohol. Moderate amounts of alcohol, no more than two drinks a day, may lower the risk of heart attack.

9. Teeth. Three-dimensional glasses that are twin TV screens in a headset will soon be available at dentists' offices.

10. Vaccines. Experimental vaccines on the horizon include: cholesterol, herpes, Lyme disease, melanoma and AIDS.

Pre-launch Checklist

Get Your Day off to a Healthy Start

Ask any physician worth his weight in golf clubs and he'll probably admit that what he can do for you has a lot to do with what you can do for yourself. An ophthalmologist can't restore your sight if you ignore your failing vision for too long. A dermatologist can't cure a melanoma once it's the size of Texas. The only way that they can help you is if you come to them as soon as you notice a problem.

And the only way that you will notice problems quickly is if you check for them—regularly. Very regularly, in fact, because to know what's abnormal, you also have to know what's normal. And the best time to do a quick health check is in the morning.

Think about it: You're rested. You're relaxed. You're buck-naked. And since you haven't yet filled your body with coffee, medications or the stress of daily life, the early morning provides you with the truest measurement of your overall health. So while you're spending time showering, shaving and combing into fine form, why not spend a few extra minutes making sure that your body actually works just as good as it looks? Here's the drill.

First Things First

You open your eyes and hit the alarm clock. What next? Bound out of bed? Roll over and go back to sleep? We have a third choice.

Check your pulse. "The first thing in the morning is the best time to check your baseline pulse because you haven't performed pulse-raising physical activities," says Robert Rosenson, M.D., cardiologist and director of the Preventive Cardiology Center at Rush–Presbyterian–St. Luke's Medical Center in Chicago. Your resting pulse rate is one of the best indicators of your aerobic fitness.

Sit up in bed and hold your left wrist in front of you, palm up. Place the first and second fingers of your right hand on your wrist, just below the thumb. You'll feel a groove between the wrist bone and the large tendon that connects to the thumb; that's where you'll get the best pulse. (If you're taking your pulse at your neck, don't put too much pressure on the carotid artery—it could leave you light-headed.) Count the beats for 20 seconds and multiply by three for your baseline pulse. Then rate your fitness according to the chart below.

50 or less	You're in excellent physical condition
51–65	Not bad
66–79	You could stand a little more exercise
Over 80	Pal, you're out of shape

In the Bathroom

After you've waited for the wife and kids to perform their daily bathroom rituals, it's your turn. So when you finally get in, take advantage of it.

Empty your bladder. You were way ahead of us on this one, weren't you? But from now on, we want you to think of a trip to the bathroom as an affirmation of your health and vitality. If all goes full stream ahead, great. But keep an eye out for a few things: color, for instance. If you urinate clear, you're in the clear. If you urinate yellow, you're dehydrated—drink some water, pronto. But the primary colors to worry about are blood red and cloudy white. Both may indicate kidney stones or a bladder infection, although red can mean bruised kidneys or even prostate problems. Either way, get to a doctor.

And speaking of the prostate, any trouble starting or sustaining the urine flow can mean benign prostate enlargement, a problem that hits one in seven men beyond age 40. If the problem becomes an annoyance, consult your doctor.

Weigh in. If you have a scale, hop on it. See that weight there?

That's not your real weight. That's your weight right now, but perform this same task tomorrow and you could be up or down two pounds or more. What you want to do is to establish some sort of norm. Weigh yourself every morning for a week, then find the average. That's your real weight. Once you know it, you can be on the lookout for unusual changes in it. If you notice any unexplained gains or losses from one week to another, there are three things to do.

■ *Look out for stress.* It makes some guys lose their appetite and others eat ravenously. If you just got a divorce, a pink slip or an eviction notice, a sudden weight loss or gain is not so mysterious, says Jonathan Robison, Ph.D., executive co-director of the Michigan Center for Preventive Medicine in Lansing.

■ *Look in your medicine cabinet.* Medications such as prednisone and some antiseizure or antidepressant drugs can stimulate appetite, slow the metabolism or allow calories to be more easily stored as fat.

■ *Get looked over by your doctor.* Many health problems, from thyroid disorders to tuberculosis, can result in fluctuations in weight. If you can't explain it away, have it checked out.

Examine your peepers in the mirror. They look okay? About the same as yesterday? Good. But keep a watch out for these problems.

■ *Bags under your eyes.* Here's one of the warning signs of high blood pressure. But before you get all worked up about them, take a look at your dad. Bags under the eyes can be just another genetic blessing, much like male-pattern baldness.

■ *Color changes.* Chronic inflammation of the eye can turn brown or blue irises green, but a melanoma in the eye can also cause a color change, says Richard Ruiz, M.D., chairman of the Department of

Ophthalmology at the University of Texas at Houston. It's not something that occurs overnight, but it is something that can be caught in the mirror and should always be examined further.

- *Puffiness.* Assuming that you haven't been worshiping the gods of barley the night before, abnormal puffiness in the lids could be a sign of chronic heart problems or kidney problems. Again, it's something that you'd want to have looked at by a professional.

Check your mouth. Here's how to tell if there's too much stress in your life: Open wide and gaze in the mirror. Inspect the gums and the inside of your lips and cheeks. What you're looking for are cold sores. These small, white, nonthreatening ulcerations are caused by a return appearance of the chicken pox virus you had as a child, explains Bruce Campbell, M.D., associate professor and vice-chairman of otolaryngology at the Medical College of Wisconsin in Milwaukee. The virus hangs out in your body and, on occasion, especially during times of stress, manifests itself as a sore.

While you're in there, look for any unusual red or white discolorations, ulcerations or lumps and bumps that last for more than ten days, says J. William Robbins, D.D.S., director of the program for advanced education in general dentistry at the University of Texas Health Science Center at San Antonio. These are signs of oral cancer, a disease that's easy to spot and treatable if caught early. Check under and around the tongue and at the back of the mouth where the soft and hard palates meet.

Under the Nozzle

Having dispensed with the basic morning necessities, it's time for the more sublime—that is, the shower. And what better place to see how fine a voice you're in?

Vocalize. Belt out a tune. If your voice sounds clear, great. If you sound like a scratchy Rod Stewart album, what you likely have is reflux, the same thing that causes heartburn. Stomach acids are backing up into your lower throat and bathing your vocal cords while you sleep. This is bad, since over time they can cause permanent damage to your voice. Try sleeping with the head of your bed up on a few bricks, says Dr. Campbell. It will allow gravity to help keep the acids where they can't reach your esophagus and vocal cords.

Make an inspection down below. Before getting out of the shower, do a testicular self-exam. You're naked anyway, and the warm water helps make the scrotum more supple and relaxed. Although testicular cancer is rare, it still ranks as the number one solid cancer in males up to the age of 35.

Roll each testicle between your thumb and the first two fingers of your hand, feeling for any lumps, hardness or other irregularities. Except for the epididymis, you should feel only the smooth surface of the testicles. Also be sure to note any pain or sensation of heaviness.

Before Getting Dressed

Dry off. There are still two things that bear investigation.

Give your skin the once-over. Look for changes in the size or color of a mole, or for once-circular moles that have developed an irregular outline. Be especially vigilant if there's a history of melanoma in your family. And don't limit your search to the ones that you can easily see. Use a hand mirror in conjunction with a full-length mir.or to check your back.

Put on a shirt. Even if you lift weights, your neck size isn't going to increase significantly in the course of a month. So if you put on your shirt in the morning and the collar is too tight, it could signify a thyroid-related problem in the lower neck, says Dr. Campbell. While you're there, run your hand up underneath your jawbone and along the big muscle that runs from below the ear to the collarbone. What you're looking for is unusual swelling, a marked difference from one side to the other or any unexplainable changes that might signal an infection or the beginning of a goiter.

Having done this, you're finally ready for work. Just remember to put on some pants before you walk out the door, okay?

The Truth about Teeth

Answers to Common Dental Questions

Most men hate going to the dentist. They don't like hearing the sound of high-speed drills or seeing a trayful of potential torture devices. There's also something highly unsettling about having a long, latex-clad finger in their mouths.

These are just a few of the things that make men cling to that dentist's chair as if it were the front car of a rickety roller coaster. When it comes to keeping teeth healthy, men just want honest, straightforward advice that will not only shorten this plunge into the abscessed abyss but also forestall the next ride.

So we went to John Dodes, D.D.S., chairman of the National Council Against Health Fraud's task force on misinformation in dentistry, located in Woodhaven, New York. He's been practicing for 25 years and has a refreshing skepticism about many of the things his counterparts foist on patients. So sit back and relax. This isn't going to hurt a bit.

Q How often do you need to visit a dentist?

A Some tooth sleuths are now encouraging patients to schedule appointments every three to four months rather than the standard six. Dr. Dodes says that if you're below age 65 and in good oral health, an annual cleaning and exam is all that you need.

Q What should a routine exam consist of?

A *X-rays.* A full set of "molaroids" taken every five to seven years so that the dentist can inspect the roots of your teeth and check for cysts and tumors. Bite-wing x-rays should be taken annually to gauge decay between teeth and bone loss.

A full cancer screening, which involves the dentist checking your tongue, mouth and throat for abnormalities.

Periodontal screening, where the dentist searches for bone loss by using a small probe to measure gaps between the teeth and gums, and a complete cleaning.

Q Are x-rays safe?

A Absolutely. According to the American Dental Association (ADA), a typical full-mouth x-ray delivers 13 millirems of radiation. To put this in perspective, federal and most state regulations permit a person to receive 5,000 millirems of radiation per year. In fact, you naturally absorb about 300 millirems annually just being outdoors.

As a result, the risk of developing cancer from a dental x-ray is infinitesimal. Nevertheless, Dr. Dodes says, you should protect yourself from possible equipment malfunction by wearing a lead apron. "If your dentist doesn't offer you one, find another dentist," he says.

Q If x-rays are so safe, why does everyone leave the room when they're taken?

A Even though an x-ray exposes the dentist and staff to less radiation than the patient, they take x-rays many times a day. Over time, this could add up to a potentially harmful dose.

Q Do you really have to floss?

A Yes, even if you go to the dentist every six months. "It's more important than brushing," says Dr. Dodes, "because most dental disease begins between the teeth, and no bristle can get in there."

In addition to dislodging debris, flossing fights bacterial growth by oxygenating the tooth surface and making it less sticky. It's best to floss once a day before bedtime, since there is less bacteria-slaying saliva in your mouth while you are snoring.

The best type of floss to use depends on your teeth. If yours are uneven or fairly close together, choose a thin, waxed brand. Or try one of the new high-tech types. Glide is a flat floss made of Gore-Tex, so it won't shred if it gets caught between your molars. Oral-B Ultra Floss is made of interwoven fibers, so it stretches and flattens when you pull it.

Q What's the best toothbrush?

A Any brand with soft, small-diameter bristles. The shape, size and design really don't matter much. The important thing is that it's labeled "soft." Otherwise, you'll be brushing away tooth and gum surfaces along with those bothersome specks of caviar.

And don't only scrub up and down. That's a vestige from the days of hard-bristle brushes that would abrade the teeth if used otherwise. Brush in all directions, once in the morning and once at night.

Q What's the best toothpaste?

A Buy the least expensive fluoride-containing brand that has the ADA's seal of approval. "The ADA has very specific criteria for particle size, abrasiveness and flavor," says Dr. Dodes. "If they've certified it, you know that it's safe. In fact, all ADA-approved toothpastes are just about identical."

Q Do adults need fluoride?

A Yes. Although it won't become part of the tooth, as it does in youngsters, it will help fight decay. Fluoride lowers the tooth's surface energy, so food particles don't adhere to it as readily—"just like Teflon," says Dr. Dodes.

Q What about mouthwash?

A If you floss and brush regularly, that's all you need to keep your mouth fresh, says Dr. Dodes. In fact, some research shows that chronic users of mouthwash with a high alcohol content may be at risk for developing oral cancer.

Q Do over-the-counter plaque rinses work?

A Essentially, no. Dr. Dodes explains that such rinsing agents have no effect on debris under the gums, and that's where the problems begin. "They're no more effective than brushing and rinsing with water," he says.

Q Is it wise to have your wisdom teeth pulled?

A Before letting your dentist torque any chops, be sure your molars are maladjusted. A wisdom tooth needs to be yanked only if: (a) it's surrounded by a fluid-filled sac that's enlarging into a cyst, (b) it's growing into the tooth in front of it or (c) it's only partially broken through the gum and is causing infection.

If you're not experiencing any pain and are skeptical of a diagnosis, ask the dentist to point out the specific problems on an x-ray or get a second opinion. "Unfortunately, extraction is a big part of many practices," says Dr. Dodes. "When you think of your wisdom teeth, think of your appendix. Just because other people have it removed doesn't mean that you have to."

Q Is bonding as great as it sounds?

A Yes and no. Bonding is a safe, useful technique for repairing chipped, broken or discolored front teeth. In some cases, a composite material is molded to the tooth,

while in others a piece of porcelain is glued on in much the same way as a fake fingernail is attached.

"It's a great way to correct simple cosmetic defects," says Dr. Dodes, "but it's not appropriate for complicated cases. Bonding is being promoted by some dentists as a substitute for crowns and an alternative to orthodontics."

In other words, when teeth are loose or poorly positioned, bonding is akin to putting an adhesive bandage on a broken arm. The bonding material, however, is not as durable as silver, gold or porcelain, so it will eventually have to be reapplied.

Q Are lasers better than drills?

A Not necessarily. Although the laser's potential is great and it lacks the fingernails-on-a-chalkboard screech, the dentist must be adept at using one, and the patient has to be very relaxed. "If you hiccup, you have a hole in your cheek," says Dr. Dodes. "The drill is much easier to control."

Dr. Dodes points out that lasers are approved by the Food and Drug Administration for soft-tissue (that is, gum) surgery only. "Although using them on hard tissue (tooth and bone) is not illegal because of a loophole in the law, it is experimental," he explains. "A laser uses high-energy photons to burn tiny amounts of tissue. No one knows how a tooth reacts to that in the long term."

Q Are there other treatments to be wary of?

A Generally, dentists make most of their money on fillings and crowns. If either is recommended by your lifelong family dentist, you probably don't have to second-guess him. But if your recent diagnosis for a full set of crowns coincides with Dr. Drillem's purchase of a new Ferrari, then get a second opinion or at least ask the twin questions: "Do I really need this?" and "What are my options?"

Other things to watch for include:

Air abrasion. A harmless tooth stain is often portrayed as a future cavity and then sandblasted and filled. "It's needless," says Dr. Dodes. Don't agree to a filling unless there's a cavity (not just a stain) present.

Electronic anesthesia. "It's time-consuming, expensive and unpredictable," Dr. Dodes says of the procedure that involves passing a mild electrical current through the gums to anesthetize the nerves. You're better off taking a needle, which should be barely perceptible.

Implants. This is the practice of drilling into the jawbone to make an anchor for an artificial tooth, commonly done after a tooth is knocked out or too badly damaged to reconstruct. The problem, says Dr. Dodes, is that any dentist can watch a video and attempt it. "There's no certification," he explains, "so ask how many your dentist has done."

Replacing silver fillings. Despite all the hubbub, including a segment on *60 Minutes*, Dr. Dodes says that there's no solid evidence that mercury in silver fillings is dangerous. So don't let your dentist replace them.

Q Is it okay to get a second opinion?

A "Yes!" says Dr. Dodes. "It amazes me that people will get a second, third, even fourth opinion on minor medical things like blood pressure medication, but if their dentist tells them that they must have their teeth pulled and replaced with bone from their ribs, they say, 'Okay, when do we start?' Get another opinion."

Q How can you impress a beautiful dental hygienist when your mouth is full of clamps?

A Two secrets, says Dr. Dodes. "Try not to whine too much, and learn sign language."

Listen to Your Body

The Right Way to Treat Symptoms

A walk down the aisle of your neighborhood drugstore tells a lot about modern medicine. Row upon row of slickly packaged pills, syrups and ointments vie for your attention, each offering stronger, quicker and longer-lasting relief than its competitors.

Unfortunately, in some cases they offer relief from the very things that your body does to protect itself. Nobody has come up with a way to cure, for example, the common cold. But what the major drug companies have done is create a bunch of "cures" for cold and flu symptoms, which, at first, sounds pretty good.

But the truth is that many of these symptoms are there for a reason: to tell you that something's wrong. "Cure" the symptom and ignore the cause, and you could find yourself laid up longer than necessary. We're not saying that feeling bad is good for you—just that sometimes you should listen when your body's trying to tell you something.

Expel the Invaders

Think of the cough as nature's way of hustling rowdy visitors from your lungs and spewing them all over the place. It's a surprisingly complex response, involving coordinated muscle contractions of the diaphragm, chest and voice box to create a forceful exhalation.

The first thing to know about coughs is that there are two types: nonproductive coughs—dry tickles triggered by colds, dust and pollen in the air, even heartburn—and productive coughs—phlegm-producers caused by respiratory infections.

What you shouldn't do: Down tablespoons of heavy-duty cough suppressants. The active ingredient that you want to stay away from is dextromethorphan. Suppressants short-circuit the brain signals that control your urge to cough.

"I have strong feelings about this one," says Richard Sheldon, M.D., a pulmonologist with the Beaver Medical Group in Banning, California. "If you're coughing up matter, you need to let your body do its work." Stop this process, and all the troublemakers stay right down in your lungs, where they can breed, prosper and set the stage for a nasty secondary infection.

What you should do: Look for an over-the-counter remedy that says "expectorant"—the active ingredient will be guaifenesin, a chemical that liquefies the crud down there and makes it easier to cough up. Drink lots of fluids to thin out the mucus. See your doctor if your cough persists for longer than two weeks or if you are coughing up anything that isn't white or clear.

Let It Run Its Course

Having the runs is sort of like coughing, only upside down. The thunder within is your body's attempt to rid itself of an infection or irritation in the intestines, notes Asher Kornbluth, M.D., a gastroenterologist and an assistant clinical professor of medicine at Mount Sinai Medical Center in New York City. It's often triggered by some type of viral infection, but you can bring it on yourself—and not just by overdoing it at all-you-can-eat wing night. Other causes include: antibiotics (which destroy the protective bacteria residing in your bowels), too much magnesium (from overuse of antacids) and sometimes even anxiety caused by performance reviews, tax audits and imminent matrimony (one more reason why you should buy, not rent, a tuxedo).

What you shouldn't do: In most cases it's best to ride out the runs. Stifling them with antidiarrheals may actually prolong the duration of an infection, says Raymond Rubin, M.D., a gastroenterologist with Atlanta Gastroenterology Associates. Remember that there are worse ways to spend a weekend than running to and from the bathroom.

What you should do: Use a gentle remedy such as Kaopectate, which contains attapulgite, a mineral found in clay. Its bulk naturally slows intestinal movement, and the mineral binds with the toxins to keep them from being absorbed. Dr. Rubin also recommends fruit juices, flat cola and sports drinks (such as Gatorade) diluted to half-strength with water as sources of electrolytes and sugar (which help the body absorb needed salt). See your doctor, he says, if you're still trotting after three or four days.

Stay Active

You did a dumb thing: wrenched your back by bending at the waist to heft that case of beer when you should have lifted it with your legs. When you hurt your back, your instincts tell you to baby it, take it easy and move slowly and cautiously to minimize the pain and damage. But as much as they hurt, most back injuries aren't the crippling kind. Simple back pain from muscle strain will usually go away in a day or two, say doctors at the Texas Back Institute in Plano.

What you shouldn't do: Quit exercising, stop having sex, lower yourself into a bed full of pillows to immobilize your back and stay there for hours watching The Weather Channel.

What you should do: Ease up a bit but stay active to keep your strained muscles limber. Immobilizing yourself will only make muscles tighter and may prolong your pain. The government's current treatment guidelines recommend light exercise, not bed rest, for simple back pain.

Crank Up the Heat

The great thing about a fever is that it offers objective proof that you're sick. There's a nice heft to a number like 102. Nobody questions it when you call in sick with that kind of backup.

But a fever isn't just a symptom; it's your body's way of killing invaders. Here's what's happening: When your white blood cells detect an infection, they respond by releasing chemical messengers called endogenous pyrogens. The hypothalamus, the part of your brain that controls the thermostat, gets the message and raises the temperature of your body, making it a less hospitable place for invading organisms. (This is good to know, because when you call your boss and tell him that you have not only endogenous pyrogens invading your hypothalamus but also a fever, he'll insist that you stay home and keep away from him.)

What you shouldn't do: Go on about your life as if it's an ordinary day. A fever is a signal that you need to take it easy so that your body can devote all its energy to fending off an infection, says Joseph DeVito, M.D., an internist and a clinical instructor in medicine at New York University Medical Center in New York City.

What you should do: While there's probably little harm in easing your discomfort with aspirin or acetaminophen, you'd be best off doing what your body wants you to do: Lie in bed, moan and channel surf. So relax.

Note: If you're under 21, do not take aspirin for fever because of the danger of Reye's syndrome, a potentially fatal brain disease.

Fevers up to 101°F without any major symptoms are generally harmless if you're an otherwise healthy adult. Drink plenty of fluids, eat when you're hungry and soak up all the pity you can. If, however, the fever lasts more than a day or rises above 101°F, call your doctor for reinforcements.

Deal with It

Stressed out? Maybe it's good for you. Anxiety is a natural part of life and one we ought to be glad we have. Think of it as your brain's self-preservation system, one of the main reasons that your ancestors furthered their genetic line while others of their ilk wound up as lunch. In their book, *Why We Get Sick*, physician Randolph Nesse, M.D., and biologist George Williams, Ph.D., note that, a few years ago, researchers demonstrated this point when they separated guppies into groups of timid, ordinary and bold fish, based on how the fish responded to a smallmouth bass. Each group was then left in a tank with the bass. After 60 hours, 40 percent of the timid survived; all of the bold had disappeared.

There's a lesson in this. Most of us are a little nervous, like those timid guppies. But that little bit of anxiety just might keep us from being eaten. Too much anxiety—that's what gets us into trouble.

What you shouldn't do: Ignore what's making you anxious. Whether your medication of choice is Valium or vodka gimlets, you're treating only the symptoms, not the stress itself. Besides, "existential, Woody Allen–type anxiety about the world or your job" is natural, says Ichiro Kawachi, M.D., an internist and epidemiologist at the Harvard School of Public Health.

What you should do: Learn to control how you react to stress, says Jerome Markovitz, M.D., an assistant professor of preventive medicine at the University of Alabama at Birmingham. "For mild anxiety from everyday stress, I tell people to sit by themselves in a quiet room for ten minutes a day and do diaphragmatic breathing, which is a fancy word for making sure your stomach goes in and out. And 90 percent of why it works has nothing to do with the technique, but just the simple act of taking a few minutes for yourself to relax. It's harder and harder for people to do that these days."

If, on the other hand, you are so anxious that you can't sleep or cope with challenges you've met before, or if your anxiety is preventing you from doing some of the things that you want to do (if you're too nervous to go to a party without a drink beforehand, for

JUST THE FACTS

A *Men's Health*/CNN survey found that only 43 percent of men are concerned about testicular cancer.

example, or if you want to make a sensible career move but are too afraid to pull the trigger), Dr. Markovitz says that it's time to seek some professional advice.

Feel the Pain

You go for a three-mile run for the first time in four months. The next day, it takes you an hour to limp from the bed to the shower. Your body is screaming at you. Listen to it.

"There's a very fine line between what you need to do to build up a muscle and overdoing it to the point of damage," says orthopedist Ben Kibler, M.D., vice-president of the American College of Sports Medicine in Indianapolis. When you exercise, your muscles build up lactic acid, a natural irritant. A well-trained muscle tends to reduce the buildup of lactic acid and flush it out more effectively. An out-of-shape muscle spends more time clearing it out and recovering.

What you shouldn't do: Take a painkiller, such as aspirin or ibuprofen, before exercising. A little muscle soreness while you're exercising is okay, says Dr. Kibler. But if you have pain severe enough to make you want to pop a pill or use one of those rub-on creams, don't even think about working out. There is a very real danger of doing more damage if you mask the pain.

What you should do: Wait a day or two before exercising to let your muscles recover, and take it easier during your next workout. If the pain feels like it is in a joint or bone—that is, if it's deep and aching rather than shallow and throbbing, if it wakes you up at night or is accompanied by swelling—you've done some damage to yourself and should seek help, advises Edward J. Resnick, M.D., professor of orthopedic surgery at Temple University in Philadelphia.

Nature's Medicines

Herbs You Should Take Notice Of

By now you're used to seeing natural-supplement ads in magazines or hearing radio commercials for herbal remedies during the morning rush hour. They give you the distinct impression that modern medicine is nothing but a big drug-company scam and that, left to her own devices, Mother Nature can cure just about anything from headaches to bad hair days. Heck, if you're lucky, there might even be a weed out there that'll cure Uncle Ralph's preoccupation with line dancing.

But what all these ads seem to lack is the research to back their claims. So we started digging. And what we discovered, surprisingly, are a few positive scientific studies that suggest that some of these herbs may be effective at treating some of man's garden-variety ailments.

Yeah, we're skeptics, but when the guys in the white coats start getting excited, well, we're more than willing to listen. Below, we list some of the areas where herbal cures hold promise—and we've exposed a few concoctions that offer little help, only hype. But before you start downing herbal supplements like M & M's, check the labels for the word "standardized." This means that the manufacturer has adjusted the potency so that it's uniform in every dose.

Rein in your prostate. Those cagey Seminole Indians originally used saw palmetto, an extract from a berry called *Serenoa repens*, as an aphrodisiac. While there's no evidence that the

Seminoles led lives of erotic frenzy, there is evidence that the plant may be an effective remedy for enlarged prostates (otherwise known as BPH, or benign prostatic hyperplasia). A big hit throughout Europe, the herb accounts for an estimated 38 percent of all medications prescribed for the problem in Italy, a bigger chunk of the market than any man-made drug can claim. "In the most recent study of 500 men, 88 percent of them experienced some relief in their symptoms," says Varro E. Tyler, Ph.D., professor of pharmacognosy at the Purdue School of Pharmacy in West Lafayette, Indiana.

The herb seems to work by preventing the conversion of testosterone into dihydrotestosterone, a more potent form of the hormone that may trigger the prostate to grow. "Plus, unlike synthetic drugs like Proscar, this herb doesn't have the side effects that can render men impotent," says Dr. Tyler. And European research suggests that it may equal Proscar in effectiveness, in terms of increasing urine flow, decreasing the amount of urine left in the bladder after urinating and reducing nighttime trips to the bathroom.

But we must also add that if you experience symptoms of BPH, you shouldn't run out and buy the extract without consulting your doctor. Your symptoms could signify problems more serious than BPH, and you'll need to rule them out. (And don't even think about parking your car off the road and hopping the chain-link fence to pick the actual berries—you won't know how much to use or how to prepare it.) Once a diagnosis is made, ask your doctor about saw palmetto. Then ask if you can try it and if he would monitor your progress.

The best way to take the herb is in standardized saw palmetto extract pills. Recommended dosage is 160 milligrams twice a day. It may take a few weeks of treatment for symptoms to improve.

JUST THE FACTS

Percentage of skin cancers that occur on the face, head and neck: 80

Halt a cold in its tracks. The next time your nose is as stuffy as a member of the Royal Family, give echinacea a try. "Because of its effectiveness on colds, echinacea is probably the most popular herbal remedy in Europe," says Dr. Tyler. "I take it myself." The herb seems to make white blood cells, the ones that gobble invading organisms, act even hungrier.

But take it only when you're sick. "You should not take echinacea for more than six weeks—after that it loses its effectiveness," says Dr. Tyler. In fact, long-term use of the herb may compromise your immune system, making it easier to get sick.

Dr. Tyler recommends taking 125-milligram capsules of the extract, standardized to contain 4 percent of the active ingredient echinacoside. When you feel a cold coming, take two capsules every six hours for two days, then two capsules every eight hours for five days. Be aware that echinacea formulations vary among products; you may have to follow dosage directions on the bottle.

Nod off to dreamland faster. Imagine finding TV sets growing wild in both North America and Europe, and they broadcast nothing but repeats of C-SPAN. Sure, it's fantasy, but we have something close to that in valerian, a plentiful wild herb that's also a potent sleeping aid. In a Swiss study, subjects were given either a pill containing valerian or a placebo before going to sleep. Those who took the valerian fell asleep much faster and experienced a better, deeper sleep than those who swallowed the phony pill. Plus, the effects seem strongest for problem sleepers.

"We have no idea why valerian works, but it wouldn't have been used for 2,000 years if it didn't," says Dr. Tyler. And, in other research, valerian not only dramatically improved the quality of sleep in a group of insomniacs but also reduced morning sleepiness—the opposite of what occurs with common sleeping pills.

A reasonable dose is a cup or two of valerian tea before bedtime, prepared with a teaspoon (one to two grams) of the dried root. Another option is 200 to 300 milligrams of the extract containing 0.8 percent valeric acid. You can buy it at most drugstores.

But there's one more thing: You'll need to hold your nose when consuming it. The herb carries a rank odor.

Calm a stormy sea. Ginger is not just the name of the sequined redhead on *Gilligan's Island*; it's also a potent herb that may be a boon for a bad belly. "Carefully done research suggests that it may be quite effective for treating motion sickness, particularly seasickness," says Dr. Tyler. "And stronger evidence suggests that it may help ease nausea that can occur after surgery." No one knows why ginger has this effect, just that it does. "It affects the stomach in a way we don't quite understand," says Dr. Tyler.

Most clinical studies have used powdered gingerroot at a dose of one gram per day. When shopping for the stuff, look for gingerroot extracts that approximate a one-gram dosage, says Dr. Tyler. For best results, take two 500-milligram capsules 20 minutes before you travel, then as needed if you start feeling queasy after a few hours. Or if you're adventurous, hit the local Asian market and try munching on candied ginger. It works, and it tastes good because it's soaked in sugar.

Sustain firmer erections. Got your attention? Good. Preliminary research suggests that one herbal remedy, known as ginkgo, may offer that very potential. Already considered a conventional drug in Europe, its best proven benefit is in improving circulation problems. "When blood flow is impaired to the legs (called intermittent claudication), ginkgo has been shown to help," says Dr. Tyler. "If tinnitus (ringing in the ears), short-term memory loss,

---

JUST THE FACTS

Percentage of Americans who say that their consumption of alcohol has decreased in the last five years, according to a Gallup poll: 41

Don't Eat These

The fact that it comes from Mother Nature doesn't necessarily mean that it's warm and fuzzy. Many natural substances are ineffective. Others are plain harmful. For example:

Ginseng. According to the radio advertisements, ginseng will make you as peppy as a *Solid Gold* dancer on a coffee jag. But here's the dope on ginseng: When researchers give it to a lab mouse, then throw the varmint into a bucket of water, he'll swim longer than a mouse that goes ginsengless. "There is abundant evidence in small animals that ginseng functions as a performance enhancer," says Varro E. Tyler, Ph.D., professor of pharmacognosy at the Purdue School of Pharmacy in West Lafayette, Indiana. "But published research with humans hasn't been convincing."

Ephedra. This herb got a bad rap when a few people died after taking it. A powerful bronchodilator and decongestant, ephedra is an active ingredient in popular asthma drugs. "But it's often promoted as a muscle-builder and weight-loss agent, and most people are buying it for those reasons and

headaches or even vertigo are caused by impaired cerebral circulation, then ginkgo can help there as well."

If ginkgo can correct impaired blood flow, researchers figured it might help fix erectile problems, as long as they're also caused by jammed arteries. In one study, 50 impotent men were treated with 240 milligrams of ginkgo biloba extract (GBE) for nine months. Some of the men also received injections of the erection-boosting drug papaverine. The extract significantly improved erections in both groups, regardless of whether they received the extra injection. Plus, in an earlier study of 60 patients who previously had not responded to papaverine injections, half regained potency after taking 60 milligrams of GBE daily for six months.

GBE can be bought in pill form at any drugstore or health food store. The recommended dosage is one 40-milligram tablet three

taking it for long periods of time," says Dr. Tyler. Long-term use can cause adverse effects, especially if you have certain underlying medical conditions. "It should only be taken for its proper use, and even then you first need to be thoroughly checked out by a doctor," says Dr. Tyler.

Comfrey. This stuff comes in many forms, all of them worthless and potentially harmful. "This may be the worst concoction sold on the market," says Dr. Tyler. Some companies tout it as an antibalding remedy, but it contains agents known to cause cancer and obstruct blood flow in the liver. "I wouldn't ingest it for anything, yet many people do," says Dr. Tyler.

Yohimbine. Yohimbine is an approved prescription drug derived from the bark of an African tree and used to treat impotence. But yohimbine, the stuff you see at health food stores sold as an aphrodisiac, is potentially harmful. An overdose can lead to paralysis, stomach problems, even death. Buy a pair of silk boxers instead.

times daily with meals. This does not mean, however, that you should treat a limp member on your own. "If the erection problems aren't due to impairment of blood flow to the penis but rather nerve damage or other problems, then ginkgo won't help," says Dr. Tyler. Talk to your doctor to see what might work for you.

Bring cholesterol down. Garlic isn't just for warding off vampires and car salesmen anymore. Allicin, the ingredient that gives the herb its notorious odor, may also help lower cholesterol. Not only does this substance cause dietary cholesterol to exit your body, but it may also shut off production of LDL (low-density lipoprotein) cholesterol, the harmful artery-clogging stuff made in the liver. One study found that eating the equivalent of one clove of garlic a day for several months can lower total cholesterol by roughly 9 percent. "The best proven benefits seemed to be for people with total cholesterol in the high (240 or more milligrams/deciliter) range," says Dr. Tyler. You may see a 10 percent drop in total cholesterol as well as a 15 percent reduction in triglycerides, another harmful blood fat.

Cooking reduces allicin's power, so look for a carefully dried garlic powder encapsulated in an acid-resistant coating. "When you take it, it releases the allicin mostly in the small intestine, rather than in the stomach or in the mouth," says Dr. Tyler. "That way, you get the benefits of raw garlic without giving off the odor to those around you."

A variety of commercial garlic preparations are on the shelves. For best results, look for products standardized for allicin or alliin content. (Alliin is the relatively odorless compound that converts to allicin once garlic is crushed.) Shoot for eight milligrams of alliin, or 5,000 micrograms of allicin, daily.

PART 5

Women and Sex

TOP TEN

Recent Sex Books for Men

The bookstores of America are seeing a wide range of sex-related books for men fill their shelves. Looking at these titles leads you to believe that there are some jaded men and women out there. We haven't checked out any of these books, so we don't know if they offer sound advice. The titles sure make them sound interesting, though. So whether you're angry at women, curious as to why women are angry at men, looking for a relationship, trying to become more sensitive or looking to go it alone, the books below will fit the bill.

1. *How to Be the Jerk Women Love: Social Success for Men and Women in the '90s* by Frank Spavlica
2. *The Stronger Women Get, the More Men Love Football: Sex and Sports in America* by Mariah B. Nelson
3. *Surviving the Feminization of America: How to Keep Women from Ruining Your Life* by Rich Zubaty
4. *Solo Sex: The Ultimate Do-It-Yourself Handbook for Men* by Robert Osborne Baron
5. *Smart Dating: A Guide for Men and Women to Dating, Romance and Sex* by Donald Black
6. *A Cuddle Is a Gift of Love* by Don Scott and Erin Scott
7. *And Adam Knew Eve: A Dictionary of Sex in the Bible* by Ronald L. Ecker
8. *Black Men Not Looking for Sex: Why They Commit Forever* by Alvis O. Davis
9. *Money, Power and the Sexes: Channeling Sexual Energy in the Workplace* by Cynthia E. Darwin
10. *Eve's Revenge* by Starr

Super**Sex**

Earth-Shaking Orgasms Can Be Yours, Too

Do you ever wonder if it's really true that women have more fun with their orgasms than the rest of us? Imagine the average guy trying to pull off that scene in *When Harry Met Sally* where Meg Ryan simulates for a restaurant full of envious observers the high-intensity, full-body climax that any man would envy. The punch line there is the patron (another woman, as it happens) saying, "I'll have what she's having." Well, as it happens, a man can have it, too.

Mind-rocking orgasms come easily to healthy teenage males, and then, as time goes on, men sometimes feel that they've lost their edge. What used to fire like a ballistic missile now, at times, seems more like a water pistol.

But this is one pleasure that doesn't have to decline with age. On the contrary, it can get better. As you mature, you can learn a few simple techniques for controlling what happens—and how great it feels—in ways that your adolescent self never imagined.

First, keep in mind that when you're ejaculating, you're not necessarily having an orgasm. They're really two different experiences. "Ejaculation is local; orgasm is global, encompassing your entire body," says certified sex educator Robert O. Hawkins, Jr., Ph.D., sexologist and professor of health sciences at the State University of New York at Stony Brook. Ejaculation, he says, is just one response to what your entire body is experiencing. "Ejaculation is just the physical expulsion of fluid. It begins when ducts in the genital organs contract and squeeze their contents—the mixture of sperm and other fluids that make up semen—into the urethra. Then muscles at the base of the penis contract, forcing the fluid down the urethra and out the penis."

An orgasm is something else. "It's the peak feeling that involves all of the above plus many other parts of the body contracting and releasing," says Dr. Hawkins. "During sexual arousal, muscles tense all over. Not just in your crotch. Your breathing rate, heartbeat and blood pressure rise. Blood collects in the penis, causing an erection, and may also swell your lips, earlobes and nipples (yes, even your breasts can become erogenous zones) and make your face flush."

When a man can let tension build to higher and higher peaks before releasing it, says Dr. Hawkins, he improves his chances that his whole body will experience the orgasm. He'll feel involuntary contractions all over: toes, fingers, stomach, back muscles. He'll thrash and make noise. Sheets will snap off the mattress. Imagine the classic female orgasm, and you have the picture for a man.

The key to having these whole-body orgasms, says Dr. Hawkins, is to delay ejaculation. That means constantly approaching, then backing away from, ejaculation. By relaxing each time as you near the point of no return, eventually your orgasmic threshold gets higher. Until finally, on that last glorious homestretch, you get the kind of rocket-power orgasm that realigns planets. Think of it as orgasm surfing, riding the waves of sexual tension all the way to shore.

Below, Dr. Hawkins lays out this approach. Give it a try and you may be in for quite a surprise (and so will your neighbors).

Concentrate on your breathing. In the heat of passion, this is the last thing that you probably want to be thinking about. But, surprisingly, changing your breathing pattern can help increase an orgasm's impact. "By training the diaphragm, the muscular partition that separates the chest and abdominal cavity, you can really increase the intensity of your orgasm," says Dr. Hawkins. Like sex, this exercise involves a bit of huffing and puffing. Here are Dr. Hawkins's instructions: "Puff out through your mouth, huff-huff-huff-huff, concentrating on bringing each out breath up from your belly, so that you feel your diaphragm contracting to force the air out." Start with

---

JUST THE FACTS

Time it takes sperm to swim one inch: four minutes

a couple sets of four huffing breaths (or one set if you feel dizzy from hyperventilating), three or four times a day. After a week, experiment with increasing the number of breaths per set gradually until you're doing ten huffs. "Then during sex, as you feel an orgasm approach, by breathing more strongly and consciously than usual and forcing each breath out from the diaphragm, you'll increase the tension through your whole abdomen and upper body, raising the intensity of the experience," says Dr. Hawkins.

Practice, practice, practice. "You can delay ejaculation and thereby increase the intensity of your orgasms by strengthening the pelvic muscles around the base of the penis," says Dr. Hawkins. You can do this by practicing Kegel exercises, named for the man who invented them. "These are the muscles you'd squeeze to avoid urinating," says Dr. Hawkins. Originally used to help women with continence problems, these exercises can also help men stave off ejaculation and make it more powerful.

Start by squeezing and releasing the muscles 15 times a day, twice each day. Don't hold the contraction; just squeeze and let go. You can do the exercise anywhere: while driving a car, watching TV, during a meeting. (Just don't announce it to everybody.) Gradually increase the number of squeezes until you're doing about 75, two times a day.

Clear your mind. At the beginning of arousal, you'll need to be in a reasonably relaxed state to get the sexual tension rolling. "Often the reasons for lackluster orgasms have little to do with our bodies," says Dr. Hawkins. "We have ten times more demands on our attention than we did when we were younger, and that makes it hard to keep the focus on pure sexual excitement."

And this is not just for the sake of mood. "Cutting out the distractions helps you relax, and that helps your erection along by widening the arteries of the penis so that blood flows in freely to swell the tissues," says Dr. Hawkins. Soft music, a little fantasizing and some serious foreplay all help get the world out of your head—and a locked door doesn't hurt, either.

Assume the position. "One of my goals in life is to reverse the national sex position—turn the man over and put him on his back, under the woman, so he can relax without having to support his weight," says Dr. Hawkins. Goals like that won't win him the Nobel Prize, but hear him out. "Because sexual arousal itself builds plenty of tension, the more you add to it in the early stage by tensing your muscles to maintain a position, the less control you have over your ejaculation and orgasm."

This position also allows you to use a technique that helps many men prolong the buildup before ejaculation. It's called "vaginal containment." The woman straddles the man or lies on top, with his penis inside her, and the man doesn't move at all; he just concentrates on enjoying the sensation of containment without the rush of friction. Of course, you don't want that to go on forever.

Pull out all the stops. When you feel it's time for the final approach, you can ensure an ecstatic orgasm by moving from a relaxed position to one that gives you ample possibilities for tension and movement. You can roll over to the standard missionary position, using your upper body muscles for support and your pelvic muscles to thrust. Or better, says Dr. Hawkins, move to what he calls the aboriginal intercourse position. "Sit up on your knees with your legs apart and lean back slightly with your heels under your butt. Have the woman scoot up so that she's sitting on your thighs, facing you. You're inside her; you can see each other clearly. You can now move freely to increase the amount of tension in your groin and elsewhere." Now that you've reached the stage of inevitability, you reverse your tactics. You quit relaxing. You thrust, you move, you breathe hard and deeply, you abandon yourself completely. "By alternately building up tension and relaxing to maintain control, you create a situation for a truly ecstatic orgasm," says Dr. Hawkins.

And when it's over, lie back and relax. Later, perhaps the next day, try to fix any broken furniture.

Kiss and Tell

Sizzling Secrets from Some Regular Guys

You could be in complete control of your life, awash in success and happiness, a master of the universe. In fact, we hope you are.

But be honest. Is there a single person you could comfortably ask, face to face, without paying any money, these vital questions: "Know any ways I could improve on the missionary position?" Or, "Have you ever figured any way to help your partner consistently reach orgasm?"

It's sad, really. Your father or doctor is probably out of the question. Your friends and colleagues would respond, at best, with a sneer or a wisecrack; sex talk among guys is mostly winks and nods, bravado and innuendo. For some reason, despite living in a culture saturated with sex (or at least the kind of faux sex used in advertising), American men don't really talk to each other honestly about it.

So a decision was made to change all that. A bunch of *Men's Health* magazine editors, writers, cronies and hangers-on got together in a conference room, kicked off their shoes and brainstormed every sexual topic a guy could possibly want to know about. Then the magazine's readers were asked for tales from the front lines. And, boy, did they respond.

Two studies were conducted. One was a printed survey mailed to randomly selected subscribers, representing a statistically valid sampling of the magazine's readership—healthy, smart, affluent, physical men like you. The other survey, which ran in the magazine itself, consisted of 12 open-ended essay questions (the kind you hated in high school). All told, about 2,500 responses were received for this one—some faxed, some e-mailed, some sent by ordinary mail, often with additional pages attached. Others scribbled their deepest secrets on yellow legal pads or the backs of envelopes. Taken together, all these responses filled two big boxes and weighed in at more than 30 pounds.

Overall, the responses were full of honesty, wisdom, humor, creativity and good-naturedness. Many of the respondents are clearly skilled and devoted lovers, eager to share what they've learned—some of which we'd never before heard.

So here's a sampling of the results.

Are you satisfied? More than half of the respondents said that their sex lives are good or excellent. Married men are far more fulfilled sexually than nonmarried men. The question: "How would you characterize your sex life?"

	Married	**Not married**
Excellent	20.0%	15.2%
Good	43.4%	36.4%
Fair	20.8%	23.1%
Poor	12.5%	13.6%
Nonexistent	2.1%	9.5%

Does being fit help? Absolutely. The better the respondents rated their health, the better they also rated the status of their sex lives.

Health status	**Excellent or good sex lives**
Excellent	65.9%
Good	54.1%
Fair	22.2%

Here's why we strike out so often: We have lousy pickup lines. The question: "Do you know an opening or pickup line that works?"

Yes	10.8%
No	60.8%

"What is it about women that attracts you the most?" was asked. Given are the percentages of those who checked the particular box.

Personality	62.2%
Beauty	55.5%
Sense of humor	48.3%
Smile	47.9%

Intelligence	47.8%
Legs	45.0%
Shapeliness	44.3%
Breasts	43.9%
Eyes	43.7%
Buttocks	42.1%
Hair	37.6%
Voice	34.3%
Height	16.9%

Top Turn-Ons

In the survey, when the question was asked, "Have you discovered any sexual aids (toys, games, lingerie, fantasies) that enhance your sex life?" the landslide vote was in favor of lingerie. Without a doubt, it is the U.S. male's favorite erotic aid.

Because it fires up a man's imagination, there's no sense in limiting its usefulness to a momentary parade in the boudoir. "It's not so much what she wears to bed," said a 36-year-old former NFL defensive back, "but what she wears under her clothes while she is out with you. Knowing that she is wearing a pair of thigh-highs and no underwear under your favorite dress makes the anticipation of getting back to the bedroom unbearable."

The only problem is that not all women share this enthusiasm. "Lingerie on a woman works magic for me," added a 28-year-old advertising executive. "But I've always felt that a woman should wear what makes her feel sexy, not what makes her partner happy. To me, nothing is sexier than a woman who feels attractive."

Many of our survey respondents said that they liked it best when their partners wore lingerie in combination with high heels and lots of makeup. Now, think about that for a second. Isn't that what many women put on every day to go to work? No wonder so many people are having sex on the boss's desk.

To hear the survey respondents tell it, about the only thing that most guys love more than a black lacy body stocking is when she talks dirty in bed.

"I think that most men are extremely stimulated by the sounds women make," said one guy. "If they sound like they are being sat-isfied and, even better, say that they are during lovemaking, most of us could go much, much longer and more creatively."

A 25-year-old attorney said, "When she is physical and also talks about how much she loves me, or how aroused I make her, or other erotic things, I always become aroused."

The Road to Great Sex

■ "I like to take fresh petals from a long-stemmed red rose and scatter them over the body of my lover just prior to engaging in in-tercourse," wrote a 55-year-old university professor. "Kissing and licking around the rose petals on the stomach, breasts, nipples and thighs add a new dimension to the experience. Finally, intercourse with rose petals between lovers provides a very sensuous addition to sex—the petals cling to both bodies because of the sweat gen-erated and leave interesting patterns when sex is over."

■ A 39-year-old bond salesman shared this titillating tip: "All women that I've used the 'alphabet game' on reach intense or-gasms—it works every time. Just make capital letters with your tongue very slowly on her clitoris. You might make it to M!"

■ A 42-year-old public-ser-vice administrator wrote, "My wife had a fantasy about being taken on the washing machine during the spin cycle. So we did—and have—many times. I am six feet tall, so I simply stand in front of my wife and she wraps her legs around my hips. We make love while the cycle is spin-ning, and when it ends I just reach behind her and start it back up again. It's like a giant external vibrator!"

- "Bringing food into the bedroom is not only erotic; it creates a more open and playful atmosphere," said one fellow. "But do something unusual. A banana is too obvious—try orange slices or melon balls." Another guy recommended "barbecue sauce to spice up lovemaking." And a 30-year-old copywriter said simply, "One word: molasses."

- A 52-year-old account executive confessed that "when a T-shirt gets old, I like to wear it during lovemaking and let my wife rip it off me."

- "Sometimes it's fun to find some board game or sport that you are both equally good at, and then play each other for control of the evening—winner gets everything he/she wants. This adds some drama to the game."

- One ingenious fellow mentioned that "a black light near the bed helps get things cooking. It gives us both a pleasant-looking tan without us having to destroy our skin in the sun."

- And finally, this technical tip from a 24-year-old computer programmer: "I have found that maintaining physical contact after an orgasm is an important step to becoming a multiorgasmic male.

After an orgasm, your body tends to want to relax or go to sleep. If you don't withdraw after your orgasm, but instead, slowly caress each other, the need to relax or sleep will usually quickly recede behind a new surge of growing arousal."

On the other hand, if this doesn't happen for you, just remember: The guy is 24.

You Did It Where?

- "In an old cemetery, at night, right on the grave of a guy who died in 1849," said a 38-year-old sales manager. "I figured he could use a lift."

- "Back of a station wagon while my wife and I were chaperoning a senior prom."

- "On a driveway with fresh-laid cement."

- "In the torture chamber at the Hohensalzburg Castle in Austria."

- "In the middle of a raging river. We walked out into the river on submerged rocks and sat with our backs against the current. The water flooded over our heads, and we were immersed in a huge bubble. It was incredibly intense."
- "Sitting in the stands during a college football game surrounded by a blanket. She was sitting on my lap and would bounce up and down when our team made a good play."
- "American Airlines flight 984 from Dallas to Indy."
- "On a ride at Disney World. Truth!"
- "In the dressing room of a department store at the mall."

Our favorite, though, was this one, related by a 55-year-old high-school biology teacher. "During our university years, on a train from Amsterdam to Copenhagen, the urge came over us—but we were in a compartment with four other people, a condition not really conducive to overt sex. My wife happened to be wearing a full skirt and, in the darkness, as the other passengers dozed off, she slipped off her panties and we snuggled in together, spooned and comfortable. We thought we were quite discreet, but when we got off the train in Copenhagen, an elderly gentleman came up to us and solemnly shook our hands. Never said a thing; just shook our hands."

Her Favorites

When asked if they had discovered anything that consistently enables their partners to reach orgasm, 62 percent said that they had. And one of the biggest revelations was the number of men who said that oral sex is the best way to ring her chimes.

"Oral sex has brought about orgasm with every woman I have ever had a long-term sexual relationship with," a 37-year-old operations analyst told us. "It is said that some women cannot achieve orgasm via oral sex, but I haven't run into such a woman in my sex life."

"You need to make sure she knows that she can give you input (harder, softer, faster, slower and so on)," advised a 26-year-old naval officer. "And you need to be careful not to overstimulate—most women need you to back off a bit just before they reach orgasm."

Next to oral sex, the thing that's most likely to drive a woman to orgasm is foreplay.

"Foreplay, foreplay and more foreplay," insisted one guy. "Touching, caressing, snuggling, sucking, licking and kissing. All this is fun and sensuous, and the more time for it, the better."

"What enhances our sex life the most is lots and lots of foreplay," agreed a young attorney. "We drive each other nuts before we actually have sex. It leads to incredible orgasms. Foreplay gets her in such a frenzy that she is halfway to orgasm before we even have sex."

But a 47-year-old academic librarian reminds us that foreplay is not necessarily limited to the bedroom. He told us that he and his wife "make love" three or four times a week, but just as important, "we are erotic and loving with each other when we aren't having sex. Many mornings, for instance, I enjoy just sitting on the bed and watching my wife dress. Or she will wash the dishes while nude, or close to it."

Fantasies Made True

Sharing a secret fantasy with your lover, or actually acting one out, turned out to be one of the favorite sexual games.

"An active fantasy life is the key to keeping sex fun and interesting," a 27-year-old law student told us. "It also eliminates all desire to cheat on your partner. Most often we make love without it, but sometimes (approximately twice a month) we do a little role-playing. Some favorites include: pirate captain/galley wench; pizza boy/bored housewife who lost her purse; Prince Charming/wicked queen; Roman centurion/Roman goddess. The improvised dialogue is usually hilarious—but laughter is an aphrodisiac, no?"

"Fantasies are very good," wrote a 33-year-old salesman. "I had a long relationship that was also long-distance. Phone sex became very necessary. When we were together, it just sort of continued.

JUST THE FACTS

According to a survey by Keebler, 61 percent of men prefer pretzels shaped like circles, while 63 percent of women prefer pretzel rods.

She would send these letters, in which she would describe some sort of scenario and then I would come home to find it set up. Ron and Nancy Reagan were a favorite fantasy in the mid-1980s."

"The key to all of these things," advised a 20-year-old student, "is respect and understanding. Feeling comfortable enough to discuss not only secret desires and fantasies, but also your fears and discomfort about them. It's enabled my girlfriend and me to try many things that we didn't originally feel comfortable with. By not demanding anything of her and by talking about them with her, I have gotten pleasure beyond my wildest dreams."

Men's Biggest Beefs

The responses said it again and again: "Men are more visually stimulated than women." This explains why you can be all hot and bothered when she's not yet. She needs to be stroked, but you've already been "stroked" by your vision of her.

"They don't understand the power of images," lamented a 23-year-old teacher. "We like to see sex." A 25-year-old real-estate investor agreed. "We want to have the lights on sometimes. We want to see them naked, not hidden under sheets."

Another big drag is that men's and women's lusts are mismatched. "What women want in bed is a romance novel," a 27-year-old sales manager told us. "Men want a pornographic movie. Isn't life set up great?"

"My wife does not understand why every tender moment with me leads to sex," a 40-year-old medical transcriber wrote. "I have tried to explain to her that my lust for her and my love for her are inseparable," he continued. "But I think that sometimes she wants me to separate the sex part from the love part so that she can be sure I love her and not her body."

One other major gripe is that just because our drive is so physical, so seemingly detached from our brains, doesn't mean that our egos aren't on the line. We get nervous. We get embarrassed. And we need love, too.

And we heard from some pretty tough guys, like this 38-year-old corrections officer, who said: "Men are just as sentimental as women are. We just need someone to help us out of our shells." And a 22-year-old graduate student made a good point about how, for most men, their relationship with a woman provides the only closeness they have. "Most of us go through the day very isolated. So when we get home or get alone with our partner, we have an entire day's worth of emotional and physical intimacy that we haven't gotten or shared yet."

A related common complaint is that most women are far too passive. "Men like to be openly seduced," said one guy. "Men want women to take more of a responsibility in love matters," agreed a 62-year-old social worker. And a 31-year-old naval aviator said bluntly: "Some of us really want a woman to take us by the back of the neck."

The Best Sex

Sure, there were some tales of youthful conquest, strange locales and unbridled lust. But as in the survey itself, sincere tales of devotion and love dominate. In all cases, material was deleted that was a little too descriptive. You can find salaciousness anywhere these days, and the point was not to compete with all that. The point was simply to revisit some of the highest, richest, deepest, most unforgettable moments life has to offer, in hopes that it might inspire you to new heights of your own.

- "I met a woman at a Halloween party, and we hit it off. We did it in a closet—masks on. To this day, I don't know who she was."
- "She was an airline co-pilot, uninhibited, insatiable. Flew for Aeroflot. Aeroflot is history. So is Ludmila."
- "The best sex I ever had lasted 3½ weeks. She walked into my life, threw me around and left as quickly as she came in. That was three years ago. I don't miss her. If she had stayed any longer, I would be dead."
- "Our 25th wedding anniversary. We had three glorious days and nights, and we used all 25 years of experience."
- "My wife is a better lover than I could ever have hoped for. The best sex I ever had will change by next week."

Fantasies
Explained

*Sexual Daydreaming Is Nothing
to Feel Guilty About*

Did you ever notice the way really, truly beautiful women shamelessly discard their inhibitions and stare right at you, right into your eyes, practically through your skull, as you're minding your own business walking down the street? Doesn't that just drive you crazy? Or the way every one of your wife's friends, even her own sister, tries to lure you away from neighborhood gatherings for a fast forbidden upstairs liaison? Why do they do that? Why do they check you out from the shoes up, then lick their moist, full lips and breathe their invitations into your ear as they press their breasts, firm and round, against your finely muscled chest . . . uhh . . . pardon the interruption, but we need to talk.

About fantasies. Sex fantasies. Specifically, your fantasies. You spend far more time daydreaming about sex than you do actually having it. We all do. Even Hefner. Even Beatty. Even men who are on their honeymoons. It makes sense. A guy could line up three real-life quickies and spend the rest of the day in a semicoma. But you can pull off a half-dozen fully developed fantasy exploits, involving women both rich and beautiful, including many grateful celebrities, and still have time and energy to neck with your wife. In fact, one study estimates that men mate in their mind an average of seven times a day. That's 2,555 times a year. Another study found that more than half of all men spend 10 percent of their time in sexual la-la land. Fantasies can worm their way into your head anywhere, anytime—driving your car, cutting the hedges, eating a peach. And why not? In fantasy, the sex is the best, you're fabulous, Fabio runs from you, women seek to please you, virgins beg you for a gentle introduction to womanhood, your wife finds you dates at motels. A guy can have fantasy sex all day and never have to re-mousse.

Yet if we're going to spend all that time doing something so irresistible, we ought to at least have a reason for why we're doing it. Do sexual fantasies have a purpose? Or are these lustful whimsies nothing more than giant psychological gnats, whose only purpose is to make us itch, to frustrate us, to force our eyes toward dental hygienists' cleavage and to make us feel that our own sex lives are as repressed, staid and stifled as a Victorian-era movie?

No. There's more to it than that. The next time your mind goes off to Tahiti with Lola from accounts payable, don't view it as a form of torment. Think of it as—well, as swell sex. Sexual flights of fancy—especially if you know how to pilot them—can serve you well in a lot of ways. They can make you a hotter lover, a better mate and a more sexually satisfied kind of guy. And with the right preparation, the right attitude and a little luck, you might even get to live out some of them.

Become a Better Lover

Long before there was Deepak Chopra, Bernie Siegel or Bill Moyers and their books and programs on the so-called mind/body connection, there was a real expert on sex—you, for instance, at age 10, wondering if the babysitter really meant for you to see that shocking triangle of white nylon panty beneath that gingham sundress. You saw that amazing sight, and you felt changes taking place in your body, both miraculous and a little frightening. It was perhaps your first introduction to the ultimate mind/body connection. But it sure wasn't your last.

Take Nikki, for example. Nikki's your ski instructor. She's 23 going on infinity and the factory ideal—your ideal—of what all women were meant to look like. Now, in your mind, take Nikki's ski suit off and turn her around a couple of times. What happens?

A Crowded Bed

Is she really moaning because you're driving her wild? Or are you a bit player, or less, in a fantasy creating her sexual ecstasy?

Like it or not (and you probably won't), studies show that women are just as inclined to fantasize in bed as men are. One study found that 84 percent of men and women at least sometimes fantasize during intercourse.

Don't be overly concerned, however. Fantasies are not a sign of a bad marriage, or even bad sex. In one study, women who fantasized reported having better sex with their husbands than those women with less active imaginations.

The kinds of fantasies that she has are likely to be somewhat different from yours. To the right is a glimpse at what sex therapists say are among the most common fantasies of lovers in the act.

The level of testosterone in your body will begin to rise. Your blood pressure will increase. Your heart will beat faster. Your breathing will speed up. You'll sweat more. Blood will rush to your genitals, giving you a feeling of warmth. Your penis will start to rise and grow, causing movement that will bring tingling. The muscles throughout your pelvis will tighten. Your nipples may harden. It's possible that your face, neck and chest will redden. And all of these physical changes occur, not through any physical stimulus, but simply because of the images racing through your mind. This biological/psychological cocktail of stimulation creates that state of being that scientists call horniness.

And while your sexual fantasies are getting you physically prepared for sex, they're also preparing you mentally. First, those erotic visions help transform you from the hardworking, hard-playing,

While you're thinking about . . .	She's thinking about . . .
Having sex with another woman you know	Having sex with a movie star (Robert Redford is still quite popular)
Making love with two or more women at the same time	You being driven berserk by her body
Her with longer legs, larger breasts or a tighter butt	You as a wounded soldier whom she has nursed back to health
Doing it in a different position	Being tied up
Forcing her to submit	Being overpowered by you
Her as a streetwalker that you just paid $30	Herself as a high-class call girl that you just paid $300
Her as a virgin	Having sex in a public place

big-thought-thinking man that you are most of the time into the ravenous sexual animal that you occasionally become. And they keep those engines revving for as long as you want, without jarring, stress-producing concerns popping up and ruining your mood. That's the reason that you fantasize about sex even while you're having sex. As long as your mind is occupied with thoughts of the silk stockings on that sales representative that you had lunch with, it won't slip back into worrying about how you're going to renegotiate that pork-belly deal that the two of you signed.

Not only do sexy thoughts melt your mind; they also prepare your body for a more powerful orgasm. That's the mind/body connection again. The increased circulation and muscle tension caused by those crazed images allow for more physical sensation and a greater feeling of release, says Robert O. Hawkins, Jr., Ph.D., sexologist and professor of health sciences at the State University of New York at Stony Brook. "Simply put, the purpose of sexual fantasy is to improve the quality of your actual sex life."

"Sexual fantasies occur most often in those who have the least number of sexual problems and the most sexual satisfaction," says Harold Leitenberg, Ph.D., a professor of psychology at the University of Vermont in Burlington. Studies also show that men with a greater variety of sexual fantasies tend to have a greater variety of sexual experiences. So dream on.

Strengthen Your Marriage

You and your mild-mannered member may live a life of quiet, solid marital fidelity, but your brain is always on the make. The male mind is simply not monogamous. Sometimes, when your body is making love to your wife, your mind is fathering the children of Courteney Cox, Jennifer Aniston and the waitress at Hooters at the same time. Don't feel guilty. "You can be in a perfectly fine relationship and fantasize about somebody that you just saw at the office," says Galdino F. Pranzarone, Ph.D., sexologist and professor of psychology at Roanoke College in Salem, Virginia. Don't worry—it keeps you from actually following through with something that you might thoroughly enjoy, only to regret later on.

But more often than not, the object of your fantasies happens to be the very same partner you sleep with every night. And she's likely fantasizing about you. "Why do you have sex with your eyes closed? It's because most of the time, you're fantasizing," says Robert Jaffe, Ph.D., a relationships counselor in private practice in Sherman Oaks, California. "You may be visualizing your penis entering the vagina, or you may be conjuring up an image of your wife's face—it's all part of fantasizing, and it's all part of raising your level of stimulation," says Dr. Jaffe. Some men, he says, also arouse themselves by imagining their partners at their most attractive—perhaps when they were younger, thinner and still wearing skirts well north of the knees. And no doubt in her mind's eye, your waistline is closer to its undergraduate dimensions.

Your True Desires

Some men fantasize about having sex with hookers. Others like to see themselves as a woman's servant. Still others fantasize about two sweaty women mutually exercising their sexual options. Nearly all men occasionally conjure up the image of the always-available woman—forever ready, willing and highly able. Pauline Reage's erotic classic, *Story of O*, involved a harem-load of women wearing dresses open at the rear. Some fantasies are but fleeting images—a breast, a thigh, a naked foot. Other fantasies are extremely intricate and detailed scripts.

What determines that one man will fantasize about Hillary Clinton while another man will fantasize about lesbian cheerleaders mud-wrestling Michelle Pfeiffer? It begins with evolution, which has seemingly wired the male brain to crave a woman who's healthy and fertile. But from there, fantasies can often be influenced by a particular society's (or a marriage's) forbidden fruits, says Dr. Pranzarone. "It's a pretty good bet that in societies where women run around bare-breasted, the men in that society don't dream a lot about boobs."

But there's more to it than taboos. Psychologists theorize that your fantasies are somehow linked to what you want in a partner. That's because we all enter the era of raging hormones with something called a love map, which is just about set in stone, according to Dr. Pranzarone. "It's a blueprint of what you desire in a mate—her appearance, personality and behavior—that is totally based on your childhood experiences." That love map, whether

you know it or not, is the invisible hand that guides your fantasies.

Our sexual fantasies offer unique glimpses into our psyches. Here are some of the more common ones, and what they reveal about you.

She runs the show. "I've had many clients who during the day have to stomp around like big, tough men—state troopers, business executives, New York City cops—and this can be very stressful. So one of the ways that high-powered men can take the pressure off themselves is by fantasizing about being in passive roles," says Patrick Suraci, Ph.D., psychologist and author of *Male Sexual Armor*. This might mean that you like her to be on top or you like to be bound up and at her mercy or you fantasize about being her servant or slave.

It's been rumored that one of New York's leading dominatrices has a rich and powerful client who leaves his prestigious Wall Street office every day and goes to her apartment, where he takes off his Armani suit, puts on a pair of size 12 red pumps and a French maid's outfit, and cleans her house before heading home to the suburbs—where, no doubt, his wife complains that he never helps around the house.

She has a pal. Lesbian-love fantasies, or fantasies in which you and your partner bring another person into bed, are among the most common erotic voyages that men take. They don't mean that you really think of yourself as some kind of superstud. (Although if you can ever actually pull this off, we'll concede you the point.) In fact, says Dr. Jaffe, for many men this fantasy may be a way for us to express the repressed feminine sides of our personalities. Subconsciously, we may be putting ourselves into the role of one of the women—and thoroughly enjoying it. Or we may also use these fantasies for education purposes—who can better turn a woman on, we reason, than another woman? On the other hand, we may fantasize about a threesome because it means plenty of sex with only half the work.

You're irresistible. For a lot of us, the early days of dating were fraught with treachery and rejection. But rejection from women started even earlier, about the time that Mom plopped us down so that she could pick up our crying younger brother. All these experiences leave a shadow of a doubt in many men's minds as to whether they're really desirable to women. So your subconscious has you conjuring up women who never, ever reject you. "Many sexual fantasies attempt to undo the early traumas to self-esteem suffered by men at the hands of women," says Wayne Myers, M.D., clinical professor of psychiatry at Cornell University Medical College in New York City.

She's a prostitute. Fantasizing that your wife is a streetwalker means simply this: You're a man. Like any man, you seek power. And in the late twentieth century, power is money. Being capable of buying sex proves the point. Paying for sex also relieves you of performance anxiety, says Judith Seifer, Ph.D., president of the Chicago-based American Association of Sex Educators, Counselors and Therapists. "If you're paying her for it, then you don't have to worry about pleasing her."

You really, really like something. Fetish fantasies, whether they involve spiked heels or leather bikinis or chocolate sauce, can come from almost anywhere. And most of them are completely harmless. Let's say that one day, when you were younger, you watched a movie in which a tender young Jane Fonda bounced around provocatively in white leather boots. You revisited that scene often in future months, maybe even while masturbating or having sex. The image of the boots eventually cemented into your brain. Now, whenever you see white leather boots, even if they're being worn by a woman with sideburns, you're still turned on. "Our sexual fantasies are based on previous experiences, and sometimes those experiences bring in certain objects that then become sexual in their own right," says Dr. Seifer.

Enter the antagonist. A common, and often disturbing, fantasy many men have is that of their wives having sex with other men. You'd be torn up if it happened in real life, so why does it keep hap-

JUST THE FACTS

Fifty-seven percent of women ages 18 to 44 enjoy giving oral sex. And 68 percent say that they enjoy receiving it, according to the survey *Sex in America*.

Fantasy Island

When it comes to creating elaborate fantasies, you're the Ricardo Montalban of sex. But wouldn't it be great to be able to actually live one out?

Okay, maybe not that one about the five roller-skating skinheads and the food processor. But how about a heated affair with your old eighth-grade teacher? Or a trashy encounter with a high-priced call girl? Or something even a little more kinky? We have just the thing for you, a plan to fully free your fancy. Think of this as a Chinese menu of sexual adventure.

"Read the list over quickly and note your immediate reactions—choose to act out those that you find most stimulating on a gut level," suggests relationships counselor Robert Jaffe, Ph.D., of Sherman Oaks, California. "To really get the most out of this exercise, make your picks early in the week, and allow the fantasy to simmer for a few days. Share it with her. Talk about it for a few nights. By the time the weekend comes, the two of you should be up for some explosive sex."

pening in your head? Simple: You like the fantasy because it says something about your worth. She's your woman. Yours. And if she's desirable, and she's yours, that means that you're a man of means and taste. Having another man bring your wife to orgasm also allows you to envision her sexually satisfied without putting the onus on you to make it happen.

The old girlfriend returns. You broke up with her—two decades ago. So why does she keep dropping in at all hours? If sex with Mary Lou was great, you want to relive it, perhaps using those memories to bolster your confidence in yourself as a lover. If sex with Mary Lou wasn't so great, you may still want to relive it—but this time so that you can make it better.

"It's the old could-have, would-have, should-have thing," ex-

You are:	She is:
A bad, bad boy	The school principal
A tall, dark, mysterious stranger	The woman in red
The handyman/pool boy/gardener	The wealthy socialite
The big boss	The new secretary
A Democratic presidential candidate	A Republican speechwriter
A traveling salesman	The bored housewife
A member of the Hell's Angels	A motorcycle mama
A football star	The head cheerleader
A patient	A dental hygienist
A rock star	A groupie
Humphrey Bogart	Ingrid Bergman
John Smith	Pocahontas
An interstate trucker	A young hitchhiker
A lion	A lioness

plains Dr. Seifer. "A lot of men will want to replay the experience—but this time to do it better—perhaps with body oil, handcuffs, whatever."

Fantasies Can Come True

If you're in a long-term relationship that's lost a little of its sizzle, or if you're in a new relationship with someone who's just really . . . well, advanced, then you may be trying to figure out how to make one or more of your wilder fantasies come true.

Some, of course, can never be lived out, especially those that go against the laws of physics, the laws of nature or the laws of your local constabulary. But with a little effort and imagination, you and your partner can make a sexual adventure that you'll never forget.

Here are some tips from the experts on turning fantasies into orgasmic reality.

Pop the question. Keep in mind that if you've been somewhat bored with your sex life, chances are that your partner is, too. For that reason, she may be more receptive to sharing your sexual fantasies than you would have thought. "As long as you have another consenting adult willing to play your fantasies out, then almost any fantasy is permissible," says Dr. Jaffe. That's not to say that you should rush in and tell your wife how much you'd like to find her best friend's marvelously tanned legs underneath the tree this Christmas. Start with fantasies that involve your wife—ones that she might enjoy playing out, too.

Get closer to your partner. Some therapists that we spoke with recommend picking a fantasy that's going to help increase the intimacy in your relationship. Many husbands and wives get off on going to a hotel room and pretending to have an illicit affair. Another great spark igniter is to park in a deserted area and pretend that you're two horny teenagers out on a date. These fantasies are fairly tame. Don't be afraid to pull the shades and engage in a little kinky sex, as well. Spankings. Bondage. Costumes. It's all okay—as long as both parties agree and it's done in fun. The only time to question living out such fantasies is when you and your partner are so absorbed in the fantasy that you're no longer relating to each other.

Proceed with caution. If your fantasy is a little bizarre (and the good ones usually are), send out a probe before launching into your deepest revelations. For example, if you think that you might enjoy wearing your new girlfriend's clothing, get her to watch *Ed Wood*, a movie that deals with this subject. Ask her, "Mind if I duck into your closet and slip into something more comfortable?" Judge from her response how receptive she might be to seeing you in her white cashmere sweater.

Rent a video. "About one-third of all hard-core video rentals are to couples and women. Many of these are obviously going home to spice up marital sex," says Dr. Pranzarone. "As far as I can tell, these videos are the only aphrodisiac on the market that really can reverse a lagging libido with no side effects."

Make it a joint effort and pick a video that you both can enjoy. Many are being made with couples in mind, often focusing on married people who work unusual sexual experiences into their lives. According to Tamar Roman, vice-president and chief product reviewer for the Stamford Collection in New York City, one of the nation's largest mail-order adult products businesses, high-quality releases that offer excellent fantasy-fodder include *Shame*, *Justine* and *Hidden Obsessions*—all of which feature couples in romantic fantasies, not men engaged in gynecological warfare. And these flicks even have plots! Other popular products for couples include: Velcro handcuffs, chocolate body cream and patent-leather teddies, says Roman. If you're into reading aloud to each other, there's always *Penthouse* Forum. Or try a more highbrow option: For example, vampire author Anne Rice wrote a trio of steamy books under the pseudonym A. N. Roquelaure (*The Claiming of Sleeping Beauty*, *Beauty's Punishment* and *Beauty's Release*).

Use your head. Reality is very different from fantasy. Imagining yourself coming home to two lustful women every night is great, but even if you could arrange such a situation, our society doesn't readily accept threesomes, and few such alliances work. Just divvying up the housework would be a real hassle. Don't expend a lot of energy trying to start relationships that are destined to fail. That includes flings with women half your age who are more interested in your credit card than in you. It's probably not worth risking arrest and busting up your life for a short visit to bimbo heaven.

New Set of Rules

Men Should Have a Say in Relationships

Admit it. You've changed. Oh, you resisted. But you can't deny that subtle, creeping transformation in the way you act and think since you've acquired a mate.

For one, you now eat chips out of a bowl. And you've actually grown to like the feel of clean sheets. And it's all because of her.

Change can be a good thing. Women, historically, are a potent civilizing force. They help us replace bad habits (murder, mayhem, maniacal laughter) with better ones (restraint, kindness, Yahtzee). It's probably good, for example, that you no longer consider spaghetti a finger food.

But if you were to cruise the self-help aisle at your local bookstore or flip through a women's magazine or, heaven forbid, take some time off from work to watch daytime talk shows, you'd start to get the impression that you haven't quite changed enough. In fact, you'd get the impression that unless you start thinking and acting more the way that women want you to, your chances of lifelong happiness are zilch. "It's the underlying assumption that in a relationship it's 'woman good, man bad.' Book titles like *No Good Men* or *Men Who Hate Women and the Women Who Love Them* reflect these assumptions," says Warren Farrell, Ph.D., author of *The Myth of Male Power*.

And now we have proof that, yes, women are indeed out to change us. It's not a conspiracy theory. It's a fact.

In a recent review of scientific studies, when a group of women were asked to describe their ideal mates, they painted a veritable Prince Charming: a strong, intelligent, economically viable and sensitive guy. Okay, fine. Then another group of women was given a series of profiles of men, all of whom had the same kinds of faults and shortcomings that you and I have. These women were asked to choose hypothetical mates from among the ordinary, imperfect men. Which they did. "And when they were asked what their imperfect mates would be like in the future, they also painted a Prince Charming," says study author Robert Cramer, Ph.D., professor of psychology at California State University, San Bernardino. The women all reported that, no matter what their mates' faults, given time, they could be—no, would be—corrected. "It's no wonder that guys are always complaining about how women are trying to change them," Dr. Cramer says. "It's because they are."

But here's the deal. There's nothing necessarily wrong with you and your distinctly masculine traits. In fact, according to new research, women find those traits so darn attractive, they're trying to adopt them themselves. In an analysis of sex-role surveys of college students during the last 20 years, psychologists found that women today describe themselves as being more "masculine"—meaning more assertive, action-oriented and goal-driven. Men, however, have remained just as manly as they've ever been. If men are in such desperate need of repair, one must wonder why more and more women are trying to act like us.

It's a revolutionary theory, yes, but maybe, just maybe, we're okay after all.

We decided to look into it. Below we've listed the typical, mindless myths bandied about on talk shows and in women's magazines—the ones that relentlessly target men for extensive overhaul. And we've countered them with a few sound, sensible, male-oriented principles that just might work better, for you and for her.

Women's rule: Set aside time together.
Men's rule: Set aside sports time.

You probably know couples who appear to be joined at the hip. They like the same TV shows, share all of each other's interests, never go anywhere alone—their entire lives revolve around each other. There's probably a reason for that. No one else can stand to be around them.

Normal people need room to breathe. They need to have their own friends and hobbies, or at the very least they need time to sneak off to swear freely, eat chili dogs and drive fast. "If you don't have time apart, you'll drive each other crazy," says psychologist Lonnie Barbach, Ph.D., assistant clinical professor of medical psychology at the Medical Center at the University of California, San Francisco, and co-author of *Going the Distance*.

"It's important to have your own life, because becoming too dependent on the relationship will inevitably break it," agrees psychologist Robert Pasick, Ph.D., of Ann Arbor, Michigan, and author of *What Every Man Needs to Know*. We're not talking about taking separate vacations with the paid escort of your choice—just a few hours apart now and then to remember what it's like to miss each other.

And that brings us to our own pertinent advice. If you like to spend a chunk of your solo time planted on the sofa watching *NFL Live*, there's no need to feel guilty. On the contrary, you're doing both of you a big favor. "We take a lot of heat for watching football," says Dr. Farrell, "but the fact is that this is one relaxation tool that really works for many men. And one key to a successful relationship is to respect each other's ways of unwinding." So the next time she complains that you're not sharing enough with her, tell her that you'll set aside some couple time. Later. Right now, you need a little quality time with Madden and Summerall. Then promise that she can watch *Dr. Quinn, Medicine Woman* when the game's over.

Women's rule: Make joint decisions.
Men's rule: Go for it and make some without her.

How often has this happened to you: You're looking through the paper for a new restaurant to try. You find two or three. And then it's like this:

"Which one do you want to try?"

"Doesn't matter to me. It's up to you."

"Well, I don't care. Whatever you want . . ."

The result, of course, is that the two of you wind up at her place of choice—a café famous for its edible flowers and tofu linguine. A few more weekends like this and your relationship is going to get old, fast.

"Sometimes, as the man, you just have to step in and make the decision, no debate," says Dr. Pasick. Men have been brainwashed by the notion that a relationship has to be an equal partnership all the time. Women don't want that. Women hate that. "Most women still like the Gary Cooper type, the kind of guy who can take a stand," says Dr. Pasick. "Although it's important to consider your mate's feelings, often it pays to be decisive."

Research bears this out. Women rate agreeable men as more attractive than stubborn ones, but that's only true if the nicer guys also possess a dominant streak. Women rate generous men as appealing if—and only if—they're strong and decisive at the very core. If those elements are missing, these nice guys come off as meek. Wimpish. Doormats.

So don't feel guilty about putting your foot down the next time both of you are making plans for dinner or choosing a movie—or, heck, deciding where to live and whether to have children. It's okay to take a stand.

Women's rule: There's more than just great sex. Men's rule: Great sex is a good start.

Relationships based on sex are often demeaned as shallow and doomed. But if the mattress is the central area of commerce for you and your mate, there's no need for concern. "It's a mistake to belittle a relationship that has sex as its primary component," says Dr. Barbach. "Great sex allows many couples to overcome other difficulties in the relationship, and even strengthen the weak points." And it may be that for some people, sex serves as a potent brainwash. "If you don't remember what you were arguing about before you hopped

---

JUST THE FACTS

Percentage of women who've agreed to a date because they like the car that a man drives: 7.5

Staying on the Good Side

If you want to remain in favor with your mate, then follow these simple rules.

1. Never eat out of cans or drink milk directly from the carton (unless she's out of town).
2. Don't refer to your wedding ring as a "magnet."
3. Avoid painting team colors on your face or belly at Giants games, especially if she's rooting for the Redskins.
4. When she fills out one of those relationship quizzes from a woman's magazine, read it.
5. Send her a postcard—even when you're home. Everyone likes to get mail.
6. Be nice to her friends, even if they irritate you. Just don't be too nice to the cute ones.
7. At parties, stay by her side for at least 30 minutes, or until you can palm her off on a group of friendly faces. Then roam.
8. Have two televisions. And one remote.
9. Have two bathrooms.
10. Never bring up her weight.

into bed, then that suggests that those problems were not as important as you and your mate made them out to be," says Dr. Barbach.

And, come on, what's wrong with two adults acting like overheated polecats, anyway? "We should celebrate relationships like that," says Dr. Pasick. "When two people are turned on by each other, what's the problem, really?"

Women's rule: Share your feelings.
Men's rule: Moping around is fine sometimes.

Perhaps you know this couple. Their relationship resembles a *Days of Our Lives* marathon. Every issue—big and small—is brought up, scrutinized, dissected and ground into a fine powder. Their reason for being together, it seems, is to talk about being to-

11. Use her name when addressing her. It makes her feel special, letting her know you actually remembered it. And just because the kids call her "Mom," that doesn't mean that you should.

12. Keep her vital statistics (birthday, anniversary, dress size, lingerie size, favorite flowers) on a business card in your wallet. Check it regularly. Don't pass it around.

13. Have one hobby that both of you can enjoy and a few that she has no interest in.

14. Never agree with her mother when they're arguing.

15. Work out. You'll look better to her—as well as to other women. And don't think that she won't notice that, either.

16. Let her pick the movie once in a while, even if it stars Daniel Day-Lewis.

17. Cook at least one thing really well.

18. Don't make fun of the books she reads or the TV shows she likes.

19. Try to express concern, instead of glee, when you hit something furry on the highway.

gether. They can't leave well enough alone. And they can't be happy without making each other miserable.

"Being able to acknowledge and share your feelings is important, but there are times when you should shut up," says Dr. Barbach. "If you can't, that suggests that you and your mate may need to define yourselves separately and get a life outside the relationship."

Men are constantly being harangued for not being open about how they truly feel. And you know what? We're not open. We're silent and sulky and difficult to read. And that's a good thing.

"We temper our responses to women for a reason," says Dr. Farrell. "Men spend their lives communicating with each other primarily through good-natured put-downs. It's our way of helping each other handle the criticism that we'll face as we struggle to succeed.

We did this at the playground, and we do it at work today. But most women haven't had exposure to this kind of hazing and personal criticism. So when your woman asks you to be blunt—the way you are with your buddies—don't take it literally. Take it slowly."

When we instinctively tone down what we say to our mate as opposed to what we'd say to one of our friends, we're not lying. And we're not hiding our feelings. We're translating into a language that's not our native tongue. So if you stumble and slip on the words, or just can't pronounce them at all, that's okay. You're just trying to be nice.

Women's rule: Talk with her about her problems. Men's rule: Her problems aren't always your problems.

She comes to you with a dilemma. She wants your honest opinion. You, a dutiful mate, give her the advice that you believe will help solve the dilemma. You're honest, sensible and direct. And, naturally, she despises you for it.

"Women aren't entirely enamored of men who can solve their problems better than they can—and do it faster," says Dr. Farrell. "More than likely when your mate approaches you with a problem, all that she really wants to do is talk about it, and for you to listen; then she'll want to make up her own mind." The process rather than the solution is more important to her, so hold off on the advice until she really wants it.

"And while it's nice to give her a hand when she needs it," says Frank Pittman, M.D., family therapist in Atlanta and author of *Man Enough*, "it's also nice to live without solving problems all the time. Most of the problems that come up, frankly, go away on their own."

So the next time your mate brings up something that's bothering her, and you think that she wants your advice, think again. "If you can draw her out, she'll often solve the problem herself," says Dr. Farrell.

And you'll emerge from the conversation unscathed and no worse for wear.

Women's rule: Learn the art of negotiating.
Men's rule: Master the art of arguing.

She remembers the 1960s as the Age of Aquarius. You remember it as a time when a lot of rich kids didn't bathe. So when the topic comes up in conversation, she starts waxing poetic about the Summer of Love. And you bite your lip because you don't want to start anything.

Well, speak up. "Men worry about voicing opinions for fear that it may set off something," says Dr. Pittman. The problem, he says, is that men are embarrassed and ashamed by the prospect of having a fight with their spouses. But sometimes, we confuse "having a fight" with the fine art of conducting an argument. "In fact, differences of opinion are the business of relationships. By debating on various matters, you learn to appreciate the fact that a conversation need not be an argument where someone must lose."

Is it important for both of you to come to a reasonable compromise on everything? Please. "While it's important to walk a mile in your partner's moccasins, you're not required to buy them when you're through," says Dr. Farrell. "Understanding her point of view is important, but agreeing with it is far from mandatory."

Arguing is good. It helps you stop talking relationship talk and start talking like friends. "With your pals, the relationship is never at stake when you debate things," says Dr. Pittman. "You can say just about anything and you're still friends. That's what you should aim for in your relationship, too."

Of course, reaching that blissful state requires a bit of decorum when debating (meaning being polite): not interrupting or distorting what she says to make your own point. Or not belittling her in front of others because she thought Bolivia was a pricey watch. "It's more important to acknowledge her best intentions even if they are not your own," says Dr. Pittman.

Hot**Spots**

Follow This Map to Better Sex

The first time he saw his wife bend over, he was hooked. Her slender waist met her hips in a wild, dead-man's curve that begged for attention. For years, he obliged. Their sexual energy was high-octane, and the smallest caress in the least-likely spot could ignite an erotic conflagration. Touch an ear, an elbow, the small of the back—it didn't matter. Their bodies were two giant erogenous zones. When skin met skin, they needed some privacy, fast.

But it's been years now and, well, like many couples, they have fallen into a rut. Where they once plumbed every nook and crevice of their bodies for erotic potential, they now head right for the same old hot buttons. The sex that once seemed original and new has become as predictable as a *Batman* sequel.

Sound familiar? "Even among the most amorous couples, sex can become rote over time," says Barry McCarthy, Ph.D., a Washington, D.C.–based clinical psychologist and co-author of *Sexual Awareness*. We spend our first months and years learning what pleases the other most, but over time, we forget to explore. Instead, each sexual encounter becomes a mad charge to the genitals. Especially if work, kids and other concerns begin to cut into our private time together. "By the second or third year of a relationship, sex often becomes mechanical, routine and focused below the belt," Dr. McCarthy explains. "And when a man and his partner lose a sense of erotic anticipation, sex can become . . . well, a drag." (*Hint:* If you'd rather spend an evening with your remote control than your lover, read on.)

The problem is that we tend to give our bodies short shrift. The human form is loaded with erogenous zones other than the penis or clitoris. And unless you stimulate all of them, you're sitting down to a Steinway concert grand piano and playing "Chopsticks." If you want to make truly beautiful music, you have to use more of the keys.

There are two main benefits that you'll derive from incorporating a longer touching session into your lovemaking. First and foremost, it can lead to firmer erections for you and more powerful orgasms for you and your partner. What's that, you say? You don't need another reason to try it? Fine, but what's also great about prolonged touching sessions is that they can lead to greater intimacy—sexual and otherwise—between you and your partner. "Everyone's different—no two people get turned on getting touched in the exact same place," Dr. McCarthy says. "And that's the fun part—discovering what really turns your partner on and learning things about her, and about yourself, that you never knew." So the next time your lover goes for your zipper, tell her to slow down, then carry her to bed for a sensual evening of body exploration instead.

For a truly titillating session, you'll need at least a half-hour. Choose a time when you're not stressed out or distracted. And avoid the late evening, when men's testosterone levels fall by 25 percent. Let your imagination run wild. Don't feel confined to the bedroom. Use the shower, a hot tub or the pool table in the rec room. Try full or partial nudity. Crank some compact discs. Use oils, lotions or lubricants. Burn scented candles. "Play to the senses. Some people react to textures. Others react to sound and smell," says Dr. McCarthy. The goal is to arouse the senses—all of them. When you get an erection, don't feel compelled to use it right away. Dr. McCarthy sometimes bars his patients from intercourse until they've had several touch sessions. The steamy lovemaking that follows is well worth the wait, he assures.

He recommends the following hot zones for men and women.

Temples. Touch your partner's temples and you'll feel veins throbbing with tension and stress. Use your forefinger and index finger to massage the temples in gentle circular motions. Your partner will melt into a state of blissful relaxation.

Ears. The cliché of blowing in your lover's ear is accurate. Stimulation from a darting tongue or a light, probing finger can be a powerful aphrodisiac—especially when combined with heavy breathing into the ear. The erotic sensation can bring some men to orgasm. Researchers call the phenomenon the auriculogenital reflex and trace its origins to a nerve in the ear canal. "Don't set orgasm as a goal, however," says Dr. McCarthy. "A very small percentage of men actually climax from this."

Mouth. Trace the outline of your partner's lips, and she'll feel the sensation turn erotic when you reach the corner of her mouth. Perhaps because the spot is rarely touched, it's all the more sensitive. Experiment to discover your partner's individual preference. Alternate hard kisses and deep, probing tongue strokes with soft, open-mouthed kisses punctuated by light, playful licks.

Neck and spine. There's a plethora of opportunities here. The thick lateral neck muscles that run from the base of the skull to the shoulders harbor tension from the chore of holding the head erect all day. Nibble or stroke them into submission, but be careful not to squeeze them—that can be painful, especially when they're tense and tired. Use the neck as a springboard for exploring the shoulders and collarbone, the fleshy area under the jaw and the soft spot where the neck meets the base of the skull. Try quick, playful love bites, especially on the sensitive collarbone. Move toward the center of the back and trace the contours of the spine lightly with your tongue. Travel up and down your partner's back, blowing and tickling lightly as you go.

Underarms. The tremendous accumulation of nerve endings here makes for great erotic potential. Using only your fingertips, stroke lightly and rhythmically from the rib cage toward the arms. Chances are that your partner will feel ticklish at first. Gradually, however, she'll succumb to the sensual feeling.

Nipples (for men). Perhaps for fear of "being like a woman," men have overlooked the sensual potential of their nipples and the surrounding areolae. Yet many men report erotic sensations when they have their partners tickle, nibble or even gently bite their nipples. Sometimes, the feeling brings men to climax. So don't be surprised if you get an instant erection when your partner finds your preferred approach.

Navel. Maybe because of the sexual association with penetration, the navel harbors ticklish and erotic feelings. Probe your partner's navel with a darting tongue while you trace the outline with your index finger.

Tanzen. Located about three inches below the navel, this region was thought by ancient Japanese to harbor a person's chi, or life force. Even if you're skeptical about Eastern spirituality, your partner will find that a stimulated tanzen is soothing and sensual. Position your partner on her back, kneel between her legs, grasp her hips with each hand and use your thumbs to massage her tanzen with slow, upward strokes.

Perineum (for men). Most men don't know that this fleshy island between the scrotum and anus even exists. Have your partner lift your testicles with one hand and use the forefinger of the other to massage your perineum with deep circular strokes. The pleasure comes not from the proximity to your penis, but from the prostate gland, which lies just inside the lower pelvic cavity. Stroking the perineum stimulates the gland, one of men's hidden hot zones.

Inner thighs. Another good argument for slowing down your rush toward the genitalia is that the inner thighs are ablaze with

---

JUST THE FACTS

Percentage of personal-computer owners surveyed who said that they kissed someone the previous Saturday night: 50

nerve endings because of their proximity to the genitals. They are a primary target for nonsexual touching. Start with strokes so light that they barely register on your fingertips, and build to a crescendo of long, powerful strokes that work your fingers deep into the tender thigh muscles.

Knees. The tender flesh behind the knee is good for both a tickle and a turn-on. Make sure that your partner's leg is fully extended, then gently trace a figure eight on the back of the knee with your fingertips or the tip of your tongue.

Fingers and toes. Yes, it's true. Suck away. And don't forget to use your tongue to probe the crevices between each and every digit.

PART 6

Looking Good

Fashion Trends

The dominant theme in current fashion seems to be "what goes around comes around." Culled from the pages of GQ, Esquire, Details *and the* New York Times Magazine, *the look that is coming back is the "wild and crazy" days of the late 1960s and early 1970s. At this rate, leisure suits can't be too far behind.*

1. Slim suits, often made from lustrous fabrics, single-breasted, one button, with broad shoulders, fitted waist and peaked lapels.

2. Close-fitting ribbed shirts and polo shirts, often with a striped collar.

3. Brighter colors for shirts, in punchy shades of peach and lime, mixed with patterned ties.

4. Loafers, possibly white, but certainly without socks. White socks with casual wear, though, are now back on the scene.

5. Trousers and khakis that have a flat front, trim cut and are often low-slung.

6. Mid-length outerwear.

7. Sleek, minimalist, cropped racing jackets in leather and synthetic fibers.

8. Plush, close-fitting frock coats and velvet coats, vests and trousers.

9. Urban prep à la Nautica and Hilfiger—young men who are a "walking oxymoron" combining giant-size coats and pants with designer shirts.

10. Outerwear made of high-tech fabrics and constructed jackets of leather.

Casual Days

Dress Right When Your Company
Dresses Down

You've had this dream before: You show up at school ready for a day of reading, writing and outsmarting bullies. But something's different. The classroom is the same, the teacher's the same, the kids are the same. It's you. Something's wrong.

Oh, my God! You're not wearing any clothes!

If you work at IBM or Du Pont or any of the other megacompanies that have relaxed their dress codes in recent years, you might be having these anxiety dreams all over again. Except this time, all the other people are dressed in trousers and pullovers, and you're wearing a navy business suit without the tie—the 1990s equivalent of showing up in your underwear. Maybe your company has adopted "casual Friday." Or maybe your company has declared that every day is Friday. Either way, things are changing. When Big Blue becomes Big Khaki, when Lamar Alexander announces his presidential run dressed like a lumberjack, you know that it's time to take a hard look at your wardrobe.

There are a lot of theories as to why casual days have become so common. Is it because aging baby boomers want to relive their youth? Because technology has made face-to-face interaction obsolete? Is it the movement toward healthy, active lifestyles? Or has our clothing changed for no other reason than, frankly, we're all just a little pissed off?

See, being a working man used to be easy. You put on your white shirt, your blue suit and your appropriately muted tie, and you put in your eight hours. And you did it over and over again for 40 years until you retired on a hefty pension and moved to Phoenix. But then those eight hours started becoming more like ten, the axes started falling and the company pension plan dried up. And the blue suit just didn't seem appropriate anymore. We're working too hard, with too little help and too little security, to spend all day and half the night constrained in a suit. Maybe the reason that casual clothes are in is that, as employees, we're sticking our collective heads out our office windows and yelling, "We're just not going to wear it anymore!"

And companies realize that letting us do our own thing is good for business. "Economics played a big part in the thinking behind our dress-casual code," says a spokesperson for Nationwide Insurance, which let down its corporate hair in 1994. "We found that productivity actually increased in this more relaxed atmosphere."

So the companies are hanging loose. The employees are hanging loose. But there's just one problem: If you're not going to wear your business suit to work, what are you going to wear?

There usually aren't any written rules, even in the stodgiest of companies. "There are no clothing police at IBM," says the company's human resources spokesman, Tom Beermann. "How 'relaxed' an employee should dress is left up to the individual." But you just know that there are a lot of unwritten rules. If you want to be taken seriously as a candidate for that next major promotion, knowing a few do's and don'ts can't hurt. So we polled executives at several major companies to find out what they expected from their employees in the way of casual dress—what's classy, what's trashy and what's going to get you into, or keep you out of, that corner office.

First, here are some warning

signs that you may have misinterpreted what "dress casual" really means.

You are mistaken on the street for one of the surviving members of Nirvana. Anything that is worn, ripped, soiled or otherwise grungy is inappropriate. Clothes should be clean and pressed. Casual does not mean funky. After you've dressed, imagine yourself changing the oil in your car. Are you dressed for that? If so, you'll have to change. And remember, nobody's going to take you seriously if you show up in Converse sneakers with naked natives on your shirt.

You're wearing the same clothes you used to wear, only differently. "Dress casual" does not mean "Take off your tie and be done with it." Those shiny black oxfords don't go with casual clothes, and you cannot just take off the jacket of your business suit and unbutton your shirt. Similarly, any silk tie that went well with a business suit probably won't go well with comfortable clothing.

Single-breasted suits, though, can look tailor-made for a relaxed workplace if paired with a banded-collar shirt and sporty shoes. Avoid double-breasted suits—there's no way to dress those strait-jackets down.

Strangers stare at your chest. Don't wear clothes with words on them, such as "Beer: Not Just for Breakfast Anymore" or "Kiss Me, I'm Irish." Do not wear the souvenir shirt you bought at last summer's Nine Inch Nails concert. You're not being paid to be a billboard. T-shirts may be appropriate in some companies, but make them solid-color, superclean shirts, perhaps with a pocket—something that will go with a pair of chinos and a sport jacket.

Other definite don'ts include sandals, sneakers (unless you work at Nike) and sports clothing such as spandex bike shorts. Jeans? Well, it depends on whom you ask. Some executives told us that jeans in good condition were okay; others frowned on them. What we gleaned was this: If you do wear jeans, dress them up. Pair them

---

JUST THE FACTS

More than half of 25- to 34-year-old American men shop for clothing at least once a month.

with, say, a pressed oxford shirt and a jacket or vest. Here are some other suggestions.

Shirts. Chambray, denim or flannel shirts are softer substitutes for your starched white dress shirt. Heavy oxford-cloth button-downs and polo or rugby shirts are also good choices. A golf shirt can work, but only in season. Don't try to pair it with a wool jacket and corduroy pants.

Sweaters. Keep on hand a few turtlenecks, some cable-knit and Shetland crew-neck sweaters and maybe a sweater vest.

Pants. Corduroys, khakis or cotton twills, gray flannels and some tan and navy medium-weight wools are good choices. Avoid overly baggy pants and anything that incorporates elastic as part of its fashion philosophy. Also look for trousers in patterns such as houndstooth check or plaid. You don't have those pinstripes to add pizzazz anymore.

Don't wear shorts until you see your boss in them, in which case it's safe to go with tan, olive or navy walking shorts cut just above the knee. No cutoffs, even if your boss wears them.

Sport coats. Keep a blazer on hand, always. Tossing it on over whatever you're wearing gives you a more authoritative appearance, and you never know when a client is going to drop by and argue about his bill. Cashmere and flannel are excellent fabrics to choose. There are even softer, fuller-cut suits available for the man who can't give up matching his tops with his bottoms.

Ties. You don't need them, but if you still love wearing ties, look for softer knits of cotton or wool. Avoid shiny silk ties and dressier patterns like foulard prints or dots.

Shoes. Business shoes were designed to carry the weight of all the layers of clothing inherent to business dress. With casual dress, look for simpler shoes, such as loafers, lug soles, chukka boots, suede oxfords, even cowboy boots. Avoid anything that can best be described by an activity that you're not going to be involved in at work: hiking boots, basketball sneakers, boating shoes. Also, wear patterned socks—not athletic socks, not solid-color business socks.

So relax, look your best and do your best. And if those dreams about showing up in your underwear start coming back, maybe you should take a vacation.

A Man of Style

Simple Steps to Sharper Dressing

When it comes to style, the difference between men and women is bolder than the check on a houndstooth check blazer. She dresses to look beautiful. You dress not to make a mistake.

Why? Simple. You don't know any different.

What did Dad ever show you besides how to throw a ball, step into a pitch and prepare for a layup shot? How to tie a tie (one way only), how to tie your shoes and how to ask for a regular man's haircut—"not too much off the top"?

Do you ever remember hearing him say, "You know, son, it's such a nice day, let's go shopping"? Or, "Why don't we go to the market and pick up some fresh fruit?" Or, "How about we find a nice Merlot and shoot the breeze?" Didn't think so. And now you're hungry, and you're thirsty, and you have really boring stuff to wear.

Well, you're not alone. It's what happens to most men when they hear the word "style." Guys were never taught what it is, so they think either that it's the same as fashion (which guarantees a free fall into panic) or it's something that everyone else seems to have more of.

But style is not about fashion. It's about the quality of imagination. It's about choice. Clothes don't have style. You do. You seem to have no problem daydreaming about a dream vacation or the perfect 18-hole golf course. You will drive a car salesman crazy about the availability of a particular British racing green. Yet, how come that same specificity and discernment fail you when it's time to edit your wardrobe, select a scent that enhances seduction or tell if your own shoes fit? The process by which you select the right tennis racket is not that much different from the one that you need to buy the perfect suit, to pack for a business trip or to care for your own skin. It's all about what suits you, makes you comfortable, makes you happy and gets the job done.

The problem is that you never explored these areas in your youth the way that you did your more obvious penchants. And now you feel silly. Well, get over it. There's still plenty of time to acquire style. All you have to do are the two things that you hate doing more than standing outside the fitting room in Better Dresses: Ask for help and take advice.

That doesn't mean that you have to go searching to find the new you. The old one got you this far. Let's just clean him up a bit.

It's Easier Than You Think

When it comes to enhancing your look, all that you have to do is follow one of the oldest tenets in clothing sales, a bylaw that any good salesman will offer you as a KISS: "Keep it simple, stupid."

Think about that KISS. Laying pattern upon pattern, stripe upon check, print upon plaid is complicated, risky and, more often than not, disappointing. What's worse is that it's a waste of time. You don't have to get so complicated.

Nothing looks cooler than combining solids with solids. Dark colors with dark colors, earth tones with earth tones. Or wearing variations of the same tone. It's not necessary to match exactly one navy blue to another. As for matching lapel, collar and tie widths, with rare exceptions, like follows like. Skinny lapel, skinny collar, thin tie—you get the idea. If you are like most men, who follow the edict of Yogi Berra, you know that if you think about it, you can't do it. Now you don't have to, so you can.

Shirts. The cleaner your choices, the better you look. When in doubt, put on the white shirt. As for collar variations, there are four kinds popularly available, but you're foolish to get yourself caught up in this multiple choice. The spread collar is fine for wide lapels and if you love big tie knots. Button-down collars look geeky and uptight, and will make even the newest suit look slightly stale. Stick with a regular classic collar, which looks fine with almost every kind of suit.

Ties. Here is a mystery to outdo the Sphinx's. The average suit sells for at least 15 times the cost of a tie. It covers your whole body. It defines you. It's designed to say more about you than any other piece of clothing you have on. Then why do men, and their loved ones, feel obliged to upstage this presentation by buying a strip of silly, goofy, cutesy, critter-filled, career-indicating, carnival candy–colored fabric that screams, "Look at this, and forget the rest"?

Listen up. The biggest compliment that you can ever hope to get from wearing a yard of ostentatious silk is "Hey, snazzy tie." The biggest compliment you can get from wearing a beautifully cut suit is "Hey. Get a load of you. You look great." Which would you rather hear? A tie, by definition, is an accessory. Let it accessorize. Now, go pick one that will show off your suit.

A Suit Makes the Man

You'd probably rather mow the lawn, sit through your nephew's third-grade dance recital or have your wisdom teeth extracted with a pocketknife. But unless you've developed technology from an episode of *The X-Files* that the rest of us missed, a new suit is not going to find its way into your closet unescorted. So get moving. No whining that you don't know how. Learn. There's a new world out there. Try dressing as if you're part of it.

Have a vision. Knowing a suit's purpose in your wardrobe will narrow your field of choices.

Business travel? Then the estimable qualities are weightlessness and the ability to lose wrinkles by being hung for ten minutes in a steamy bathroom.

Year-round wear? Remember that corduroy has a tendency to retain beach sand.

Know your fabrics. This doesn't mean that you have to know the percentage of wool or silk in a blend. Common knowledge and common sense will do for openers. Traveling while on business? Then linen is out. Find low maintenance appealing? Then linen is out. Want your money's worth with a year-round garment? Then linen is out.

Here's what you do need to know.

- Wool blends de-wrinkle quickly, wool crepe being the quickest and the most comfortable.
- Cotton weighs next to nothing, so it's nice for summer travel.
- Corduroy makes your butt look bigger.
- Polyester, born again as "microfiber" but with the Sybilline capacity to adopt personalities as varied as viscose and ramie, is now pliable, resilient, occasionally luxurious and no longer the flag bearer of cheesiness. Wash-and-wear, however, looks and remains as cheesy as it sounds.
- Linen is for remaining totally cool while looking fabulously carefree. You can, however, sustain the effect over long periods only if you never sit down. In fact, avoid leaning, reaching and turning too quickly.

Shop at the right place. You don't know what wool crepe, viscose or ramie is, do you? Don't worry. You'd be amazed at how many guys reading this don't even know what linen is. That's okay, too. The only things that you really need to know are how to find one good men's store that doesn't make you feel as if you're being judged on whether you're worthy of its time, and how to find a salesperson in that store who likes his work, does his homework and, most of all, listens.

A savvy salesperson is the most desirable accomplice to have in tow when you're shopping, far more valuable than being accompanied by a male friend, which practically ensures purchasing either nothing or a duplicate of something you already own; or by a female one, which guarantees your dressing the way that she sees you and permanently quashes any attempts at indulging in secret sartorial daydreams for fear of looking foolish in her eyes. As for blood relations, shop with them when you're looking for a burial plot.

By the way, you know that you're in the right store if:

- The salespeople are wearing clothes that they like, perhaps have even bought.
- They ask what you already have in your closet.
- They knock before they open the dressing room door.
- They don't tell you that you look good—they show you why you do or don't.
- They provide three-way mirrors.
- The staff recognizes you the next time you're there.

On the other hand, you're probably in the wrong store if:

- The lighting was inspired by *Tommy*.
- You've been wandering for five minutes, and no one has yet said, "May I help you?" or at least, "Good afternoon."
- The staff members dress as if they could veto your promotion and behave as if they'd seen you on *Hard Copy*.
- The salesperson tells you that you're "hard to fit."
- You don't recognize any artist on the sound system.

Slip on a high-priced suit. Good-looking suits can be found at all prices, but expect to pay at least $500 retail for a suit that flatters you and offers enough quality to provide a full-day's-wearing level of comfort. But before you put up your price ceiling, even if you have no intention of parting with this much of your paycheck, try on an expensive suit, if only to provide you with a frame of reference as to what a suit should do for you, what it can look like on you and what you ought to feel like in it. It's why a struggling law student test-drives a Porsche. It's the reason that we have museums. You can't devise standards unless you know the range of possibilities.

Ensure that it fits in some key areas. Great tailors can work magic. But if a suit jacket does not fit in the shoulders—if it puckers, drops too low or is too restricting—or if a jacket's too short or too long, take it off. Here are some other points to consider.

- There should be no puckering or bulk where the shoulder insets to the sleeve. If there is, it will not iron or steam out. If a salesperson promises you that it will, ask to see another salesperson, permanently.
- If the desired fabric is plaid or striped, look at the way the pattern is matched at the seams and how it is handled on the lapels, at the shoulders and especially down the center seam in the back.
- A felt backing, not a backing of matching fabric on the underside of the lapels, is what you want.
- Look at the quality of the buttons—plastic, wood, horn—and how they're sewn on. If there is thread wound round and round between fabric and button, the buttons were probably sewn on by hand. Very good.
- Is the lining of comparable quality to that of the jacket? Is it fully sewn down? Is it sewn to the fabric at any point other than the edges, compromising movement?
- Flap pockets look best on business suits.
- All pockets and buttonholes should work.
- The back of the jacket collar should be flush with your neck. No dead space.

Caring for Your Other "Suit"

Okay, you look great in that new suit. But as for what's holding it up, well, we may still have some work to do. How much did your dad teach you about skin care?

You didn't think that it mattered, did you? You wash, you dry and you're out of there. Your skin? What about it?

The mirror has stopped sending you off with a "Looking good, kiddo." The media's harangues about the ozone layer, ultraviolet rays, tretinoin (Retin-A) and the dramatic rise in melanoma are getting to you. Your skin's a little flaky. Sometimes, it's itchy. You burn. Face it, you're getting older. She is, too. But she's getting better. You? You're not so sure. It's time you knew.

A man can't afford to treat his skin any differently than the way that a woman treats hers. You don't want to hear that, do you, macho man? Well, keep scratching if you want. Tell others that it's from bewilderment. But you can still stave off prune season if you act now.

- Stop washing with those banded quartets of detergent soaps sold in discount drugstores for next to nothing. This is all the skin factory that you're ever going to have, and—like it or not—it's in the first stages of a work slowdown. Try gentler glycerin soaps such as Neutrogena Original Formula Cleansing Bar.
- When you wash, pretend that it's someone else's skin. Go easy. Squeaky clean is for dishes.
- You can't go without moisturizing anymore. You don't need gunk, but you do need help. Most men's hydrating products are either oil-free or have low oil content; are light and absorbed almost instantly; and have savvy, nonthreatening packages—usually in austere steel blue or charcoal gray.
- Look at the faces of those actors who have had work done and look incredible. Then look at their hands. Hands are nature's way of saying "Gotcha." Better moisturize them, too.
- For clean, healthy, younger-looking skin, as much water as you can drink is not enough.

This simple skin-care regimen will add 15 minutes to your daily routine, which finally gives you somewhere to put all that time that you claim to be saving on baked potatoes with your new microwave. That's a quarter of an hour for looking a few years younger. You've made worse deals.

On the Road

Going away again? Ah, think of those stone bridges, quaint inns, warm fires, lucrative contracts. Nice. Just remember severe wardrobe edit, indifferent cabbies, dehydration, wrinkled linen,

snapshot junkies, foreign customs, U.S. Customs. Here are some
essentials for business travel.

- Reservations. Confirmations. Aggravations. Why bother?
  Find a good travel agent. They know nice hotels. They ask
  questions that you don't until you get there. They know people, make deals and save money, because it often costs you
  nothing. That's right, nothing. In case no one has told you,
  most commissions come from the other side.
- A travel agent who doesn't get you boarding passes in advance is not a good travel agent. Next.
- Renewing a passport is as much fun as visiting the Department of Motor Vehicles. Unless you're dying to finish that
  new Tom Clancy novel, there are people who will endure this
  for you. They're listed in the phone book under "Passport and
  Visa Services." For what it will cost you to wait, it's a bargain.
- Pack using the Jelly Doughnut Theory—hard stuff on the
  outside, squishy stuff on the inside. But line the flat sides of
  the suitcase with semi-unwrinkleables like sweat clothes,
  jeans and socks so that protruding heels and hair dryers
  don't jab when you're lugging.
- For short business trips, stick to black or gray, and white,
  plus one color.
- Most business travelers pack more pants than sport jackets.
  It should be the other way around. You're at meetings. Who
  sees your pants?
- Turn your jackets inside out.
- Roll your ties. Then put them in jacket pockets.
- Cotton sweaters are more versatile than wool.
- The most versatile item of sportswear is black jeans.
- Interlock your belts around the inside circumference of the
  suitcase.

JUST THE FACTS

Number of American men who wear contact lenses: 8 million

- No matter how warm the weather, wear your topcoat onto the plane, then fold it inside out and stow it in the overhead. It eats up too much of the suitcase and unpacks as if it has been chewed. Wear your boots on board as well.
- Your carry-on luggage should contain: your cash and traveler's checks, checkbook, passport, tickets, jewelry, personal effects, toiletries, reading material, work, gifts (maybe), medicine, house keys and a change of clothes.
- Tags fall off. Paste your name and address inside your luggage as well.
- It's just an observation, but handlers throw tapestry luggage harder—and don't catch it. Look at it. Can you blame them?
- If you're not going straight to the meeting, why are you wearing your suit on the plane?
- Learn how to say, "Where's the bathroom?" in the correct language before you get there.
- People who need people are called houseguests. If you're staying longer than four days and your friends don't have a mortgage on the Ponderosa, be a pal; check into a hotel.
- If you're in town on business, even for only one night, check into a hotel. Let the business pay. Let your friends take you to dinner.
- Why stay in better hotels? Because they can launder in a few hours, and they have room service when it's 3:00 A.M. but your stomach thinks it's dinnertime. Because they sew buttons, press faster, have clout with maître d's, offer feather pillows and remember your name.
- Don't live out of the suitcase. Stake a claim. Unpack as soon as you get into the room. Ask for two dozen hangers. Put your books on the nightstand. Rearrange the furniture. Take a shower that lasts way too long, then use every towel in the bathroom. There are lots more.
- If you're going through more than one roll of film a day, you may be on a vacation, but everyone with you is in hell.
- If you buy art, or would like to think that it's art, have the dealer write "one of a kind" on the receipt and you won't have to pay duty on it at customs.

The Face of Youth

Get a Healthier Look with This Advice

Okay, maybe you're no longer the fairest of them all. You're older and wiser, and you have a few lines. Every time you look in the mirror, you see the kids and the mortgage and the job and the stress and all the bad things that you did to your body during college, all written right there, on your face. It's the story of your life. But you don't necessarily have to live with it. Here are some quick and easy steps, and some long and arduous ones, that can give you a younger, healthier visage, starting today.

Forehead wrinkles. A facial peel can remove some stubborn wrinkles that exercise, tretinoin (Retin-A) and drugstore alpha hydroxy acids can't handle. "A facial peel is a chemical burn that induces healing—old skin peels off, and new skin replaces it," says Melvin L. Elson, M.D., medical director of the Dermatology Center in Nashville and co-author of *The Good Look Book*. A light peel will sting for only a few minutes, but the result is permanent on mild to moderate wrinkles. (Of course, new ones can crop up.) One word of caution: Have the procedure done by a physician such as a dermatologist or a plastic surgeon. In some states, salons can offer this procedure. Uh-huh. This is a surgical job, and it comes with risks. The cost is anywhere from $650 to $1,500.

Crow's-feet. If you're not up to surgery and just need a quick fix, try whisking an egg white and gently applying a light coat over your wrinkles. The egg white tightens your skin and flattens wrinkles. It works as well as any $100 wrinkle cream.

Light wrinkles. Go for a brisk daily walk. Exercise flushes your skin with blood. The result is denser, thicker skin that springs back to its original shape after being stretched. This translates to fewer wrinkles and bags around the eyes, says James White, Ph.D., an exercise physiologist in San Diego and author of the exercise book *Jump for Joy.*

Dry eyes. Change deodorants. If yours contains an antiperspirant, that could be what's making your eyes dry, according to Dan Nelson, M.D., chief of ophthalmology at the St. Paul Ramsey Medical Center in Minnesota. Antihistamines can also cause dry eyes.

Dark circles under your eyes. If you look like Robert De Niro in *Raging Bull,* you might want to check out a surgery called Fresh Eyes. Developed by Dr. Elson in 1992, this procedure lightens your dark circles by placing a layer of collagen (the natural connective tissue within your skin) between the skin and the muscle. It lasts up to 12 months, and the most pain you'll feel is a slight prick from the needle, he says. The average cost of this procedure is $400.

Chapped lips. Switch toothpastes. Some can cause dry, chapped lips; tartar-control products and dyes are the most common irritants. Switching to a baking-soda formulation can solve the problem, says John E. Wolf, Jr., M.D., chairman of the Department of Dermatology at Baylor College of Medicine in Houston. Or grab a lip balm. On second thought, use a lip balm anyway. One with a sun protection factor of at least 15 will minimize your risk of lip cancer, a common male malady. (Women don't get it as much, since they often wear lipstick.)

Razor burn and bumps. If razor burn is a problem, apply a layer of light moisturizing lotion before your shaving cream, suggests Marina Valmy, a cosmetician at Christine Valmy Skin Care School in New York City. Then wait two to three minutes. Your face will be softer and more likely to give under a razor.

Sunspots. Use a cotton swab and dab fresh lemon juice on your sunspots twice a day. The citric acid safely and painlessly peels away the skin's uppermost layer, says Jerome Z. Litt, M.D., assistant clinical professor of dermatology at Case Western Reserve University School of Medicine in Cleveland and author of *Your Skin: From Acne to Zits.* Be patient: You should see results within a month or so.

If you use sunblock, you'll help keep new spots from forming.

Oily skin. The more you wash, the more oil and acne you seem to get. It could be because your cleansers and moisturizers are oil-based. You don't want to add oil to what's already there. Keep your facial products oil-free, and moisturize only skin that is dry.

Monobrow. You don't have to shave between your eyes. Electrolysis will remove the hair and stop it from growing back. During electrolysis, the hair follicle is zapped by an electric current that travels through a very fine needle. The discomfort level is mild, the risk of scarring is minimal and you'll probably need only a few sessions for the hair removal to become permanent. Each session ranges from $15 to $100, depending on the time that it takes.

Bags under your eyes. You shouldn't have had that V-8. Canned vegetable drinks and tomato juice are loaded with sodium, which can cause your body to retain water. The bloating that results will often announce itself around your eyes, says Julius Shulman, M.D., assistant clinical professor of ophthalmology at Mount Sinai Hospital in New York City.

Dry skin. Toss out your soap. The key ingredients in many soaps are detergents, which can be too harsh for dry skin, according to *Men's Health* magazine adviser John Romano, M.D., a dermatologist at New York Hospital–Cornell Medical Center in New York City. Instead, use a soap-free cleanser and top it with a moisturizer. If it contains a mild alphahydroxy acid, all the better. These acids help slough off the dead upper layer of skin. (Hey, do you want to look like your old man?)

Double chin. If you have an extra chin or two that can't be budged by slimming down or pumping iron, consider liposuction. It isn't only for women's thighs. A lot of men are having it done to their chins as part of a face-lift procedure. "I call it a neck-lift. It's not a full face-lift, and the only incisions needed are two unnoticeable ones behind the ears and maybe a small one under the chin," says Chicago cosmetic surgeon Richard T. Caleel, D.O. The muscles and skin on the neck are tightened and suspended to give the whole neck a leaner look. "The pain is equivalent to what you may feel after a tough workout," he says. The difference, of course, is that a workout won't set you back $1,500 to $3,000.

Grooming through the Ages

Look Your Best at Any Time

There are two roads leading from here to Geezerville. One road is wide and smooth: It simply demands that for the rest of your life, you try to look as young as you are right now—or, if you're more than, say, 25, as old as you were when you looked fabuloso. It's an easy road to follow: You just go straight uphill all the way.

The other road twists and winds and takes you through the decades of adulthood as if each year were an interesting sight to see. On this road, you forget trying to look 25 forever. Instead, you concentrate on looking as good as anybody your age—or, with just a little effort, much better than most.

Both roads lead to the same place: six-oh, the gateway to wisdom, where you pick up all your lovely parting gifts. But on the first road, you cross the line looking like a chemical-filled mummy held together with spandex and black hair dye. On the second road, you arrive in the best style possible—your own. And that's not bad. Heck, that's not even old.

"Being 50 is not what it was 20 years ago," says J. Stanley Tucker, fashion director for that monument to impeccable grooming and sartorial splendor, Saks Fifth Avenue. "Today," he says, "50 is young." True enough. Men are staying in shape longer. The youth culture invented by today's half-centenarians has sustained a limited trickle-up effect, and older men in car ads no longer drive

Oldsmobiles, which they can afford, but flashy luxury coupes accompanied by beautiful women, which they can't.

Most guys know that looking great isn't simply a matter of absorbing youth vibes. For one thing, after a certain age, looking young doesn't guarantee looking good. According to Tucker, to present an image that's sharp, clean and sophisticated, you have to work for it, at any age. We're here to tell you how, with the big picture being this: Your body's not the same from one decade to the next, and your grooming and clothing objectives aren't either. Here's what you need to watch out for as you reel in the years.

The Early Years

Nobody understands the twentysomething guy. Older men think that he has it made, with his full head of perfect hair, taut skin and lean muscles. Actually, guys in their twenties tend to think the same way: assuming they can do—or suffer from—no wrong. And that's where most of the problems lie.

Your hair. It's healthy; it's manageable; your stylist says it even has a "sheen," a term coined for a family of male movie stars— Emilio, Charlie and Martin—all of whom have hair deluxe. But in your twenties, hair takes a lot of abuse. Playing outdoors exposes it to the elements; multiple daily showers using whatever shampoo (even, admit it, soap) is at hand makes hair dry and robs it of proteins; applying a second coat of gel causes product buildup. It all amounts to what the guys with the scissors call "styling stress." "The overall effect is that hair can appear dull and frayed-looking," says Damien Miano of Miano–Viel Salon and Spa in New York City. "Even a good haircut suddenly won't look so good."

The best protection is simple: Use gentler cleansers that are low in detergents but high in emollients to prevent hair from getting

JUST THE FACTS

According to a survey of dentists, 81 percent of the patients they see who have bad breath are men.

dry and brittle. For a bit more body, use a gentle "leave-in" conditioner that you apply after towel-drying. "It provides a light grooming effect that a lot of men prefer to gel," says Christina Griffasi, style director of New York City's Minardi Salon.

Your skin. Postpimple, prewrinkle: Your skin will never look better. The only question is, how much foresight do you have? Exposure to the elements, particularly the sun, takes a toll on skin as well as hair. The only difference is that skin damage won't show up for another 15 years or so, in the form of premature leathering and lining of the face. Avoiding sun exposure is just as difficult for a guy in his twenties as saving money for retirement, but the rewards are just as great if you make an early investment.

To rebuff premature aging, wage war. Wear protective clothing (hats and the like). Avoid the sun between 10:00 A.M. and 4:00 P.M. Regularly wear sunscreen. And don't skimp on the stuff. "Most people apply it too thinly," says Susan Detwiler, M.D., clinical instructor of dermatology at Stanford University School of Medicine. "Put it on so that an entire area is white, then lightly remove the excess."

Your clothes. It's a form of natural balance (older men might say justice) that being in peak form physically is generally offset by being in middling shape financially. You can't afford true finery—but then, you don't need it like a 40-year-old does. Older members of the great big brotherhood of men understand this, so it's still possible to make a good impression on a budget in your twenties. "You can buy a pair of $60 Florsheim shoes that come pretty close in style to a pair of $200 Ferragamos," says *Men's Health* magazine clothing and grooming editor Warren Christopher. And in a more casual business environment, you don't have to match power suits with the Head Gorgonzola. Combining khakis from familiar stores like Gap or Banana Republic with a shirt from Tommy Hilfiger and jacket from Haggar makes it easy to succeed in business dress without really trying.

Special concerns. It's time to stop jawboning about your teeth and consider getting serious, if you haven't already. "By the twenties, major bone and tooth development is complete, so it's an ideal time to make an assessment of what might happen down the road," says Robert Bray, D.D.S., spokesperson for the American Association of Orthodontists in St. Louis. If you have a problem with appearance or alignment, now's the time to take care of it. "Don't wait to have orthodontal work done," says Dr. Bray. "Younger bones recover and adapt better than older ones."

Catching Your Stride

It's a period of transition, this decade between carefree youth and full-bore adulthood—which is great. You're young and mature at the same time. But maturity entails some changes.

Your hair. Uh-oh. It might not be noticeable at first, but your hair may be thinning. That doesn't necessarily mean that your hairline is changing. In fact, the number of hair follicles rooted in your cranium may be the same, but each individual strand is less thick than before. What does this mean to you? Your hair dries more quickly. It has less shine: It's sheenless. It appears flatter. It may not feel as good to women who might want to run their fingers through it.

Fortunately, thinning isn't uniform but usually concentrates at the top of the head, says Griffasi. She recommends letting the hair on top grow out a bit, while reducing bulk at the back and sides. "It makes your hair look balanced and more consistently full," she says. If you also happen to be losing hair, don't wait to use Rogaine, the only balding treatment proven to work. It produces best results for young men who've been balding less than five years.

Your skin. The skin concerns for a man in his thirties aren't significantly different than for a man in his twenties, especially if you've done a good job of controlling sun exposure. In some men, however, oil-making glands just below the surface start cranking up production during this decade, giving skin a greasier, thicker appearance, says Barry I. Resnik, M.D., clinical instructor of dermatology and cutaneous surgery at the University of Miami School of Medicine.

The obvious way to deal with this is to wash more often with soap and water. The trouble is that healthy-looking skin needs some oil for moisture, and soap strips it away. Here's a solution: Use a soap-free cleanser, then follow with a light moisturizer. You may want to try oil-inhibiting pads, which help regulate the amount of oil allowed to percolate to the surface without stripping it. "That will keep skin looking smooth and clean, and also feeling more comfortable," Dr. Resnik says. Top it all off with a sunscreen.

Your clothes. In your thirties, you're a pathfinder, exploring and setting the courses that will carry you through the rest of your life professionally, socially and personally. You're established in a career, you may be getting married and you may be accepting leadership roles in your community. In all of this, clothes become more important, says Tucker. Not incidentally, you probably have more discretionary income than you did in your twenties. It's a time, Tucker says, to upgrade to quality garb that will last for years, especially if you foresee income-diverting children in your future.

So trade the Florsheims for Cole Haans. Get a serious watch to replace the Fossil that you've been wearing. Stylewise, the world's your oyster, but you still don't have to spend a fortune: With suit and sportcoat lines such as Assets/Andrew Fezza or Hugo Boss, you can get quality European styling at reasonable prices.

Special concerns. You're hitting the leading edge of the aging curve. Don't make the mistake of shrugging off loss of flexibility, as most men do. For one thing, the tapering of resilience starts sooner than other symptoms of aging. It's already been happening for ten years or so.

There's no need to enroll in a yoga class to stay limber. Just make a point of gently stretching major muscles once or twice a day. Here's just about the simplest stretch we know, courtesy of Bob Anderson, author of *Stretching*. It works much of your body, especially your back: Lie on your back on the floor with your legs straight. Extend your arms overhead. Now reach as far as possible in each direction, extending your arms up and legs out as far as they can go. Hold for five seconds, then relax. That's it. Repeat five times.

At the Peak of Your Game

For a lot of guys, the forties are the peak. The long, hard climb to success is nearly over. That's the good news. The bad news is that when you're at the top—well, let's just say that it's not as difficult to go from 40 to 50 as it was to go from 30 to 40. On the other hand, you've gained lots of experience, you know what you're doing, you know who you are and you have a good idea where you're going. You don't need to ask for directions in life because you've already been down most of the pertinent paths. You have that inner boy whipped into shape. Now you need mastery of the external you.

Your hair. The big question is what you're going to do if you're suffering significant hair loss. There are plenty of options, but not many real solutions. Wigs, weaves, wunderkind surgeries—all can help, but all entail risks of making you look foolish, if not permanently scarred. The most sophisticated solution, Griffasi says, is to work with what you have. "Cut the hair much shorter and closer to the head," she advises. "It looks dramatic and has a much younger effect than trying to comb it over." Think about growing a closely cropped beard and mustache to balance the short hair on top. "When a beard is kept short and the edges are neatened daily with a razor, it looks wonderful," Griffasi says. Console yourself with this rule of thumb: Your age roughly corresponds to the percentage of guys who are bald or balding. At 40, you can figure that 40 percent of men your age are skin-tops. At 60, only 4 in 10 men have significant follicle foliage.

Your skin. Age spots are likely to start appearing in your forties, especially if you've had a lot of sun exposure. Try removing small spots with an over-the-counter hair bleach for women. Make sure that it contains at least 30 percent hydrogen peroxide, and dab it on with a cotton swab. If this doesn't work, you'll need stronger, prescription solutions containing hydroquinone (Melanex or Eldoquin) or tretinoin (Retin-A), which gradually return skin to its normal state.

For faster results, you have the higher-technology options of having a specialist freeze spots with liquid nitrogen or erase them with lasers. If spots become rough, change color, grow bigger than a pencil eraser, lose their round symmetry or bleed, have a doctor check for melanoma, a form of cancer—but one with an extremely high cure rate if caught early.

Your clothes. You've become experienced, worldly and—with any luck—richer. You want to project an image of elegance and sophistication because your business dealings are now with presidents, not vice-presidents—but also because you've spent two decades making serious clothing decisions, and the time for delaying gratification on expensive quality and style is past. Good thing: Your body has also chosen this moment to sandbag you with a little extra padding that good clothes can go a long way toward hiding. "Stick to muted solid colors," advises Christopher. "They're not only authoritative, but they create an illusion of thinness because they don't draw attention to the body the way that, say, a glen plaid would." Unless you're built like David Letterman, avoid double-breasted suits, which can make you look stuffed. But don't shy away from sleek designer lines such as Armani or Donna Karan. You may have gone Republican, but that doesn't mean that you have to be conservative in your own domestic policies.

Special concerns. Maybe you never look at your fingernails, but the divestiture lawyers from that company that you're acquiring might. No, it may not seem like a big deal, but it blows your elegant image if, when dislodging that stray piece of spinach from between your teeth or pointing to your complex legal documents, attention goes not to your nutritional wisdom or the contents of Paragraph 24(b), but to your ridged, broken, scaling fingertips.

All these problems start to afflict nails in your forties, but they're easily remedied with a trip to a manicurist. She'll buff and polish nails to get rid of ridges and retard peeling. Taking care of them afterward is your job. "Nails should be jewels, not tools, we always say," notes Gaby Nigai, co-owner of Ellegee Nail Salon on Manhattan's Upper East Side. Remember that: jewels, not tools. It's a good thing that Gaby's not a urologist.

Reaping the Benefits

Older doesn't mean old, but the most blatant signs of physical maturity, like wrinkles and gray hair, can no longer be postponed or ignored. The whole key to aging "gracefully," as people who are not aged like to call it, is to make your age an asset, not an enemy. Where guys in their twenties have a thick head of hair and T-shirts, you have wisdom, wit and spending money.

Your hair. Some men's hair keeps its original color well beyond the fifties, but not most. It pays to bear in mind that gray is a color, too, and not a bad one. Gray goes with anything.

If you choose to color your hair, however, invest in professional coloring: Over-the-counter products can give hair that's still naturally dark a blue-green or purplish hue. The idea isn't to get rid of all the gray, anyway, but to tone it down in selected areas for a more natural look. "If you're 60 percent gray, we might make you 30 percent gray," says Miano. Expect to spend about an hour in the chair. And make sure that you see a stylist or barber often for trims. "In your fifties, you need to be more fastidious about clean necklines and sideburns, because becoming at all unkempt can make you look haggard," Miano says.

Your skin. A number of prescription topical solutions have been found to erase wrinkles by making the skin's top layer shed cells, exposing smoother skin underneath. All the attention lately has gone to one of them: glycolic acid. "It works pretty well," says Clay Cockerell, M.D., clinical associate professor of dermatology and pathology at the University of Texas Southwestern Medical Center at Dallas. "Retin-A is still better." This tried-and-true treatment is more effective at removing wrinkles, he says, and if used in the right solution for your face, isn't necessarily harsher than glycolic acid.

Some men in their fifties also suffer from an inflammation in the face caused by rosacea, a reaction to the skin's oil production. "The effect is like having a W. C. Fields nose," says Dr. Cockerell, although the redness can also affect the ears and forehead. Treat afflicted areas with a 1 percent solution of hydrocortisone or an over-the-counter anti-inflammatory cream, or consult your dermatologist.

Your clothes. Would you really trade the power, money and know-how that you've accumulated to be 25 again, staying up all night, hanging out with twentysomething women and sniping at guys in their fifties by calling them "sir"?

Okay, okay. Still, there's a yearning for youngish trappings, even if it's something as simple as looking natural at the office in casual-Friday clothes. "To reclaim your youth, you don't have to go for bell-bottoms and unconstructed jackets," says Christopher. What you should do is stock up on high-quality sweaters and turtlenecks, wool trousers and a modest selection of sport coats. Tone down the shiny silk ties and opt for softer woven or knit ties. "By dressing down smartly, you project an image of being open to new things, yet you retain a casual elegance that will be the envy of younger men," says Christopher.

Special concerns. Varicose veins can make their first appearance before 50 but usually don't become bothersome until now. As many as half of us get them. (It's a vascular trait that you can inherit from either parent.) The first step in dealing with them is to wear support socks or what's known as gradient compression stockings, which apply pressure to the leg to keep veins from swelling.

If this doesn't provide acceptable results, consider surgery. One operation involves stripping problem veins out of the legs while you're under a local anesthesia. This is usually reserved for larger

JUST THE FACTS

Number of soaps, shampoos, razors and other bath products found in the average American shower: 8

veins, however. Smaller veins are erased with an injected solution that makes vein walls collapse; then they're absorbed by the body.

Taking It Easy

Life after 60? There's plenty of it. Most of it is swell, and all of it is better than the alternative. But the secret to looking great at any age is just as true at 60 or 70 as it is at 25 or 30: Look your age with the most style and charm that you can muster. Nothing ages a man quite as much as an obsessive worry about age. And nothing looks better on a guy than a few well-worn, highly polished, smoothly finished, extremely comfortable years.

PART 7

Man to Man

Movies That Make You Proud to Be a Man

Here are some movies that are universally considered to make you say, "Boy, am I glad to be a man."

1. *The Pride of the Yankees* (1942)—Superb biography with Gary Cooper starring as baseball great Lou Gehrig, who is afflicted with a progressive neurological disease.

2. *The Bridge on the River Kwai* (1957)—British soldiers in a Japanese prison camp during World War II build a bridge to keep their morale up.

3. *Ben-Hur* (1959)—Epic-scale production of the "tale of the Christ." Charlton Heston and Stephen Boyd star as friends who become enemies because of their convictions.

4. *The Alamo* (1960)—Starring John Wayne, this saga is a classic of courage in the face of hopelessness.

5. *The Magnificent Seven* (1960)—Townspeople pay gunslingers to run out bandits devastating their small town.

6. *The Great Escape* (1963)—Allied prisoners of war plan a massive escape from a Nazi prison camp. Based on a true story.

7. *Goldfinger* (1964)—Exciting James Bond adventure that has nefarious villains and a hair-raising climax inside Fort Knox.

8. *Rocky* (1976)—Story of Rocky Balboa, a two-bit fighter who gets his big shot for fame and self-respect.

9. *The Right Stuff* (1983)—Offbeat look at the birth of America's space program and the first astronauts. Filled with solid performances and exhilarating moments.

10. *Stand by Me* (1986)—One of the best movies for capturing the spirit of boyhood. Four youths spend a weekend on an adventure in a time when things were simpler.

Fatherly
Advice

Salvage Your Kids' Love and Your Self-Respect

In the past two decades, with the rise of the sensitive man, fatherhood has been depicted in the media as an uninterrupted series of Kodak moments. Here's Dad at Courtney's first birthday party, helping his beloved toddler smash open her piñata, loaded with hand-carved, hand-painted German dolls that cost more than a trip to Aruba. Here's Dad at Jared's first soccer game, beaming as his son kicks the winning goal just as time expires. Here's Dad at Jasmine's piano recital, grinning from ear to ear as she tiptoes her way through Tchaikovsky for Tykes and is rewarded with thunderous applause.

Lamentably, as with virtually everything else in this obstreperously cheerful society, the myth of Kodak-moment fatherhood is largely that: a myth. Not every Kodak moment is going to turn out quite the way you may have envisioned it. At Courtney's first birthday party, five will get you ten that either Tiffany or Brittany will storm out in tears because she couldn't bust open the piñata, while Alison, Allison or Allisson will become hysterical because her party bag didn't contain jewelry or T-bills. At that soccer game, your son will reach down to pick a daisy when he should be tending goal, and you'll have to watch in horror as another ball whizzes past, making the score 8–0. And at your daughter's first spelling bee, she will miraculously figure out some way to misspell the word "town."

When yuppies seized control of American society 15 years ago, the notion of fatherhood changed dramatically. When kids grew up in the 1950s, it was commonly understood that the role of the father was to stay home, drink beer and watch baseball games until the kids were old enough to join the army or get married. The fiendish notion of "quality time" had not yet been invented. All that changed in the 1980s, when children suddenly became the emotional focal point of the sensitive father's life. Fathers were expected to spend a lot of time with their children, time that was supposed to be filled with moments of peerless rapture, all captured on videotape.

Inevitably, this put a lot of pressure on the kids. In previous generations, it didn't matter if Courtney's birthday party was a bust, because fathers weren't expected to do much more at their kids' birthday parties than just show up. Today, all that has changed. Today, Dad is involved everywhere: at cultural events, at science projects, at track meets, at the zoo.

The emotional freight that children now carry around with them makes their lives all but impossible. Take these true tales from some men that we know. One daughter's soccer team went seven weeks without scoring a goal, and several of the dads had the entire season captured on videotape in case any of their grandchildren wanted to sit back and watch a history of unparalleled athletic futility. At another's daughter's piano recital, one of her classmates became so distraught at fumbling a few notes that she burst into tears and ran and hid in the kitchen. Then, when she was finally lured back into the living room to finish her performance, she played the piece flawlessly but became so distraught by the absurdly enthusiastic standing ovation she then received that she burst into tears and ran back into the kitchen.

The point in recounting these tales of woe is simple. Fathers want to ensure their children's happiness. Fine. Fathers also want to ensure their own happiness. Terrific. But fathers cannot hope to ensure anybody's happiness if they continually place their children in situations where they are bound to fail. Therefore, we've compiled the following tips on how to survive contemporary fatherhood.

1. Encourage your kids to play musical instruments that they're likely to be good at. Tubas are wonderful, because you only have to play one note at a time and nobody can tell whether you played the note correctly. Easy guitar can be mastered in a few weeks. Bongos are, of course, the best suggestion: Everyone can play the bongos. On the other hand, actively discourage your kid from joining the

school band or orchestra, using financial incentives if necessary. Violins, saxophones, cellos and clarinets all have been linked with innumerable homicides all across the United States in recent years. Another thing about bongos: If your kid takes up this harmless instrument instead of the piano, you won't have to spend the next ten years listening to him or her playing the theme song from *The Bodyguard.*

2. Count your blessings. Moments of sheer boredom can be mollified by simple rationalization. Take musical performances. As your daughter warbles her way through "Feliz Navidad" at the school Christmas pageant, coax yourself through the performance by remembering how many afternoons she practiced her rendition—at school, away from the house, with no effort on your part.

3. Encourage your kids to develop an interest in something that you're interested in. The stock market, for instance. Make a big deal of opening your child's first bank account. Explain the seductive notion of compound interest. Take photographs of your child purchasing his first Series E Savings Bond.

4. Don't be a perfectionist. Most men think that they have to be perfect when they're with their kids. Not only is this too much effort; it's also a bad idea. Better you should just continue being a screwup. Fall off your bike. Drop an easy pop fly. Order a really dumb product from some lame infomercial that you saw on TV. Make a fool of yourself on the ski slopes. The sooner that kids understand that you're not perfect, the sooner that they'll realize that they don't have to be perfect.

5. Steer them in the right direction. If your children are born with fat legs, then discourage them from taking up ballet. If your children are born extremely short, as most children are, encour-

age them to imitate Muggsy Bogues or Spud Webb rather than Shaquille O'Neal or Patrick Ewing.

6. Instill in your children a healthy contempt for the sport of soccer. Unless you want to spend every weekend for the next ten years ferrying your kids all over the county to soccer games that always end in a 0–0 tie because your kids stink and the kids from all the other teams stink, start dissing this vile European import before your children can even walk. You can start this surreptitious brainwashing program by hanging pictures of Babe Ruth in the nursery and playing the kids inspirational tapes with subliminal messages like: "Grow up to be like Ty Cobb or Chris Evert, not that Argentinian lowlife who knocks the ball into the goal with his hand when the ref's not looking." And if your child does get lured into soccer, or any other contrived "quality time" activity, remember to stay flexible and creative. Do not buy in to the myth. When a co-worker's daughter was six, she played on a mixed boys-and-girls soccer team that lost its first six games of the season. Not only did the kids lose every game; they never scored a goal. As they were coming off the field one afternoon, his daughter started crying.

"Why do we lose every week?" she asked.

"Do you really want to know the truth?" he inquired.

"Yes," she said.

"You stink," he crisply replied. "You guys are all cadavers. If we dug up the corpses in Sleepy Hollow Cemetery, we'd have a better chance of winning a game."

To the father's astonishment, his daughter was not miffed by his candor. Neither were her teammates. They were actually kind of amused by his comments. They knew that they were terrible; at least now they could acknowledge it without feeling embarrassed.

Right then and there, he told them that if they scored in either of their final two games, he'd buy everyone pizza. If they managed to win a game, he'd buy pizza and take them to the movies.

They won the final game of the season by a score of 1–0, triumphing over a team of seemingly dead amphibians.

Now that was a Kodak moment.

Command Respect

Tips to Make You the Envy of Others

Respect used to come easy to guys. You went off to war, came home with a few medals, took a job in the factory and earned an honest wage. Your wife made sure that you had clean T-shirts and meat loaf every Wednesday, the dog knew that it was his responsibility to fetch your slippers and the kids understood that your belt served a higher purpose than just bolstering your Bermudas.

But things aren't clear anymore. There are, thankfully, no wars to go valiantly off to, the rivet factory has been retooled to make bottle caps and it's no longer possible to support a family on one paycheck. Your wife says that you have to do the laundry and make dinner whenever she works late, the dog growls when you tell him to get off the couch and the last time you raised a hand to your kids, they threatened to call Johnnie Cochran.

Like fortune and the occasional free lap dance, respect is something that every man desires. But there are no instructions for assembling it. There aren't even any classes at the community college. In fact, the closest thing to an authority is some guy named Dangerfield.

This despite the fact that 83 percent of the respondents to a *Men's Health* magazine fax poll say that men are less respected today than 20 years ago. Some point fingers at feminists who have succeeded in stereotyping us as deadbeats, abusers and harassers. Others criticize themselves, citing materialistic attitudes, loss of traditional values and a willingness to do what's popular instead of what's right.

"It no longer means anything to have a man's word," says one reader. "What used to be done on a handshake is now all contracts and legalities. We've lost respect for each other and for ourselves."

Part of the problem is the media microscope that politicians, celebrities and other potential male role models exist under, says Ken Kragen, career consultant and author of *Life Is a Contact Sport*. "So many leaders and heroes have been shown to have feet of clay that there's a tremendous skepticism in society. And that's hurting us."

The other part is that men are losing their self-esteem. We're tentative where we were once confident, anxious where we were once in control. It's not a man's world anymore, and the dislocation that many men feel is taking its toll. "Self-esteem is the health of the mind," says Nathaniel Branden, Ph.D., author of *Six Pillars of Self-Esteem*. "It gives you a clear sense of identity, competence and worth. And the greater the number of choices and decisions we need to make, the more urgent our need for it."

But the simple truth is that to get respect, you have to give respect—to yourself and others. Then, once it starts, it's contagious. Do it here, do it there, and before you know it, you'll be getting more than you ever thought possible. So here's how to command respect from a variety of people. People like:

The cop who stopped you for speeding. Have your license and registration in hand. And when that state trooper asks if you know how fast you were going, say the following: "Well, I do now, sir. Although my mind was being diverted with other problems I won't bore you with, when I saw your lights in my rearview mirror, I looked at my speedometer and realized how fast I was going. You got me. I shouldn't have been driving like that, and I won't do it again."

"Remember that cops are people, too," says Joseph M. Dwyer, professor of human behavior and a certified protection professional with MVM Risk Management in McLean, Virginia. "They're dealing with persons that they don't like much all day. Because you cooperated and admitted guilt, you may get off. You're making the cop's life easy."

Guys in the gym. So you're pale, out of shape and terrified of getting sucked into the treadmill. How can you overcome the intimidation and look like you belong? Bill Pearl, five-time Mr. Universe, says that there are three things you should do:

Seek out knowledge. "When you're in an unknown world, humble yourself and ask for help," says Pearl. There's just one simple line that you need to master: "Can you show me how to do that?" People will respect you for asking.

Wear appropriate clothes. Don't wear spandex bike shorts that make you look like a large sausage in a medium casing. And despite their name, tank tops are not appropriate for the double-barrel chested. Instead, "dress in a way that makes you and everyone around you comfortable," says Pearl. If you're not happy with your physique, wear a sweatshirt and sweatpants. It'll stop the snickers and your self-consciousness.

Pass out the compliments. A simple compliment will go a long way. "Hey, great biceps, man. Anything special you do to build them?" Not only will you make a new friend, but you'll also get some free training advice.

Anyone. Want to *instantly* earn respect? It doesn't take much, but these simple things can go a long way in most situations.

Shake hands. Make your grip firm and confident, and pump no more than three times. Look the other person in the eye and smile.

Stand three to four feet away. This is the normal interacting distance. Get closer, and you'll make the other person uncomfortable. Farther away, and you'll appear detached and disinterested.

Square off. Face the person directly instead of standing slightly to the side. This suggests that you're giving your full attention.

Gesture. Occasionally extend your arms with the palms facing upward. This says that you're being honest and have nothing threatening to hide.

Reach out and touch. If it's appropriate, punctuate or end the conversation with a pat on the shoulder or a touch on the arm. This connotes friendliness and warmth, especially if you're of a higher status. Be careful patting women, though. In fact, it's better not to touch them at all.

Salesmen. There are three principles to remember: Look smart, act smart, be smart. "All salesmen are experts at sizing you up," says Herb Denenberg, a consumer investigative reporter for WCAU-TV, a CBS station in Philadelphia. "You have to let them know that you're not a soft touch, whether it's by how you dress, act or talk." Here's how to make sure that you don't get the bad end of a deal.

Drive the deal. The key is to do your homework. Every April, *Consumer Reports* divulges what dealers pay for the car (along with any options). This is called the dealer invoice. Once you know this, you've taken away the salesman's advantage and you're on equal bargaining terms. Offer him a fair profit (anywhere from $100 to $500 over invoice depending on the make and availability of the car), and if he balks, head for another dealer. Armed this way, Denenberg says that he's never paid more than $100 over invoice for a new automobile.

Hack your way to a computer deal. Leave your hair unwashed, wear a pocket protector and pull your pants up so high that you have to open your zipper to talk. Just kidding. Actually, the same "homework" strategy that works for buying a car is effective here, with two notable exceptions. First, there's a better chance that the salesman is incompetent, given the swiftly changing technology and the fact that he still might be awaiting puberty. So don't swallow everything he says. Second, realize that it may be impossible to buy the perfect computer the first time.

"It's kind of like law school," says Denenberg. "You don't really know what it's all about until you start practicing. Buy a computer with the understanding that if it's not exactly what you want, you can always upgrade later."

Make sure the goods are real. Any guy can tell if a car is quality. You slam the door, kick the tires and check out the cup holders. But a diamond? It could be a piece of glass for all you know. To make sure that you're getting the most carats for your quarters, Denenberg says that there are two things you must insist on: the right to get it independently appraised and the right to return it unconditionally within 7 to 14 days.

"If you talk this way to the salesman," says Denenberg, "you'll earn his respect, and he'll be a lot more careful about what he tries to sell you."

A guy with a gun. Your goal is to make the gun inconsequential. Of course, this is difficult to do under the circumstances, but it's the only escape. To deflect the focus from the weapon, Dwyer recommends doing exactly what you've seen in the movies (*Die Hard* notwithstanding). "Get him talking," he says. "The more someone talks about what's bothering him, the less it bothers him." And while you're at it, try to get him to realize that it's not just your life that's ruined if he pulls the trigger; it's his, too.

If your adversary has dilated pupils, rocks back and forth on his feet or points a finger at you with the rest of his hand balled into a fist, you may not be able to reason with him. These are animal actions that hint that he is deranged. It's time to pull a Bruce Willis.

Punks on the street. Very tricky. But here are the rules, according to Dwyer.

Don't:
- Challenge them or try to establish superiority through force, unless you can do a very impressive Terminator impersonation.
- Try to bluff your way out with macho talk like: "Be careful, I know karate and seven other Japanese words."
- Agree with everything they say, otherwise they'll consider you worthless and deserving of additional abuse.

Do:
- Give them money or valuables, if that's what they're after.
- Pay attention to what they're saying and paraphrase it to keep them talking. For instance, if they say: "Man, I hate guys like you with fancy new clothes. You're a have, and I'm a have not." Then you say: "Hey, I've been there. I understand. At least I think I do. Why are you so mad?"
- Empathize. Listen to what they say, and express a genuine understanding of their side.

"What you're seeing is anger," explains Dwyer, "and all anger has its foundation in fear. Diffuse it by letting them talk about it." If you can actually engage them in a conversation about something other than what they'd like to do to your face, you're in good shape.

An irate, 350-pound NFL noseguard. "If a guy feels that he's been wronged and goes ballistic, I tell the team captain to get him under control," says 54-year-old Gerry Austin, a National Football League

(continued on page 230)

Respect Defined

In an issue of *Men's Health* magazine, readers were asked to send in what made them snap to attention and salute. Here's what they said about respect.

In order of importance, name the five qualities that you respect most in other men.

1. Honesty
2. Integrity
3. Intelligence
4. Humor
5. Loyalty

Are there any qualities so bad that they negate all of a man's good qualities?

1. Lying/dishonesty
2. Sucking up
3. Cheating/infidelity
4. Selfishness
5. Arrogance

Do you respect your boss?

Yes	69%
No	31%

What makes for a respectworthy boss? "He respects me," one reader wrote. Other comments include:

"He sets clear principles, encourages creativity and autonomy, and is honest."

"He is communicative and works as hard as we do."

Here's what you told us about the boss that you don't respect.

"[He provides] no positive reinforcement."

"He does not confront the people he has a problem with."

"[He] treats employees like children."

"[He] doesn't recognize his own shortcomings."

Would you work for someone you didn't respect?

Yes	70%
No	30%

Most readers said that they'd do it for the money, but some of you pointed out that you don't have to respect someone to want to work for him. "Even people that you don't respect can teach you something," one reader commented.

Are men more or less respected than they were 20 years ago?

Less	83%
More	10%
Same	3%
Undecided	4%

A pretty overwhelming consensus about a disturbing trend. Why are men suffering so much in society's eyes? You named three main factors: the feminist movement, the media and the breakdown of traditional male values.

"Women in the workforce have taken 'traditionally' male roles, so now men are less valued."

"We live in a society where accomplishments are immediately suspect and weaknesses are sought out and publicly revealed."

"We know our heroes too well today."

"Religion and family breakdown are to blame."

Not everyone, however, bought the party line. In fact, some believed that the feminist movement has helped men pull together. "Men respect each other more because of the growing tide of women's issues," one reader says. Others said that men were still respected, but for the wrong reasons: "I wish respect for men wasn't always tied to work and success. I'd rather get respect for crying with my 16-year-old daughter over problems in our relationship."

What's the one characteristic you wish you had that would earn you more respect from others?

1. Confidence
2. Assertiveness
3. Patience
4. Communication skills
5. Ambition

official for 13 years. "You want to give him the chance to walk away. But if he persists or makes it personal, especially in the presence of others, then you can't turn away or you'll never get respect. You have to flag him for unsportsmanlike conduct.

"It works the same way if a coach goes off the deep end," continues Austin. "If he calls me a name, I ask: 'What did you say?' If he's willing to repeat it, then he's willing to spend 15 yards. If he's willing to back off, I let it go."

Your boss. Why is it that whenever you meet with Mr. Big, you're never able to express yourself as forcefully as you would like? Don't despair. There are many other ways to subtly earn the big guy's respect beyond an eloquent summation of third-quarter stationery expenses.

"When we communicate with another person, only 10 percent of the communication is through words," says Stephen J. Holoviak, Ph.D., author of *Golden Rule Management: Give Respect, Get Results.* "The rest comes from voice and body language. These things add power to your words."

Here, then, are five ways to make a positive impact without opening your mouth.

Be on time. Being late shows disrespect. Being early by more than five minutes shows that you don't having anything else to do or that you're anxious.

Keep your eyes on his. Look up, and it'll seem like you're not paying attention. Look down, and you'll appear guilty like a child. Your eyes should be on his about 80 percent of the time, says Leesa Dillman, assistant professor of communication at the University of Nevada/Las Vegas.

Look comfortable. Don't sit perfectly erect, because you'll look stiff and nervous, and don't lean forward as if you're hanging on his every word. Instead, lean slightly to one side or cross your legs, with one ankle atop a knee. This suggests that you're comfortable and at ease, says Dillman. Taking up more space is also a sign of credibility and dominance.

Lose the nervous habits. Don't play with your tie, tap your notepad with a pen or jiggle your foot. All this hints that you're anxious and lack self-control.

Say "cheese." Women smile too much; men don't do it enough. And precisely because of this, it can have more impact if used at the proper time. In fact, facial expressiveness generally connotes sociability and better character, says Dillman.

Your co-workers. What most men forget is that all the things that garner respect from the boss also work with peers. "To get respect, you have to give it away first," says Dr. Holoviak. In other words, treat others the same way you'd like to be treated.

For instance, when you're talking in your office with Stan from accounting, don't interrupt the conversation to answer the phone. Listen to other people instead of thinking of what you're going to say next; and compliment your co-workers on promotions, sharp new ties and thoughtfully bagged lunches. But don't be insincere or self-effacing. People resent this, and it backfires.

Your mother-in-law. First, the simple fact that you're her son-in-law means that she'll forever view you as a child, so accept it. Then understand that if she's quietly warring with you, it's probably because she has some support from the home troops.

"The only time in-laws are a problem," says Michael S. Broder, Ph.D., a clinical psychologist in Philadelphia and author of *The Art of Staying Together: A Couple's Guide to Intimacy and Respect,* "is when someone in the family, your wife, collaborates with them. They rarely meddle without collaboration. If your wife agrees when your mother-in-law complains about you, then you'll never get respect."

Rather than confront Mom, enlist help from your partner. Ask her to explain to her mother, "the more you push my husband away, the more you push me away." That should end it.

Your mate. Well, for starters, stop getting your soiled briefs mixed in with the good linen, quit demanding that she wear a fake Cindy Crawford mole during sex and don't wander around her company clambake with any more capers stuck to your nose.

What you need next, according to Dr. Broder, is empathy.

"Never demean her," he explains. "Listen to her. Try to understand her for who she is, not for who you want her to be. Look for positives and try to help her develop these positives. One of the classic mistakes that men make is assuming that respect comes without giving it back. Actually, it's the other way around."

Your ex-wife. If there are children from the relationship, never put their mother down in their presence, recommends Dr. Broder. Also, follow the rules regarding visitation, alimony and child support, while setting some rules of your own that will keep you from being pushed around.

"You can resent someone and still respect them," he explains. "I wouldn't go too far out of my way to gain approval, though. You'll negate yourself. Just stick by the rules of the agreement, be respectful yourself, and you'll eventually gain it."

Your child. Here's what you have to do to rear a child who will respect you, according to Ron Taffel, Ph.D., parenting columnist for *McCall's* magazine and the author of *Why Parents Disagree.*

Do the little things. Put them to bed each night, help with their homework, go to their soccer games and generally do all the things that you're too "busy" for. Dr. Taffel says that many fathers operate on the periphery of their kids' lives, stepping in only to bark out disciplinary orders ("Go to your room") or abstract commandments ("Play fair").

"It's easy to talk like that," he says, "but unless you know the details of a child's life, how can you give him good advice? By doing the ordinary, you build respect from the ground up, and you develop a bond that won't be broken when you have a disagreement."

Fess up when you're wrong. When you punish or yell at a child more because of your own irritability than his or her wrongdoing, apologize. "It shows them you have enough faith in yourself that you can admit you're wrong," explains Dr. Taffel. "I can't think of a more respectful thing a man can do."

Hit the books. Most men know more about their 401(k)'s projected growth curve than their kids'. "Fathers don't know as much about normal child development as mothers do," says Dr. Taffel. "That's why we're so unsure of ourselves when it comes to discipline, often giving punishments for behavior that's totally appropriate for a child that age."

There are many books and magazines on parenting that can be helpful, or it may be as simple as chaperoning your third grader's field trip. Comparing your child with others the same age adds perspective, which promotes patience and wisdom.

Uncooperative people. If you're not getting any satisfaction from those you're dealing with, go over their heads. Ask to speak to a supervisor, a manager or the president of the company. If you know what you're entitled to and show the resolve to get it, usually just threatening such action will settle the dispute.

When all else fails, Denenberg recommends enlisting the help of your local state representative. "One thing politicians do well is constituent service," he says. "They have whole staffs sitting around with nothing to do but help people. They're wonderful about it."

Situations to Master

Now that you have gained the respect of everyone in your life, here are some tips to skillfully conduct yourself in some important, common situations, and thus, earn the respect of others.

Voicing respect. At one end of the spectrum, there's James Earl Jones, whose deep, booming voice makes us want to own multiple phone books. At the other is Alvin of the Chipmunks, who may be a great harmonizer but is certainly one who never commanded much respect. Here's how you can strike the perfect vocal chord.

Get a grip on breathing. When you're upset, your breathing becomes shallow, and spoken phrases get short and hurried. This conveys nervousness. What you want is for each breath to originate deep in the chest so you can speak slower with longer phrasing. This suggests confidence and control. To achieve a perfect blend of oration and oxygenation, Bonnie Raphael, Ph.D., the voice and speech coach for the American Repertory Theater at Harvard University, recommends reading aloud from a newspaper, telling stories to children or practicing with waitresses or phone solicitors.

Relax your jaw. Dr. Raphael says that you can enrich your voice by keeping your jaw relaxed. "There should be a little cushion of air between the top and bottom teeth," she explains. "Think of your tongue as belonging to the bottom of the jaw, rather than just being stuck in there. Always have a half-yawn in the back of your mouth so that there's room for the sound to come out over the back of your tongue."

Enunciate your words. If you can't be heard or understood, you won't be respected. "People who mumble get undervalued," Dr.

Raphael explains. "Clarity and articulation command respect."

Be assertive but not pushy. An assertive voice elicits respect, whereas an aggressive one induces fear. "Assertive is not whispery or shouted," says Dr. Raphael. "There's a certain sound to it that says, 'I don't have to shout because I know that you're listening.' When you're speaking aggressively, you get yappy, talk louder and faster, and interrupt. You're trying to force other people to respect you."

Act like a singer. Although a deeper, richer voice generally suggests elegance and class, a bad impersonation of Burl Ives will cost you. More important than pitch is the amount of music in your voice. "You want to get rid of the noise," says Dr. Raphael. "You want more depth, amplification, resonance. It's closer to singing, actually, and that's what you should do to develop it. The more music in your voice, the less noise in your voice."

Pay attention. Listening doesn't have anything to do with speaking, but if you're good at it, it'll earn you more respect. "When we speak and know we're being heard, we tend not only to respect that person but also to admire him because he's taking the time to listen," says Dr. Raphael.

Getting an audience in the palm of your hand. If you think you have trouble formulating an impressive, convincing presentation, consider the challenge facing Lisa Schiffren, former speechwriter for that Rodney Dangerfield of politics, Dan Quayle. Here's her best advice for winning respect from a roomful of skeptical strangers.

Be wary of humor. Open with a joke only if it's funny and appropriate and you can deliver it well. Otherwise, launch immediately into your topic.

Tolerate nervous habits. Don't worry about sweating, looking stiff or what you're doing with your thumbs. In a large auditorium, no one is going to notice, unless you're addressing binocular salesmen.

Keep it simple. Never make more than three major points. Anything more won't be remembered. And buttress each one with relevant statistics that are succinct and insightful.

Weave in a story or two. They're usually more effective than jokes because they're more relevant. Often stories are the most memorable part of a speech, especially if they illustrate your main point.

Practice, practice, practice. "Success is a function of work," says Schiffren. "A great weakness of a lot of businessmen and politicians is that they presume that they have a natural gift for public speaking. Use video equipment, coaching, whatever tools are available to improve. Do the hard work, just like any acting student would."

Cooking a good meal. Most men get into trouble by being too ambitious—trying to make chicken cordon bleu, for instance, instead of just chicken for two. Weekend Graham Kerrs who are out to impress should keep things simple, says Robert Shoffner, wine and food editor for the *Washingtonian* magazine. Buy a nice selection of greens for the salad, serve a cold first course and make a steak or roasted chicken for the main event. "Never try to go beyond your abilities," he says.

Controlling a dog. If Bowser treats you worse than a fire hydrant, then it's about time that he realizes who buys the doggie treats. Wayne Davis, president of the West Virginia Canine College in Buckhannon, offers the following suggestions.

Stare him down. Just as with humans, you command respect by making eye contact. To stare at a dog and make him avert his gaze means that you're dominant. But be careful. Unless you follow all our instructions and have full mastery of the animal, he may challenge or even bite you. "All you have to do to get respect is understand the psychology of the animal," says Davis, who has trained more than 3,500 dogs. "I never have trouble with dogs. In fact, the same principles work with people."

Calm him with petting. To settle an active dog, slowly stroke him across the top of the head, pulling his ears back and down. This calms, whereas a pat on the rib cage excites.

Speak some German. Correct unwanted behavior and reward good behavior. But instead of saying, "No!"—something you probably yell at the kids a hundred times a day—say, "Aus!" This is Ger-

---

JUST THE FACTS

Nearly half of the 12 to 20 million Americans with tattoos want them removed.

man for "out" or "off," but more important than its specific meaning is the deep guttural sound it produces. It actually mimics the low growl mother dogs use to chastise their pups. Use it as a command to stop bad behavior, giving a sharp jerk on a choke collar to reinforce it. Use "Phooey!" as a milder form of correction.

If you're walking or running and a Rottweiler mistakes you for a mobile bone, turn around and walk toward him, says Tom Rose, owner of the Dog House Training School near St. Louis. Make yourself as big and aggressive-looking as possible by waving your arms and yelling in a deep voice.

"The dog's motto is: 'If it runs, I chase it,'" explains Rose. "It's a rare dog that will bite you when you're coming at it. You're just too big."

Dog most likely to respect you: A spayed female golden retriever.

Dog least likely to respect you: A non-neutered male Doberman.

Male Bonding

Name-Calling Is What Friends Do

Male friendship has three great traditions: going to the game, taking a bullet for a pal and busting each other's chops. The last one—relentlessly ridiculing those you like and respect—predates the other two. Long before bleachers or ballistics, best buddies were needling each other mercilessly. Huck and Tom on the river, Butch and Sundance on the range, Hope and Crosby on the road. All of them made a friendship of mockery.

Now, some people who—what's that phrase?—*just don't get it* say that this is a pathetic way to show affection. They throw around phrases like "arrested development" and "adolescent aggression." They wonder why men can't be as open, straightforward and intimate in their conversations as women are. The answer is simple: Sisterhood may be powerful, but it ain't a laugh a minute. Just try spending a weekend with three people who are respectful to and supportive of each other. No yuks there. You'll be checking the train schedule by lunchtime on Saturday.

No, you're going to have much more fun with a guy who can eviscerate your haircut and your heritage by suggesting that your ancestors didn't have opposable thumbs. And there are other benefits, too. Consider what a great gift you've given when you launch a scathing insult at a friend.

You're fighting against snobbery. We hate it when a guy thinks that he's better than we are. It's no accident that the roast, the institutionalization of insult humor, was invented at the all-male Friar's Club. It's a chance for the vassals to give the king a symbolic wedgie. It's our way of making sure that nobody gets any fancy ideas about moving out of the neighborhood.

You're keeping things under control. Think of the opening sequence of *2001: A Space Odyssey*. It doesn't take a Margaret Mead to see that our verbal jousting has a baboons-competing-to-be-alpha-male component. No question, when we pillory a pal, we're saying that we're cooler, stronger and more desirable as a dance partner than the dear friend that we're destroying. Yet everybody lives to get even. The Visigothi, for example, probably weren't bad people. They just couldn't think of anything witty to say.

You're marking your territory. Our ribbing ropes off a boundary between us and the rest of the world. It's cowboy talk, announcing that we ain't beholden to nobody. Our need for autonomy and self-reliance (or rather, the appearance of same) is brain stem–deep, so the closer we get to a real bond, the harder the unconscious forearm shiver we give any guy who threatens to matter.

You're trying to be one of the boys. The fact is that the only thing more important than having our freedom is being part of a group. Men will suffer all manners of ignominies to get on the team. Does the word "hazing" ring a bell? In fact, it's kind of cozy inside the satiric, smart-aleck circle. Better to be a target than just another anonymous kid from the chess club.

You're satisfying an ancient urge. Safer than skydiving, cheaper than helicopter skiing, more orthopedically sound than rugby at middle age, it offers the same adrenaline release that Cro-Magnon guys got from chasing down dinner. Now we're reduced to doing our hunting and gathering when the deli-counter guy calls our number. But old urges die hard. We still need the rush, a little danger in our lives. What better to keep a guy on his toes than a completely unprovoked attack by his nearest and dearest?

General George Patton said it for all of us when surveying a battlefield: "God help me, I do love it so." That's why you like to go

---

JUST THE FACTS

Percentage of men who say that supporting their wife's career is very important to being a good father: 78

out with the boys more than she likes to go out with the girls. That's why male friends have the annual Memorial Day Weekend Tequila and Golf Festival, but there's no traditional Lady Buckeyes Class of '85 Pre-Christmas Lingerie Spree and Grouse Hunt.

Now, let's consider two phenomena: First, the pop-psychology types tell us that we'll have stronger relationships if we can learn to express our affection more adroitly. And, as we've shown, busting on each other is how men express this supposed affection. No argument yet, right? Now let's make one great leap for mankind. It therefore follows that the more adept you are at verbally disemboweling your fellow man, the closer and more prosperous your friendship will be. Therefore, let us offer a few tips on sharpening your saber.

What Mies van der Rohe said about architecture is true about making fun of somebody: God is in the details.

If you're not scoring with your jabs, it's probably because they're not specific enough. Don't just make generic fun of his personality, pick up on a particular quirk. Does he have a word he uses like a crutch to get him through conversations? One guy we know (we'll call him Dave) used to use the word "action" constantly, as in, "Want to catch some pub action?" His pals descended mercilessly. ("Hey, Dave's got a date tonight. He's hoping for some action action.") Not only has the hapless fellow dropped the word from his vocabulary, but he now has a wonderful collection of Action Jackson memorabilia in his office, courtesy of his mates.

For an insult transfusion, spend some time with the magnificos of verbal massage. If a hitter's in a drought, he should watch Boggs

The King of Insults

Don Rickles became the sultan of slander by honing his skill with hecklers. "It became a duel of who could win," he says. "That doesn't happen anymore. If it does, they'd better have Blue Cross." Here's Rickles's crash course in cut-downs.

Don't cut on someone you dislike. "If you don't like the guy, it's not going to come out funny," he says. "It just comes out hurtful. And you look like an idiot."

But be sure he likes you, too. "My favorite line," says Rickles, "was what I said to Sinatra: 'Hey Frank, be yourself and hit somebody.' " Sinatra's a pal, which is why Rickles is alive to talk about it.

Make it funny for him. "When I size a guy up, I look for stuff that he can laugh at himself about," he says. "So now we're both laughing at him." Sinatra had a penchant for pummeling, and Rickles simply pointed it out.

Be confident. "When I'm talking, I believe that I'm right," he says. "I say everything with confidence. It's like a fighter. If you go into the ring and think that the other guy can beat you, you're toast."

Be gracious in defeat. Once you've been torpedoed and you're at a loss for a funnier comeback, smile and live to fight another day. "If you get hit, be a good sport and laugh it off," says Rickles.

or Gwynn take batting practice. If you're in a satire slump, pick up anything written by Shakespeare, Mencken, Twain or S. J. Perelman. These guys were titans of the taunt. They used great, old-fashioned insulting words—words like "yokel," "knave," "mountebank" and "starveling." Shakespeare once described a guy of girth as "a stuffed cloak-bag of guts." Not bad. Spend a little time reading them and you'll get a slanderous second wind. You'll find yourself calling somebody a "jackanapes" instead of plain old "jerk."

But remember, tweaking egos is dangerous stuff. There must be limits. A joke's only a joke until it becomes fisticuffs in the parking lot of a 7-Eleven. Here, then, are the unwritten rules of the Gotcha game. There's no protective padding in the world of insult, so follow them closely.

■ No secrets, pally. You don't rib a guy about something private—about the fact that he didn't really resign because the agency took that cigarette account; he actually got an hour to empty his desk. No, you only fire a shot about something that's already out there for the world to see—that spineless prayer he calls his jump shot, that eyesore he calls his car, that patch of Tobacco Road hardpan he refers to as his lawn.

■ No gut shots, ace. You never go for the jugular. Flesh wounds only. You don't mention that your friend Jeff is a third-rate father; you libel him for his prized collection of Lee Majors memorabilia. You don't notice that Brian is a philanderer; you describe his golf swing as a serious medical disorder.

In short, you work the edges. You ride a guy about his habits, not his heart; his quirks, not his character.

■ Master the "I bust you 'cause I love you" inflection. This lacerating lilt requires perfect pitch. But not to worry. Most of us have it down cold. We learned it from our dads.

■ Pick on someone your own size. You don't go after a guy who can't defend himself. It's unseemly, like Tyson fighting "Tomato Can" McNeeley or Reagan invading Grenada. You don't attack unless it puts you at some risk, unless there's a reasonable chance that you'll take a short, stiff counterpunch to the solar plexus. Only fire at a buck; don't take a shot at Bambi.

■ Take as good as you dish out. What's the lowest form of male life? The guy who can dish it out but can't take it. When the next guy's bald spot is on the griddle, our man is a Benihana chef, slicing, dicing, coolly carving up a compadre. But when a jab jolts him, Lenny Bruce turns into Little Lord Fauntleroy. He's suddenly as sensitive as he was sharp a moment ago.

Dads'
Wisdom

There Is Much to Learn from Their Experiences

Many men are still waiting for their fathers to talk to them about sex and success, money and marriage, religion and rearing kids. It's not that our fathers are bad fathers. But even in the best father-and-son relationships, there's that uncomfortable familiarity that inhibits us from talking like friends.

It's not that our fathers had too little to say to us, but rather, too much. They lived through the Depression, fought Nazis, loved women, lost women, reared difficult kids and met every manner of person, good and bad. They witnessed the trajectory of their own careers and lots of others; watched heroes, fads and politicians come and go; learned what's important and what's not. They've been to so many places that we have yet to go. But since neither father nor son knows where or how to start these conversations, we talk about sports and cars instead. The shame of it is that most of us feel as if we're navigating life without a map. Our fathers may not have all the directions, but they sure know where a lot of the potholes and detours are.

There's a lot of wisdom out there, if only we can ask and listen.

"No matter how much you love your wife, another woman is going to come along and bring something alive in you that you thought was dead or never knew existed. She is going to fascinate you and obsess you and fill you with desire. You are going to want her, and it is going to feel natural.

"Whenever I feel a surge of attraction to a woman, I think of my

left leg. I broke it several years ago when I slipped on a patch of ice. Unfaithfulness snaps a relationship as surely as that fall snapped my bone. At first it may seem like nothing. Over time, you may even be able to mend the break so that the relationship is stronger than ever. But it is not healed. The scar remains, and it will haunt you forever."
—*Kent Nerburn, Ph.D., author of* Letters to My Son

"When you're young, you think that nothing you do, no choices you make, will have a long-term impact on your life. But they do.

"After I got back from the war, I fell for a woman whose husband had been killed fighting in Italy. We really loved each other, but I couldn't commit. She had two kids, and I thought I wasn't ready to become a father. Like a fool, I started seeing another woman. It was my cowardly way of escaping, and it worked. I lost the woman I loved, and the other affair didn't last six months.

"That was 50 years ago, but the strange thing is, hardly a month has gone by in all that time when I haven't thought about her and regretted the path I took."
—*Joseph Gold, 73, retired textile executive, father of three*

"I regret smoking. I've had two episodes of congestive heart failure, and I'm very close to a third. I didn't recognize what was happening because I was always in good shape. But I understand now how stupid I was."
—*Joseph McFadden, 72, diplomat, professor, father of five*

"Men get worried because they hear that there's no sex in old age. Well, my first 20 years of life weren't bad, and there was no sex then, either."
—*Moe Turner, 76, retired military scientist, father of five*

"I'm not a dummy, and I guess that the people around me know that. So they often ask me

Robert N. Butler, M.D., 68

If there's anyone that you'd expect to be vibrant, inspirational and wise at an older age, it's New York City's Dr. Robert N. Butler. Founding director of the National Institute on Aging, Pulitzer Prize–winning author of *Why Survive? Being Old in America* and nationally recognized expert on senior sex, he has made an illustrious career out of studying life's progression. In fact, he has never had any major health problems, and after rearing three children in one marriage, he has a 15-year-old daughter from a second.

Early retirement: "Those young men who think about early retirement are in a fantasy world. It's better to think of how you'll remain productive later in life. More people are having three and four careers. Keep learning and, if you retire, then retire to something that gives you a sense of purpose. Studies show a relationship between purpose and living longer."

Friendship: "Men need to maintain their friends, nourish them, strive for some of the same intimacy women have in their friendships. For instance, rather than sending a card, I call each of my friends at Christmas."

Regrets: "As a gerontologist, I do a lot of listening to older people. Their biggest regret is not what they did, but what they failed to do. They regret not standing up for something, not expressing an affection."

Sex: "There are two languages of sex. The first reflects our reproductive function. It's explosive, highly emotional, and it comes naturally. The second language is something that you acquire. It involves becoming more sensitive to your partner, more concerned with his or her needs. It's the secret to having a continuing love affair."

why I didn't become a millionaire. And I tell them that I didn't have the time."

—*Carl Campbell, 70, retired high-school art teacher, father of three*

"I used to think that my father was a hypochondriac. He had a string of doctors that he'd go to. I realize now that he was just taking inventory. He wanted to know where he was at. And while he was testing himself, he was also testing doctors. That was wise. He lived to be 84, and I get a thorough physical exam every 18 months."

—Joe Drake, 73, retired lawyer, father of four

"I've had a few hairy experiences. I survived three plane crashes and got blown out of a foxhole during World War II. I was bayoneted between the eyes in Korea. And I had five heart attacks between 1979 and 1988. After the last one, I had open-heart surgery and was on the table for 15 hours. But that was years ago, and I feel great now. In fact, I bench-pressed 225 pounds five times on my 69th birthday. People call me an inspiration, but I've always just tried to keep a cool head. If you get too excited, the adrenaline starts pumping too fast, and you do stupid things."

—Sam Jerzak, 71, 26-year army veteran, father of six

"To stay out of trouble, stay sober. You have no judgment when you're not. Listen to your instincts, too. You know that it's not quite right to cheat on your taxes or fudge on a loan application. That's the start of trouble."

—Aaron Binder, 67, millionaire entrepreneur
who served 44 months in prison for fraud

"Develop something outside of yourself, a burning interest in Napoleon or the Civil War or anything that inspires the same kind of passion that kids have with ease but adults somehow forget about. I've never known an unhappy person with a stamp collection."

—Wilfrid Sheed, 64, author of In Love with Daylight,
father of three and survivor of polio, addiction and cancer

"I have six kids, five of them daughters. I survived it. And I was a New York City police sergeant, and I survived that. I also survived occupation in Japan in the 1940s, and I survived the Korean War as well. I went back for that and served. I was just a dog soldier— nothing heroic, nothing too famous. . . . Me? Give advice? Never! I'm still looking for people to tell me what to do."

—James Curtain, 67

"When my sons were growing up, I was interested in carpentry, so I gave them tools. The problem is that parents usually give their children little kids' tools. Even skilled carpenters couldn't do diddly with kids' tools. I gave mine professional tools. And they took care of them, too. To this day, they're all pretty skilled with their hands, and none of them looks down on any person or occupation."

—Dean Dimick, 69, physician, father of six

"I've been a millionaire two times now. I didn't know how to use all that money. In the mornings I'd be either drunk or stoned, and I'd buy a $500 leather jacket. Then, not remembering, that night I'd buy the same jacket in a different color. If anyone said that they needed $1,000, I'd wire it to them. I got the biggest kick out of that. I thought I was Frank Sinatra or something.

"When people say to me, 'I want to be rich,' I ask them what they mean. Then they say, 'I want to have millions,' and I'll ask again what that means. Finally, they'll say, 'I want to have all the money I need.' Ahh, all the money I need. That's the key, because you don't need much."

—Aaron Binder

"When you're negotiating, don't go for the jugular. Keep a fall-back position and be able to let your adversary reach his fall-back position. Everyone has one. In diplomatic situations, strength is knowing where it is and being able to reach it with a smile."

—Joseph McFadden

"You've got to be awfully lucky to find the right mate. At that time of life, at that age, very few men are wise enough to make a decision on any logical basis. There's no advice that I can give. It just takes an enormous amount of luck."

—Gene Cooper, 79, professor, husband for 51 years and father of two

"We adopted a baby girl named Samantha who died when she was four months old. It was a crib death. We put her down, and the next time we checked she was cold as the devil. It was devastating. The death of a child doesn't make any philosophical or religious sense. I found out that among parents who lose children, more than

John D. Cahill, 71

John Cahill of Salt Lake City spent most of his life building a law practice in Milwaukee, then walked away from the money and the tedium to study Spanish literature and become a hotelier. Now he travels between hotel properties in Colorado, Utah, Wyoming, Montana and Hawaii; climbs mountains such as Kilimanjaro, McKinley and Aconcagua; and is obsessed with breaking three hours in a marathon. Perhaps most rewarding, many of Cahill's nine children run, climb and work with him.

Satisfaction: "If you're happy, if you feel good about what you're doing, then tell the rest of the world to go to hell. Don't let society pressure you."

Health: "You don't wake up at age 55 with a trashed heart. You start trashing it with pizza and cheeseburgers at age 20. Begin a health regimen as early as you can."

Sex: "Change partners every eight to ten years."

Success: "Totally personal. It's achieving the goals that you set for yourself and having the discipline to reach them. It's an inner thing. It's possible to be a success on your terms when everybody else thinks that you're a failure."

Regrets: "That I'll die before I see what happens to the world in the next 50 years. I'm fascinated with the speed at which technology advances, and I can't imagine what the world will be like in 2050. My regret is my inability to satisfy my curiosity."

50 percent eventually divorce. That's because they're so devastated they can't support each other. I was guilty of that. I was thinking about my own loss so much that I couldn't give support to my other children or my wife.

"I was 39 at the time, coming up on my midlife crisis, and it made me examine myself a bit more. As it turned out, it was a starting-over point. I left the research lab to become chairman of medicine for a hospital. Maybe in periods of great pain and crisis you get rid of the crap in life, the stuff that's totally meaningless, and refocus on what's important."

—*Dean Dimick*

"My family had to leave Poland in 1941. We took the Trans-Siberian Railroad to Vladivostok, then went on to Kobe, Japan, because Jews were allowed to use that territory to come to America. But when Japan joined Germany in the war, we were shipped to Shanghai and became displaced persons. We lived in the ghetto until I was 13. I always thought that I missed my youth. While other children were playing baseball or riding bikes, we were looking for a piece of bread. There was much disease in the ghetto. I saw bodies piled ten feet high. I think you have to see inhumanity like that before you can appreciate humanity. Later, I decided to become a rabbi to try to improve humanity a little."

—*Rabbi Israel Wolmark, 61, father of two*

"In general, most people think of old age as a frightening thing. Old people look the way we never want to look. As it happens, I feel perfectly natural at every age I'm at. No one ever told me how little you change inside. One's 12-year-old self and one's present self feel exactly the same."

—*Wilfrid Sheed*

"I regret wasting so much time. It's amazing how little value we put on it when we're young. I wasted so much time staring at junk on television, reading dumb books, talking about unimportant things with people that I didn't particularly like, chasing women

---

JUST THE FACTS

Eighty-three percent of men over age 50 know the function of a woman's ovaries, but only 42 percent know the function of their own prostate gland, according to the American Foundation for Urologic Disease.

Norman Vaughan, 89

In 1929, Norman Vaughan was part of Admiral Richard Byrd's expedition to the South Pole. In fact, Byrd named an Antarctic peak—Mount Vaughan—in his honor. A few days before his 89th birthday, Norman realized a dream by climbing to the summit of that 10,302-foot ice-covered mountain.

This was only the latest in a lifelong string of adventures for Vaughan, a gregarious character who dropped out of Harvard, sold chain saws to lumberjacks, was decorated for numerous heroic search-and-rescue missions during World War II, competed in 13 Iditarod Trail Sled Dog races, taught Pope John Paul II to mush, has been married four times (most recently at 82) and just published an autobiography aptly entitled *My Life of Adventure*.

Thrills: "Most men have zero adventure in their lives, and that's sad because it takes you away from the humdrum of life and helps you see other people's points of view. Some men go on these fancy two-week bicycling trips. They come back and say that they had a great time, but it's still just a bike trip. An adventure is not knowing which way you'll go on that bicycle. You come to a corner and see some trees in the distance, so you take that road. Then you see a brook, so you go that way and you end up fishing with a fellow you meet. That's adventure—facing the future without any given plan. Try it. It'll make you feel great!"

Divorce: "If you're not happy, and you realize that you never will be even if things straighten out a bit, then it's best to correct it. If you do this early and don't wait until it's forced on you, then you'll end up being comfortably associated with your former spouse."

Life's most underrated thing: "Manners. I was brought up strictly, and it has stood me well. Manners are a matter of respect—one human being to another. It's a very undertaught part of life, one that we should emphasize more."

Getting what you want: "Dream big and dare to fail."

that I never caught. I'd like to have back half the hours that I spent on office politics that didn't amount to squat. When you get older, time gets a lot more valuable, and you start thinking about all the things that you wanted to do with your life that you could have done if you'd used your free time a little more productively. At least if I had spent it golfing, I would have broken 100 by now."

—*Mike Strehren, 68, photographer, father of three*

"The secret of happiness is to get sick. . . . After each of my illnesses, I have felt not only undiminished and unready to die, but quite goofily elated. . . . Every cheer comes with an asterisk, but so does every groan, as the will to live keeps pounding back. And there's a certain excitement to be had just from living on the edge: You are more fully alive than you have ever been and getting more out of each day. If the will to live can't have quantity, then it will have quality, seizing on one great year in exchange for 10 or 20 dull ones."

—*Wilfrid Sheed*

PART 8

Men at Work

Business Etiquette Faux Pas

Much of the career advice that you see these days tells you how to acquire the right skills to avoid the downsizing ax. But what about the little things you do every day? The way you carry yourself and interact with bosses and co-workers plays a significant role in whether you get that corner office. We consulted some etiquette experts and asked them for some everyday slipups in the office.

1. Not saying "Please" or "Thank you" enough. And these words are to be used for all co-workers, not just ones above you on the corporate ladder.

2. Not apologizing when you've screwed up.

3. Rejecting compliments, as well as not giving enough compliments.

4. Forgetting names and botching introductions.

5. Being observed talking to yourself.

6. Not holding doors open—hold them open, including elevator doors, for everyone regardless of gender and rank.

7. Losing your sense of humor about your mistakes.

8. Getting "caught" in an awkward position, like searching through the wastepaper basket, ripping your clothing on an obstruction or kicking a malfunctioning copying machine.

9. Misplacing important items or papers, or realizing that you've lost important documents in the middle of a meeting.

10. Criticizing another person, or analyzing an issue, only to realize that you've got the wrong person or the facts wrong.

Bridging the Gender Gap

*Overcoming Miscommunication Mishaps
with Women*

You are an insecure, overbearing macho sexist jerk. No, really, you are. It says so right here, in this handbook on gender sensitivity in the workplace. Well, not in so many words, but that's the gist of it.

The common belief is this: As more women enter the workplace and gain power, men feel threatened. And because our security is on such shaky ground, we react by flaunting a whole bunch of male evils, such as boorishness, sexism and really bad aftershave. How do you overcome the rising tension between men and women in the marketplace? Gender-sensitivity training.

Hooey. Whatever tension that's arising between men and women at work has little to do with sexism or insecurity. It has to do with simple misunderstanding in our habits of communication. It's the little things that men say and do that are misconstrued by women (and vice versa). "Slight differences in our biology tend to create different communication styles," says Jayne Tear, a consultant who specializes in the mysterious art of gender dynamics. "When these innate communication patterns clash, misunderstandings occur. And while they have nothing to do with stereotypes or sexism, they're often mistakenly perceived this way."

These small misunderstandings are as common as Post-it notes, and result from seemingly innocent stuff: silly jokes that you tell, the way you sit during meetings or how you like to talk sports in the halls. Sure, they sound innocuous, but all can be taken the wrong way. And after a while, you can become a marked man. Women will stop consulting you. They'll go over your head. They'll leave you out of the loop. They'll bad-mouth you to other women in the company. And you'll be left wondering why you never got that promotion or an invitation to the company croquet tournament.

So it pays to know how to detect these areas of potential crisis and avoid them. We're not necessarily saying that you need to dramatically change your behavior at work. Just be aware of the subtle signals that you're sending to the women around you, and the subtle signals that they're sending back. Here are a few simple steps that may help you work better with the opposite sex.

Poke fun at yourself. It's your Monday-morning meeting, and Begley is wearing a tie that's busier than a condom store on Madonna's birthday. So you and the rest of the guys mercilessly goof on him until he removes the repellent thing and slides it into his coat pocket. Harmless fun—even the Begster is laughing. But the women at the table aren't. Why? Is it because we're being mean?

"When it comes to humor, men banter and poke fun at each other," says Tear. "Women, though, are more likely to make fun of themselves. So during the male banter, women back off." The result is that women feel excluded.

Here, and elsewhere, it pays to be bilingual. A man who can make fun of himself as well as poke fun at a pal appears far funnier

to women. "If you can interchange both on a dime, women are more likely to engage in the same kind of interchange," says Tear. And you will be more engaging, more persuasive and, on the whole, even more competent around the cubicles.

Gab about your new sofa. For us, small talk is simple. We like to talk about the Knicks, the Flyers, the bootleg video of Tonya Harding's honeymoon. For women, though, small talk is more about personal self-disclosure. "They like to talk about what's going on at home, with their family or in the community," says Tear. Men do this too, but not as much. The solution is to master both. "If you can be as comfortable chatting about the home as you are about sports, then you'll seem much more approachable and less exclusionary," she says.

This is not to say, however, that you should start talking and thinking like women. Phil Donahue has retired, so now it's officially okay for men to think and act like men again. "Just talk about things, now and then, that appeal to more people than just your pals," says Jonathan Segal, a Philadelphia lawyer who provides employee-relations training to judges and private-sector managers across the country.

Save the rough stuff for the playing field. Your boss is carrying a cup of coffee in one hand and a stack of files in the other. You give him a playful whack on the shoulder. He, in turn, merrily bodychecks you into the wall and moves on. No problem. You love the guy. He thinks that you're the best. "Hitting your male boss may be seen as a sign of affection," says Segal. "Bodycheck your female boss, though, and the odds of her perceiving this as an affectionate gesture are slim to none."

There's a biological reason why men use playful aggression to show affection. "Men are less sensitive to touch than women, so it makes perfect sense that men would develop a set of physical habits and gestures that are much more physical," says Tear. "Pushing and hitting aren't unpleasant for most men, but they are for most women."

The problem is that women don't understand this. They're likely to interpret our roughhousing as macho posturing—that somehow putting a peer in a headlock is our way of proving that we're up to the job. And then when women overreact if we touch them ever so slightly, we assume that they're either oversensitive or uncomfortable around men. Neither is right. "It comes down to sense of touch, nothing more," says Tear, "although it's amazing how many idiotic interpretations result from this."

Meet their gaze. In the loony landscape of pop psychology, we're

I'm Not Lost!

Ask any woman what most annoys her about her man and, somewhere at the top of the list, right below "obsessed with football" and right above "scratches himself inappropriately," will be this old chestnut: "He won't ask for directions."

And why? Because, she'll say, men have fat egos and an overripe machismo that prevent them from admitting that they're lost. Well, next time someone lays this myth on you, crush it like a bug. Although men may be less likely to ask for directions, it has nothing to do with egos or gender politics. It's all biology.

"In terms of getting from one place to another, women use visual cues, finding their way based on landmarks," says consultant and gender specialist Jayne Tear.

Women know that they're supposed to make a left when they recognize the doughnut shop on the corner. If they don't see the doughnut shop, they're lost, and so they feel that it's appropriate to ask for directions.

Men are different. We make our way using vectors, navigating based on how far we move in one direction before we feel it's right to move in another. When we sense that it's right to take a left, we will. We may not know exactly where we are at all times, but we usually have an idea of where we're going. And we find our way through a process of trial and error, so it naturally takes us longer to acknowledge that we're off course.

"Refusing to ask for directions is not proof of infantile machismo," says Tear. "It simply means that you don't feel that you're lost yet. And why should you ask for directions if you don't feel lost?" Good question.

told that men don't listen, women do. Actually, men just don't listen to pop psychologists. Who does?

We're great listeners. We just do it differently. When we listen, we tend to shift eye contact frequently. Women maintain steady eye contact with whomever is speaking. There's nothing deep about it. It's simply a behavioral difference that carries no psychological luggage. "Because men rarely return the eye contact, women think that they aren't listening," says Tear.

The solution is simple: When a female co-worker is talking to you, fix your eyes on hers longer than you normally might. Nod once in a while. "It's a useful tool at certain, but not all, times," says Tear. Stare too long (at a guy, girl or small pet) and you'll give them the heebie-jeebies.

Rein yourself in. You're in a meeting. You're comfortable, sitting diagonally with your elbows resting on the chairs beside you. The female co-worker sitting next to you, however, is becoming visibly uncomfortable. She shoots a few glances at you. She clears her throat. You sense that she might be annoyed. Finally she asks you to move. You move your arm, but you wonder what's bothering her.

No, her problem isn't political, psychological or chemically induced. It's *visual*. Men and women have slight differences in their sense of sight, and this is why the co-worker got so unnerved. "Men are better at judging distances in front of them, whereas women have slightly sharper peripheral vision," says Tear. The sharper peripheral vision allows women to see that elbow, and it's distracting to her. "Although you did nothing wrong," says Tear, "a problem occurs if the woman assumes that you're using subtle body language to distract her. She may get mad and say something."

So next time, be aware of this simple visual difference, and don't put it through the pop-psychology meat grinder. Just assume that you're in her line of fire and pull back. You don't have to sit up, put your arms at your sides and maintain a glazed, stoic expression. Instead, just relax without unfolding like an emergency life raft.

Take a breather. Strident feminists will claim that men constantly interrupt women as a sign of their oppressive nature. But if these lasses would shut up for a moment, they would realize that this interruption is just our way of conversing. Interruptions allow us to take turns talking. If we didn't do it, then each office meeting would be like Oscar night: an interminable series of long and painful monologues.

A Tough Assignment

The downsizing ax may have grazed your skull, but your workout compatriot two cubicles down took a direct hit. To make matters unbelievably worse, he's your direct report, his jumper cables are still in your trunk and you have to fire him before 10:00 A.M.

Ugly situation.

But you can survive it. And so can your friendship, says David A. Laney, senior vice-president of Manchester Partners International, a human-resources consulting firm.

Here are some tips on handling it professionally and delicately.

- If there's time, ask advice from someone who has terminated a colleague.
- Role-play the termination with a neutral party in advance, preferably someone from your human-resources.
- Be honest with your feelings. Recognize that this will put a major strain on your friendship. And then remember the different roles we all must fill and that you are not the ruination of your friend's life.

Men tend to talk *over* each other, cutting in and out like commuters at rush hour. "Men will speak in a steady stream of verbiage until they're interrupted," says Tear. Then we'll cut back in when the time is right. There's no underlying psychobabble here. It's pure linguistics.

Women take their turns differently. "Their rhythms of speech are different," says Tear. "Women speak with frequent pauses, allowing time for others to interject." That's why, in a normal business meeting, you find a lot of silent women waiting for a pause—and a lot of men wondering why women don't speak up more. This clash of styles can lead to resentment on their part.

Again, the simple solution is to be bilingual. "Women must learn

- Schedule the termination meeting for early in the week. Avoid a Friday firing—this way, your friend could start looking for a job immediately.
- If possible, meet with your friend in a neutral and private setting on company premises instead of your office, and always speak to him face-to-face.
- Keep the meeting between five and ten minutes. Forgo small talk. Get right to the point, giving your friend a clear, significant reason for his termination.
- Be prepared for his reaction. Listen to his response, and let him express his emotions. Be empathetic and understanding. Treat your friend with respect and dignity.
- Help your friend by telling him exactly what to do next. Assist him in a compassionate, responsible way when it comes to bringing his relationship with the organization to a close.
- Remain a friend. Alert him to job openings, and offer to serve as a reference if company policy allows it.
- When things are almost back to normal, return the jumper cables.

to interrupt more, and men should use more pauses when talking to a woman," says Tear. Pausing has another benefit: You'll appear more self-assured and as less of a know-it-all.

Figure out the real meaning. A female supervisor approaches you with a request. "If you don't mind," she asks politely, "would you please call Ezekiel Coogan about the cattle prods when you have a chance?"

You never get around to it. So she gets ticked. But hey, if she wanted you to make the call, she would have said so. Instead, she softened her language with "if you don't mind" and "when you have the chance." Maybe you do mind and maybe you didn't have the chance. If she's your boss, then she has to make it a priority, not you.

Women tend to be much more oblique about giving direction. "But a supervisor has to realize that we're all more comfortable with orders," says Segal. And men need to peel away the effluvia that can mask a female boss's request.

For example, she might use qualifiers ("probably"), inclusive pronouns ("our" instead of "I") and end with confusing tag questions ("don't you think?"). We, on the other hand, just raise or lower our voices or gesture to make a point. So when a male boss tells us to do something, we get the point. When a female does the same, we hear all the probablys and the maybes, and we doubt whether the speaker really means what she's saying. Similarly, when women hear us convey our ideas forcefully, they consider us hardheaded.

Women need to understand that men operate more directly— and it's not because we're arrogant. It's just our style, probably originating from the evocative grunts of caveman days. And men need to pay more attention to the idea and ignore all the stuff swirling around it. "Do this and you'll find that men and women will agree more often than not," says Tear.

Reveal her true feelings. You ask the saucy temp Tallulah out for a date. She says, "I can't, I'm busy." A few days go by and you ask her out again. This time, she says, "I can't, I'm going out of town." You try one more time. She says, "I can't," and points to her cranium. "Brain surgery." You make one last attempt—and she goes to personnel to file a complaint.

Which, from your point of view, doesn't seem fair. "In this case, what you hear is her saying *why* she can't go. But she never says *no*," says Segal. "This makes it sound to you like she wanted to go, but couldn't. Even if she didn't want to hurt your feelings, she should have been honest."

So the moral is to be as up-front as possible. "If the woman seems to be making excuses, then ask her if she is," says Segal. "Say,

---

JUST THE FACTS

When 500 men were asked in a survey, "What would lighten up your life?" 70 percent replied, "A month's vacation from work."

'Hey, this is the second time I asked you out and you've been busy. Are you really busy, or is this a nice way of saying *no*?'" If she says that she was just being nice, accept it. And better yet, boil it down to one rule: Don't date anyone from work. But feel free to ask if they have sisters.

Watch out for their smiles. When you told that joke about the farmer and the front-end loader at the staff meeting, sure, a few women in the room smiled. And you took that to mean, yeah, they thought you were quite the wit. But later, when these women band together into a coalition to have you demoted and demoralized, you realize that sometimes a smile is not a smile at all. "When men are angry, they tend to raise their voices," says Segal. "But when women are angry, they often become quieter, and sometimes they smile because they are uncomfortable."

So, as a preventive measure, you might want to watch the off-color, dirty, mildly dirty, slightly dirty or vaguely soiled jokes in general. Even if you're just with the guys, you never know who's listening. This is reality. Before you get the urge, ask yourself if you'd say the same thing in front of your mother. And if you do happen to tell a joke and the woman across from you pulls a Mona Lisa, don't think for a minute that you're safe. She might be uncomfortable—even furious. Recognize it, and be more careful next time.

Balancing Act

A Guide to Getting It All Done

We're all struggling with the issue of balance, at least in the larger, whole-life, metaphorical sense (as opposed to the literal, isolated, late-night-with-Old-Grand-Dad sense). We're all fighting to keep our feet amid all the pushing and the shoving; we're looking to do our jobs well, to raise our kids right, to romance our wives over the long haul. We want to spend time with our friends, time with our family, time with ourselves. We want to take care of our homes, our cars, our bodies, our heads. We want to play sports, enjoy hobbies, nurture outside interests. We want all this, and we want, on top of it all, more money, more power, more respect, more recognition, more possessions, *more*.

Well, we can't have it.

"There's a very specific point where we reach overload, where the demands on us exceed our limits," says Richard A. Swenson, M.D., associate professor at the University of Wisconsin Medical School in Madison and author of the time- and stress-management book *Margin*. "We have, as a culture, crossed that line. History is happening to 250 million Americans. We're all hitting the wall together."

Dr. Swenson is not just a medical doctor but a physicist as well, and it's his belief that the demands on our time and energy, and our ability to cope with these demands, can be mapped and plotted with the same kind of accuracy as the path of a comet or the growth of the gross national product. Simply put, the human race has never progressed at the rate it's been progressing for the last few decades. And we, as men, are gradually losing our ability to cope with the myriad demands facing us.

Consider that, in the meager lifetime that you've been allotted, you'll spend:

- Six months at traffic lights waiting for them to change
- One year looking through desk clutter for things that you've misplaced
- Two years calling people who aren't in or whose lines are busy
- Five years waiting in lines, and three more years sitting in meetings

That's a lot of time being drained away from us. And it's not just time we're running out of; it's energy—mental, emotional, physical. By the time they close the lid on you, you'll have learned how to operate 20,000 different devices, from can openers to camcorders. By the time you put in your 8 or 10 or 12 hours on the job tomorrow, your work will have been interrupted an average of 73 times, by bosses, underlings, clients, peers, debtors and cronies; the average manager is interrupted every eight minutes. You have voice mail, e-mail, cellular phones and fax machines. You don't have the resources to get done what you need to get done. How can you do the things you want to do?

Balance. It's what you want to see in yourself. It's what you admire in other men. A recent survey commissioned by *Men's Health* magazine asked men what qualities they admire in others. Sixty-five percent of the respondents said that they admire a man who can strike a balance between work and leisure.

But like other admirable traits, balance is hard to achieve. And it involves asking yourself some tough questions.

What Does Balance Mean?

Balance is not about living life as if it's a TV commercial, where you effortlessly go from the office to the home, gathering admiring glances from smartly dressed women as you pass because, hey, you're in control, you're a nurturer and a provider and you're wearing the right deodorant.

"Balance is internal," says Peter McWilliams, co-author of the best-seller *Do It! Let's Get Off Our Buts.* "Society tells us that having balance is about having a spouse, 2.3 kids, a house, a station wagon, civic activities, a career, church, physical fitness . . . just looking at that list makes me tired," he says.

"That kind of 'balance' is fine for those who want it. But living your own personal balanced life takes a great deal of courage. And experimentation. And sometimes those experiments fail."

In fact, McWilliams says, balance isn't about spending the right amount of time and energy on each part of your life. It's about whether you enjoy spending that amount of time on each. "The definition of having balance is thinking about what you're doing and enjoying it. If you work 14 hours a day, and you're concentrating on and enjoying those 14 hours, you're in balance." Similarly, if you'd rather quit at 3:00 P.M. and take care of the kids, and you're enjoying that time with them, you're in balance. On the other hand, if you're here, and you'd really like to be there, you're out of balance.

"There's a simple way to know if you're in balance," says Walt Schafer, Ph.D., professor of sociology at California State University in Chico and author of *Stress Management for Wellness.* "You want to be healthy, fit, contributing to the well-being of the larger world, having a positive impact on those around you and enjoying yourself. If you have those things, you have balance." If, on the other hand, you're out of shape and miserable, and tend to bite others' heads off at the slightest provocation, maybe you have a little adjusting to do.

Am I Still Learning?

There's a great story about Lee Iacocca during his tenure at Chrysler. One of his senior vice-presidents was heard bragging about the fact that he hadn't taken a vacation in two years. His reward? Iacocca fired him. "Anybody who can't take a vacation in two years," the chairman said, "has something seriously wrong with him."

That hard charger got rubbed out for a reason. He was working so hard that he hadn't paid attention to what his boss really thought. He wasn't taking time to listen and learn. As a result, his life had fallen completely out of balance.

It's an ego thing: Keep pushing. No time for feedback. We put so much into what we do that we don't take time to figure out what we're getting in return. "You're always in danger when you come to the point on the learning curve where you're putting in more than you're learning," says John R. O'Neil, president of the California School of Professional Psychology in San Francisco and author of *The Paradox of Success*.

By "danger," he means any unexpected event that throws us off track, sometimes far off track. "I see it all the time, men who rush through life not paying attention. They become mindless. Then, one day, they get fired. They didn't have their antennae up." The clues were there all along, but the march of progress is loud, friend; it's hard to hear above all those high-stepping boots.

The same thing can happen at home. Did you ever fake hearing what she said? She said it right to your face: Uh, let's see, something about somebody and Friday night and I have to do something. "Oh, um, uh-huh, okay." It happens to all of us. She's right. You don't listen. We need to get our antennae up.

Arrange fixed events. There's too much going on around us, and too much going on inside us, to really pay attention. That's just a given, so don't fight it. You'll have time to sit down and really listen about the time your hearing starts to go. As for now, the short-term solution is to set aside particular times—ritual times—when you're just there to pay attention.

"Set aside an hour or two each week to talk with your spouse," says O'Neil. "Have lunch with your boss once a month. Make it a regular, scheduled event." Don't bring an agenda; remember that you're there to listen. You'll probably get feedback about your personal and professional life you might otherwise have missed.

Look up to someone. You need someone in your life who's been where you've been and who can clue you in if

Tug of War

When you were single, every night was a night out with the boys—hitting the bars, playing basketball, going to ball games.

Then, you met her. And suddenly, life is a balancing act, a struggle for a comfortable equilibrium between her and them. It's a toughie, because whether you know it or not, there's a battle going on—and you're the one who's being fought over. Below is a handy checklist to find out which side is winning.

You're spending too much time with the guys if:

- You can remember your pals' birthdays, but not hers.
- A conversation with your mate usually starts with "What's wrong?" instead of "Hello."
- You get two tickets to a very cool concert, and she's choice number five.
- When your friends call, she hides your messages.
- She starts going out with her friends more, and makes a point of staying out later than you.
- She tries to involve herself in your guy activities, with disastrous consequences.

you're starting to veer off track. Unfortunately, mentors are hard to find. Bosses aren't always good choices because you never know their agendas. It's better to find someone in your field whom you admire, call them up and say, "I'd like to talk with you." "They'll probably be flattered," O'Neil says.

Defuse the dullness. Listen to yourself. If your head starts telling you, "This job is getting stale," take it as a warning sign. Start paying attention. You're in trouble. Look around the office for new responsibilities, or look outside it for new opportunities. Take care of this problem, or someone will come along and take care of it for you.

Same thing at home. If playing board games with the kids gives you all the thrill of a *Golden Girls* marathon, that's okay. You don't have to keep playing. "Being a parent is about learning, too," says O'Neil. "If you're bored, admit it. Sit down with your spouse and

- You find yourself cutting dates short, forfeiting opportunities for certain sex, just to meet up with your friends.

You're spending too much time with her if:

- You've traded in the pronoun "I" for "we."
- The only men you hang out with are either married to or dating her friends.
- You know more about salad dressing than you do about beer.
- All your luggage matches.
- It comes as a shock to you that Lawrence Taylor is retired.
- You've purchased a car for its high safety rating.
- You haven't seen a movie with a big explosion in it for a long time. But if anybody needs to know which Meg Ryan film to rent, you're the man.
- You find yourself envying guys in prison. At least they get out more.

say, 'Look, I can't do this "Chutes and Ladders" thing anymore.'" You ought to be in the business of learning to be a more compassionate person. And if your kids can't teach you that, then who can? Ask yourself if you are learning, and if you're not, start looking for new ways to spend time with your kids, ways that both of you will enjoy.

Beware of stale habits. Do you really need that 10:00 A.M. Monday meeting? Sure, you've been running it for years. But is it really the best use of your time and energy, or is it just a way to slide safely into the lunch hour without doing any work? "Psychologists call it 'repetition compulsion': the drive to repeat that which is familiar," says Dr. Schafer. "To achieve balance, we need to recognize that we often rob ourselves of time and balance out of habit." Take a hard look at your daily habits. What are you learning? Nothing? Then change.

Do I Have a Long-Term Goal?

What are you working for? Retirement? Get real. Retirement isn't about balance. Retirement is about them yanking a big load off one side of the seesaw and you plopping down into the dust, trying to figure out what's going to come along to lift you back up.

If you want real balance, you need to set goals, and that's not easy to do. Goals are frightening. They're freestanding measures of our shortcomings. Avoid goals; you'll avoid disappointment, right?

Well, you'll avoid specific, easily defined disappointment at least. Fuzzy, amorphous, free-floating disappointment, on the other hand, is a practical guarantee. That nagging sense that you've failed to accomplish something. But what?

"Americans are notoriously myopic," Dr. Swenson says. "We tend to live connect-the-dot lives. We need to learn to build five-year goals, even ten-year goals. That way, we can monitor whether we're in balance by how well we're progressing toward those goals."

Start slow. You may be a connoisseur of single-barrel bourbons, but you started out drinking beer. This whole goal-setting thing can get heady, too. Take small sips. Mark Riesenberg, president of the consulting firm Human Resources Unlimited in West Orange, New Jersey, has a few suggestions for those just learning to find their focus.

Plan ahead 30 days. Go get a pencil and paper. No, it's all right, go ahead.

Okay. First, write down one or two personal goals that you'd like to achieve in the next 30 days. Make them simple—you only have a month. Need to get the tires rotated? Buy a watch? Send that love letter to Tipper Gore?

Second, write down two or three family goals. Attend Jimmy's soccer practice at least twice, perhaps.

JUST THE FACTS

Percentage of Americans who take their shoes off at work, according to Dr. Scholl's: 49

Third, write down four or five business goals (hey, you have bills to pay). Learn how to use your e-mail. Clean out your in-box. Lock in that client.

Be precise. Any goal you pick is fine, but it has to be specific and measurable (in other words, you'll know for sure if you've gotten there or not). And it has to be attainable in the allotted time, which isn't very long, so no saving-the-world stuff, okay? Continue this goal-setting practice for six months. By taking one month at a time, you'll become accustomed to goal setting. It's like overcoming a fear of heights, except you're still standing on the bottom rung.

Break a big goal into little pieces. When you're ready to take the next step, sit down and write out exactly what you want to accomplish in five years. Again, make it specific and measurable. Fuzzy goals lead to fuzzy results. Don't be afraid to dream big here. If you want to make vice-president, that's great.

Now, start breaking down the time frame. If you want to be a vice-president in 5 years, where do you have to be in 2½ years? A department manager? Okay, to be a department manager in that time, where do you have to be in 18 months? To get there, what do you have to achieve in the next 6 months? And so on. What's your goal for the next month? The next week? Today?

Make it your little secret. Goals are private. Tell your mentor, the person who's helping you move toward your goals. Tell the people whose cooperation you need in achieving them. But around everybody else, shut up. "People are uncomfortable when those around them try to better themselves," Riesenberg says. You're getting the upper hand in life. They know it. They don't like it.

By the way, make sure that you have family and personal goals as well as career goals. As long as you're walking straight toward them all, you have balance.

If I lose my balance, who's going to be there to pick me back up?

Know who your friends are. Cherish them. The traffic can get heavy out there.

Backstabbing
Protection

Steering Clear of Friendly Traitors

Otto and Willie were the best of friends. They left a large corporation to found a hot company in the go-go 1980s. Then, just as they were about to hoist each other into the stratosphere, business flattened in a very fast, rough way. Five years of planning, money raising and general butt breaking were heading down the tubes. Time for the founders to fight together to save the company, right? That's what Otto thought, anyway. Fifteen or 20 seconds after the trouble became evident, dear Willie strapped on his parachute and bailed. Otto stuck it out, turned the company around and sold it a couple of years later. But the boys haven't talked much since.

Otto's doing well now. He's taken the whole episode with Willie bailing rather philosophically. "However good you think your friendships are, you can't tell what people will do when the going gets tough. The most unexpected people will pull through, and some people you expect to hang tough will turn and run. I'm lucky it wasn't uglier, financially or emotionally. Plus, I got a good lesson about going into business with your friends: Don't do it."

Let's face it, guys. In the daily battle that is our lives, we try to betray each other. We compete like the 400 million sperm swimming madly for that one fresh and glistening egg. Sure, it's harsh, but if we didn't struggle to win, nothing would get accomplished.

Within that matrix, you assemble a battalion of trustworthy friends and relations who fight alongside you, and you're stronger for it. Trust is the pact that binds you. This is the tacit code of the battalion.

The truly tough problems arise on an intrabattalion basis. Forget the guys who are admittedly trying to kill you—we know what they want. The truly deadly event is when somebody close—an office mate, a brother, your best pal from college—violates your trust. Such events can take on huge, toxic proportions precisely because they occur at such close range. Your soft belly and your weak chin are just crying out for a punch, and nobody can see and reach them like those closest to you. But you have to keep your friends, family and office allies in fighting shape, for support and protection. What you need is a strategy for dodging the blades meant for your back and healing the wounds that you've already suffered.

So let's talk about saving some friends. What could be useful is to draw a sort of road map so that we can avoid the most dangerous intersections. The discussion that follows is by no means complete—there are as many ways to get betrayed by friends as there are friends in your card file. But there's also a way to train for these eventualities, an instinct you can develop. It won't stop you from being betrayed, but it may save you from having to give, or receive, a deadly blow.

The best pal traitor. Among good friends there is a kind of rough rivalry that can be good for us in an athletic sort of way, making us better competitors and possibly even better human beings. If it's within the bounds of your friendship to draw blood, steal women and welsh on bets, so be it, but you won't find us hanging with boys like that. So to each his own, but the caveat here is this: The rougher it gets, the rougher it gets.

Try to analyze why, exactly, your old buddy Biff told your girlfriend that he turned down a job you took. She thought it was a transparent ploy to get her into bed. Funny thing. It was. So, when you and Biff are next enjoying a casual Gatorade-rehydrating postworkout moment, let him know that you know. If it doesn't make him uncomfortable enough to begin to build an apology, Biff is no friend.

The corporate stabber. Deadly politics are the very stuff of office life, and there is more than a little tolerance for betrayal. The higher the stakes in money and glamour, the higher the tolerance. Betrayal is often a good corporate tool, ensuring that mere human considerations don't get in the way of profit. It also helps keep a competitive edge among the foot soldiers. You have to be prepared to give, and get, as the circumstances dictate. But you can still conduct yourself with class, even if it is the office. Sometimes a stab can work out for everybody. If you have integrity, you'll see that it does.

The touchy-feely traitor. Some backstabbers are aware of their transgressions in a debilitating way. Knife wielding eats at them. If you have a friendship in this status, level with whomever it is that betrayed you. It's possible that he'll respond indignantly or that fireworks will be set off that can't be called back. But most of the time, it will come as a relief. People know at some basic level when things are wrong. You must make your approach with absolute calm—you do not want to whip out your six-gun and shoot up the saloon. As usual, the experience will be valuable. His response will allow you to measure whether the friendship is truly worth the work.

Familiar traitors. Members of families have been betraying each other since the dawn of time, and so there is some historical kick to this variety of betrayal. Agamemnon, Orestes and, of course, Cain are our violent and cautionary paradigms. For the moment, let's define family as the people with whom we grew up—as opposed to the people with whom we now live.

A guy we know in Florida lost his grandmother's precious beachfront apartment to his dysfunctional brother because the brother claimed he was chronically unemployable and needed a free place to live. There is a weird sort of prodigal-son element to this—the guy who goes to the trouble to leave and suffer is the one who gets the biggest welcome when he comes back. Meanwhile, the dutiful son gets the dark meat on Thanksgiving afternoon. Your job, if you want to avoid this sort of betrayal, is to speak up when the bird is carved. Stake your claim.

Stabbed and loving it. There is the rare experience of betrayal that makes us feel extremely lucky. It's complex, but there is a peculiar feeling of relief that comes with a good betrayal by the right people.

Take the story of James, for example: Blofeld, a college friend of his, had managed to hang on to their friendship for a few years after they finished school. But he made James uncomfortable. What had been merely obnoxious around the dorm room became boring and weird in the real world. But James could never figure out a way of ditching Blofeld. Then James's business took a spectacular turn, resulting in a sudden deluge of financial and media attention. Blofeld instantly began representing himself as James's "agent." He insulted several people with whom James had business. James heard about it and formally severed the relationship. "Somehow," James explains, "he'd never managed to do enough wrong for me to wield the ax. I finally had the excuse. I got the bastard out of my life."

There are many time-honored ways in which men betray each other. But *mano-a-mano* betrayal carries a special number of what we'd call debt dollars that need to be repaid before there can be some kind of resolution. It is a question of revenge. The tacit question after every betrayal of one man by another is: How's he going to pay? Will there be a calling out, however crazed, to satisfy the debt? You might not expect the chief executive officer of a major international corporation to be pummeled on a dance floor, but it happened to one such executive at a fancy Long Island fund-raiser last summer. Despite his number one social position, the fact remains: The guy is not immune to a fistfight. He's a man, and fighting's part of his job, whether he knows it or not. Now he knows.

Fistfights aren't the only way to settle a score, of course, especially if you have some hope that the relationship can be repaired. But recovery is hard work, because the fundamental unfairness of the initial transgression—you trusted them, they betrayed you—means that the rules are out the window. It also means that you have to resolve the conflict through the rules of mutual trust, while operating in territory where no rules and no trust exist.

How does it work? It doesn't—at least, not very often. But it's worth trying if you get the chance, because when it works, you regain more than just a friend who has somehow not been lost. The stink of betrayal is swept away, you gain a better friend/co-worker/relative out of the deal and you gain extra camaraderie because you've weathered bad situations. It's worth it. You need all the friends you can get.

We do not lead perfectly ethical lives. There are, within all of us, little daily betrayals with which we can or cannot live, which we do or do not admit. It is best, in general, to find and uncover betrayal and call it by its name. That is, painful as it sounds, the way to make it go away.

Do yourself a favor. Call in your betrayers now. Resolve the issues that separate you, or clear the bastards from your life. Then you can resume building bonds with the men who've earned your trust.

Stress Busters

Call on These Tips to Ease Your Woes

It's Monday afternoon and your boss has just appeared in your doorway to inform you that the report due next week is now due Thursday; he'd like it to be better organized than your last one and, by the way, he's pulling your secretary for the next three days to help on a hot project that he's in charge of. Before you can even reply, he's gone, shuffling down the hall like some satanic factotum, trying to remember which pant leg he tucked his tail into today.

Although the rational part of your brain is stunned, the chemicals inside your body have already gone to battle stations. The two small adrenal glands atop your kidneys are gushing stress hormones like a fire hose. Your pupils dilate, the better to see your enemy. Blood is shunted from your stomach toward the muscles in your arms and legs, preparing you to fight. Even your clotting factor is on the rise, adding protection from the inevitable wounds of close combat. There you sit, all stressed up with no place to go.

In an ideal world, each of us would follow our bliss, get paid for doing what we love and be recognized for our unique talents. Then we would close up shop at 5:00 P.M. sharp and effortlessly transform from Bill Gates into Mister Rogers.

But it doesn't work that way. You need a few strategies to help you leave behind the stress of the workday and throttle down so that you can enjoy home life. And the best decompression technique for you probably includes three critical benchmarks.

- It's pleasurable. No surprise there.
- It's distracting. In other words, it involves concentrating on something besides work.
- It's satisfying. Whether you go for a run, sit down and do a crossword puzzle or enter a co-ed mud wrestling tournament, it should float your boat.

"It doesn't matter how weird it is," says Allen Elkin, Ph.D., who is program director at the Stress Management and Counseling Center in New York City and advises corporations such as IBM and Pepsico. But it should be something that you do and then finish doing and feel as if you've accomplished something.

Here, then, is a list to get you started.

End-of-Day Tasks

Before you blast off, remember that the object is to travel light. You want to park as many worries as possible at the office.

Wipe your desk clean. The experts say that there is a magical correlation between clutter and stress. Take the last 15 minutes of your day to organize your desk to the fullest extent consistent with your toilet training. Creating order out of chaos gives you a sense of closure for the day and fools people into believing you actually know what you're doing.

Plan for tomorrow. This is a big one. Making a "to do" list is more than a way of remembering things. It's a way of dealing with them. Go beyond the basic checklist of phone calls and appointments, and include the really gnarly things that you need to do tomorrow, such as "confront Bob about how he interrupts me in meetings." The reason is that the human mind is a worry machine. At home, when you should be relaxing or asleep, it will scour your memory like a hungry shark looking for trouble. The "to do" list helps appease the beast. When it discovers Bob, tell it to relax. You've already got him scheduled.

Let your family decide. Okay, despite your Herculean efforts, you couldn't get all your work done during normal hours. This happens a lot and eventually leads to: (a) your family complaining that you're always at work and never at home, or (b) your family complaining that when you're at home, you're always doing work. The solution is often simple: Call the family and ask whether they'd rather you work late or bring work home and spend the evening ignoring them. They won't be happy with either, but at least they'll feel that they have a choice in the matter.

Stretch out in your cubicle. You can shake the fatigue that has set in during the last eight hours with a simple stretch. First, check to make sure that Sally, the sassy executive secretary, has left for the day. Coast clear? Okay. Now stand two feet away from your chair with your feet 12 inches apart, knees flexed. Bend over from the hips (keeping your back as straight as possible) and place your hands on the chair seat, elbows bent. Point your butt at the ceiling and slowly straighten your knees without locking them. Round your back and drop your head between your arms. Breathe evenly as you drop your head, allowing it to sag. Feel the stretch in your spine, sides and back.

To come up, bend your knees and bring your hands to your thighs. Push on your thighs to finish the rise, lifting first your head, then your chest, trying to keep your back straight. Repeat. Five minutes of this will re-establish the mind-body link you need to descend stairs without falling.

The Commute

You're out the door. This is a great moment. Most guys cut it short and make an unthinking beeline for the car, bus or train. Don't. Remember that the transition from work to home is a process, not a contest. Savor the moment of liberation as one of its highlights, a prime time for you to regroup mentally.

Stop and smell the flowers. If you're taking a bus or the subway, walk to the next stop. If you're headed for your wheels, stow the keys and walk around the block first. Look at the sky. Check out the skirts. Enjoy the nonfluorescent light, the unforced air against your face, the fact that you're out of range of e-mail.

Regain control. Stress comes from the feeling of not being in control, so remind yourself that you're still the boss in your life. Window-shop. Browse in a bookstore. If you're really hurting, go into a department store and try on the most expensive suit there. Dig yourself in the mirror, smile at the salesperson and tell him you like the cut but were looking for something in a tasteful orange plaid. Then leave.

Refuel your body. Many men eat a big, sleep-inducing lunch, stave off fatigue through the afternoon with caffeine and crash at the end of the business day. Instead of a few 12-ounce curls after work, revive yourself with a trip to the local salad bar for a little protein/carbohydrate combo: half a chicken or turkey sandwich, or a salad with a little Parmesan on top. The protein will wake up your mind, the carbohydrate your body.

Remember that stress is a response to something, not the thing itself. Traffic jams and packed commuter trains are God's way of telling you not to take the universe too personally. Since you can't control them, you might as well use the time to your advantage.

Release the stress. Here's a technique that Dr. Elkin teaches his clients. Press together firmly any finger and thumb on either hand. Now inhale through your nose and hold the breath for several seconds until you feel a slight discomfort. Then exhale deeply through slightly parted lips, as you release the tension in your finger and thumb. Let a wave of relaxation spread from the top of your head down to your toes. Repeat.

Try "beach ball" breathing. Stress causes you to take shallow

---

JUST THE FACTS

Times of day when you are at greatest risk for being hit by a sleepy driver: 2:00 A.M., 6:00 A.M. and 4:00 P.M.

breaths, which impedes the proper oxygen/carbon dioxide exchange your body needs. To counteract this, imagine a small beach ball behind your navel. Slowly fill it as if you were breathing directly into the ball through your navel. Empty it with a slow, measured exhalation. Repeat until the desire to kill the guy tailgating you passes.

Diversionary Tactics

Feel like you're digging a trench between the office and home? Maybe you need to break out of the rut. Once a month or so—say, the day that the sales reports come in—surprise yourself by doing something that a guy like you wouldn't ordinarily do.

Blast away the stress. Go to a pistol range and remove your credit card from your wallet. They'll do the rest, supplying you with a shooting iron, shells, safety glasses, ear protection and instruction. Get the human silhouette targets. Visualize. You'll be shocked by how much you enjoy this. Ducks will begin eyeing you warily.

Knock some pins down. Head to a place that you probably haven't been to in years: a bowling alley. The multicolored clown shoes alone are worth the price of admission. Devise your own scoring system in which gutter balls count as four points and your actual score is the number of pins that remain standing.

Play some games. Go to an arcade, roll up your sleeves and swat a few balls in the batting cage. Take a roller-coaster ride, if you're the type.

Get back to nature. Carry a pair of old boots in your trunk and pull over when you see some woods. Take a walk, then quietly stand stock-still until the birds and squirrels forget about you and resume their lives. Remember that you are the one who decides what's important in life.

The Home Front

Stress experts say that the biggest mistake people make is unconsciously bringing their worries home and displacing them onto their partners and children. Doing this alienates people so fast that you'll have Mark Fuhrman calling to ask for your secret.

Warn your family. "People will put up with a lot if they know where it's coming from," says David Fischer, M.D., a Washington, D.C., psychiatrist who counsels a lot of men in high-level government positions. "If you come right out and tell your family, 'Look, I had a bad day and I'm gonna bite your head off if you look at me cross-eyed,' you've accomplished two things," he says. "First, people around you will cut you more slack now that they know you're not angry at them personally. Second, the very act of owning up to your feelings lessens their intensity, making you less likely to explode."

Establish a pattern. Stress experts say that many people find that some sort of ritual helps them get back to a relaxed state of mind. You may want to shed your work duds and change immediately into comfortable clothes. Some men like to spend some quality time with the junk mail. Other guys need to sit on the edge of the bed and stare at nothing for a few minutes until the stress-o-meter in their head slides down into the green zone.

Appreciate your better half. "The deal in a relationship is for each of you to get what you want," says Dr. Fischer. "Men—though a lot of us aren't aware of it—basically want to feel nurtured by our mates. What women want from men is to feel valued and desired." It's easy to forget this under the weight of a 9-to-5 life punctuated by dirty socks and mortgage payments, dust bunnies and French-bread pizza. But you're helping yourself when you find ways to let her know how important she is to you.

Flowers, which are expensive, ephemeral and totally nonfunctional, somehow get you an awful lot of goodwill. Send her a note saying that at 11:45 on Wednesday in the middle of a meeting you were thinking about how happy you are to have her in your life. Grab her when you come in the door, take her to the bedroom and begin undressing her slowly without saying a word. In the afterglow, tell her you were stressed out about something earlier but now you've forgotten it entirely.

Cool Careers

Check Out These Great Ways to Earn a Living

Maybe you're pretty happy with your job. The pay's okay, the boss isn't a cretin (usually) and there's little chance of you being injured at work, unless an unusually deep paper cut happens to sever an artery. All in all, you're pretty satisfied.

But sometimes you can't help but think that there's a better job out there. One that would require you to visit exotic places, traveling incognito with celebrities, spies and international beauties. One that would pay you to be pampered, employ you to be entertained and cut you checks so that you could catch some rays.

You probably think that jobs like this are few and far between. You're right. They are. But after an exhaustive search, we were able to round up a few first-rate positions we believe to be the best jobs in the world. Jobs so fun that you can't believe people get paid to do them.

Hotel Snoop

Jeff Stokes, 30, gets to go to some of the most exotic vacation destinations in the world and make the people there very nervous. Stokes is a spy. A pampered spy. He spends his workdays being catered to by concierges, valets and bellboys; chefs, waiters and maître d's; golf pros and caddies; personal trainers and masseuses. Stokes is a mystery shopper, a service evaluator. A mole of the leisure class. Posing as a typical customer, he anonymously evaluates the service at first-class hotels, restaurants, health clubs and golf courses for Bare Associates, the Alexandria, Virginia, company of which he's a vice-president. Hotel and spa owners use guys like Stokes to see if their operations are up to snuff.

How he landed the job: This is a case of combining interests to fill a particular niche. Stokes was a business major and physical-education minor in college. He then went into the health club industry as a personal trainer. After moving up into sales and then management, he learned what resorts needed and how to market himself as their solution.

Why he'd never quit: Stokes holds the power that all of us wish we had: to complain about service and be taken seriously. "And I can write my reports on my laptop while I'm sitting at poolside." And everything is written off.

Downside: Fear of discovery by an angry mob of bellhops.

Model Shutterbug

When video crews started tagging along on the annual *Sports Illustrated* swimsuit-issue shoots, the world got a glimpse of what Walter Iooss does for a living. And so did his wife.

"The opening scene was of me drinking margaritas in the pool," recalls the 52-year-old photographer, who shoots sporting events for *Sports Illustrated* the rest of the year. "Then I was waxing up my bodyboard to go surfing. Then there were the girls." The "girls," in-

cidentally, have included Christie Brinkley, Elle MacPherson, Kathy Ireland, Carol Alt, Angie Everhart . . . you name her.

How he landed the job: He started young and worked without pay. Iooss began as a freelance photographer for *Sports Illustrated* at the green age of 16, after showing his portfolio to a photo editor. The editor was impressed enough to get him press credentials for a game but would pay him only if the magazine published his photos. It did. Lots of them. Now he frolics with women on the beach. Did we say gorgeous women?

Why he'd never quit: "I live sort of the male fantasy," Iooss says. "I'm either with Michael Jordan or Vendela." But he also admits that there's one guy who has a better deal: the makeup artist who has to dust sand off Stephanie Seymour's butt. "And she has one of the most beautiful butts God's ever made."

Downside: You can only take pictures.

Sporting-Goods Tester

Look through the L.L. Bean Sporting Goods catalog and you'll see that it's loaded with active-guy gear that most of us would love to have the time and the money to play with: fly rods, kayaks and canoes, ice skates, cross-country skis, backpacks. Top-of-the-line stuff, the kind of gear that you'd treasure and take care of and pass down to your grandkids. Unless you were Dave Teufel. He'd rather waterlog that canoe you've been ogling just to see if he can sink it, ride those kayaks right into a river's rocks to see how they handle the impact or trundle down an embankment with fly rod in hand never worrying if he might snap it against a streamside oak.

As a copywriter for the catalog, his job is to play with the equipment. Play hard. "We take the gear out and see what it can do. Push it to its limits. And when we're done, we act like total idiots and see if we can break it," he says. Tomorrow it's a pair of in-line skates, which he'll spend the day in, hopping curbs and racing the other employees around town.

How he landed the job: Teufel worked to learn a particular skill, copywriting, then found a creative way to apply it. A journalism degree from Lehigh University in Bethlehem, Pennsylvania, led to direct marketing work in New York City, which gave him the experience he needed to go out and land a fun job.

Why he'd never quit: He doesn't have to explain to anybody how he ruined his expensive new toy.

Downside: It's hard to come up with something fun to do on vacation.

Demolition Man

As kids, the first time we lit a firecracker, we understood the true joy of controlled mayhem. Some of us outgrew the need to make loud noises. Others—Yoko Ono, for example—didn't. Or take Allen Hall, 49, who gets paid to make a mess on a huge scale as a movie special-effects coordinator. His credits include *Backdraft*, *Top Gun* and *Apocalypse Now*. He also won an Oscar for the exploding napalm during the Vietnam sequence of *Forrest Gump*. And recently, he hobnobbed with real pirates in Thailand and blew a pirate ship to smithereens. And he still has all his digits.

How he landed the job: What else? He knew someone. A friend of the family was Glen Robinson, four-time Academy Award winner and the special-effects man who did the flying monkeys in *The Wizard of Oz*. But what really paid off were the chemistry and physics classes that he took in medical school. "I understand what momentum is and how to set up a safe stunt so that we don't kill a man," he says. Yes, well, it's important to keep the client happy.

Why he'd never quit: It's hard to argue with a job where you're encouraged to blow up at your boss.

Downside: Relatives are always after him to throw Fourth of July parties.

Beachcomber

For the past seven years, Stephen Leatherman, Ph.D., has been getting paid for doing what normal guys like us do on vacation. No, not buying tacky commemorative T-shirts. Dr. Leatherman hits the beachfronts and rates them for travel magazines such as *Condé Nast's Traveler*. He lies on snow-white sand, swims and surfs in turquoise-blue water and lounges under palm trees—all for the betterment of mankind, or at least for the betterment of white-collar criminals who need to decompress before indictments. Dr. Leatherman is a 47-year-old University of Maryland geography professor who also studies beach erosion and other coastal geological features. It's a nice area of science to explore—you never know when a billionaire out scouting islands to buy will need an expert's opinion.

How he landed the job: He hit the books. Dr. Leatherman started with a bachelor's degree in geology, then went on to earn a Ph.D. in coastal/environmental science. It was after 20 years of teaching that he acquired the lofty title of "Doctor Beach."

Why he'd never quit: He's well-traveled, well-tanned, and tenured.

Downside: That's a lot of schooling just to surf.

Spy-Gizmo Maker

Every man with a desk job fantasizes about a life of intrigue. If you're stuck in the office late at night among the dark, empty cubicles, suddenly that file in your hand no longer contains the Filberstein account; it conceals satellite photos of the world's largest rocket factory. And you're not making copies; you're saving the world!

Gregg Graison, 45, vice-president of Quark Research Group, doesn't have to play make-believe. He runs a company steeped in intrigue—designing and selling tools that secret agents use: bulletproof umbrellas, sunglasses with video cameras built into the lenses, wristwatches that turn into knives. He fits BMWs with secret control panels that trigger smoke screens, tear gas, oil slicks and blinding lights. A plumber for life's nasty clogs, Graison sells equipment that he can't name to government branches that he can't discuss. "Confidential," he says, "but exciting. You have a problem and I solve it."

How he landed the job: "Sorry, that's privileged information."

Why he'd never quit: It's an excuse to do insidiously sneaky things while also helping people. "Once, a client was going through a messy divorce, and he was afraid his wife would skip town with their kid. So we built a tracking transmitter into a handheld Nintendo game, then gave it to the kid as a gift. It worked great." Not James Bond, but still cool.

Downside: Hard to keep any secrets from co-workers.

Sports Fan

Sure, you have to endure the endless chatter of talking heads such as Chris Berman, Roy Firestone and their blow-dried brethren, but that's a small price to pay for a front-row seat to the Stanley Cup, the World Series or almost any major sporting event that you can think of. As ESPN's Los Angeles bureau producer, it's

Steve Peresman's duty to coordinate coverage of West Coast sporting events and feed footage to the hungry network's news programs. "It's remarkable to be on the field at the World Series and look up and see everybody, and think to yourself, 'Gee, look where I am. And I wasn't even a good athlete.'"

How he landed the job: Peresman, 31, worked as an assistant at a Pittsburgh television station and eventually rose to sports producer. After a discouraging stint as an on-air personality in Altoona, Pennsylvania, he moved to Philadelphia and took a post at Group W Newsfeed, which provided networks with programs to air. One network was ESPN.

Why he'd never quit: Famous people sometimes tolerate him. "At the NBA finals one year, Michael Jordan came in the room to talk to us, and he just said, 'Hey, can I just stick around here? The pressure of all the other media is so intense.'"

Downside: Annoying network theme music.

Hero of the Universe

When video games made their debut in the early 1980s, John Amirkhan took to them like a socially challenged 12-year-old. "I would start playing a game right after dinner, and then after a while, I'd stand up and think, 'Ooohhh, I'm feeling kind of stiff.' I'd look out the window, and the sun would be coming up." If you're going to spend that much time chained to a desk, you ought to get paid for it, reasoned Amirkhan. Now he does. As a video-game tester for Sega of America, this 48-year-old spends eight hours a day annihilating monsters, decapitating warriors and drinking Jolt. In the meantime he's looking for glitches and bugs, then reporting back to the programmers who design the games.

How he landed the job: It helps to be obsessed. Then again, it helps to have really good hand-eye coordination.

Why he'd never quit: Most people need a hobby to let them blow off stress and take out the frustrations of the job. But Amirkhan's career is all about blowing off stress and taking out your aggressions. Plus, he saves the universe on a daily basis.

Downside: Has more in common with a pimply faced adolescent than with guys his own age.

PART 9

Men at Play

Mail-Order Fun

Look forward to getting something in the mail every month by considering some of the many mail-order clubs. We haven't tried the products, so be sure to shop wisely. Prices may vary.

1. Coffee. For $16.95 per month plus shipping, you get two pounds of gourmet coffee. Call Coffee Quest at 1-800-205-5282.

2. Wine. You receive two bottles from little-known vineyards. Cost is $19.95 per month plus shipping. Call International Wine Cellars at 1-800-205-5282.

3. Beer T-shirts. For $12.95 per month plus shipping, Brew Tees will send you a T-shirt. Call 1-800-585-8337.

4. Boxer shorts. Memberships start at $208 for a year. Call Boxer-Shorts-of-the-Month Club at 1-800-746-7875.

5. Salsa. For $14.95 plus shipping, you get two jars of salsa, tortilla chips and more. Call Salsa USA at 1-800-897-2572.

6. Chocolate. For $14.95, you get up to three-quarters of a pound. Call Chocolate Indulgence at 1-800-901-9910.

7. Flowers. Make a relationship blossom by sending flowers. Call 1-800-356-9377 (or 1-800-FLOWERS).

8. Panties. Subscriptions start at $79 for a three-month plan that includes gift-wrapped undies with a personalized note, perfume and candy. Call Panty-of-the-Month at (515) 469-6800.

9. Beer. For $15.95 per month plus shipping, you receive two six-packs from different microbreweries. Call Beer Across America at 1-800-205-5282.

10. Meat. Choose from one of three plans that will deliver all kinds of meat to your house on a monthly basis. Call Omaha Steaks International at 1-800-228-9872.

Mentally Tough

Training Your Mind to Give You an Edge

From the day you turned five or so, gave your mom a kiss on the cheek and clambered onto that big yellow bus, you've been training your mind to work better. You've crammed for thousands of tests, sat through thousands of hours of lectures and spent tens of thousands of your own, your parents' and your fellow taxpayers' dollars to achieve the elevated state of mental acuity that you boast today.

And it has paid off. For the most part.

But if you're like us, you've occasionally let that highly developed organ between your ears take over a little too much, especially when it comes to sports and fitness. You've let it talk you out of making a crucial free throw. Let it conjure images of blown chip shots that somehow came to be. Let it convince you to quit and hit the showers when your body was ready to press on.

Face it, whether you're working out, playing tennis or taking a leisurely run during lunch, you're using more than your legs, lungs and deodorant. Your mind is always present, guiding your every move, telling you what you can—and can't—do. And sometimes, if your head isn't as determined as the rest of your body, you'll fold like a savings and loan. "The mark of a truly tough competitor is a tough mind," says James E. Loehr, Ed.D., president of LGE Sport Science Center in Orlando, Florida, and author of *The New Toughness Training for Sports*. "Talent and skill are important, but without mental toughness, you'll never achieve your very best."

Unfortunately, there aren't a whole lot of accredited colleges offering master's programs in mental toughness. So once you've accumulated all the knowledge, reason and logic that you need, how do you learn toughness? How do you make your mind as formidable and unyielding as your body? Is there a Cybex for the cerebellum? A NordicTrack for your neurons?

Not quite. But research in the area of sports psychology has uncovered some simple yet surprisingly effective tools to help build an ironclad mind so that you can perform better and reach your fitness and sporting goals faster. And these tricks will work in plenty of nonathletic situations as well. You can call on them when faced with an overheated boss, an angry mob of in-laws or a deadline that's coming down on you like a brick wall. With a buffed-up mind, you'll make it through any tough situation that might cause weaker psyches to crumble.

Master the Weights

You're staring at the weight resting on the rack. It's eyeing you back. If it could talk, it might say, "Fat chance, buddy." Sure, you think that you might be strong enough to lift the darn thing, but you can't get beyond the fact that, yes, this is a lot of weight. So how do you get over the mental willies? "You need to forget about the weight completely," says Jack Curtis, Ph.D., health education professor at the University of Wisconsin–La Crosse who has helped toughen the minds of Olympic, college and professional athletes, including some players on the Milwaukee Brewers, and author of *The Mindset for Winning*. Rather than psych yourself out, Dr. Curtis suggests using some simple distraction techniques.

Stare at something. Lie back on the bench and focus on a spot on the ceiling straight above you. "Concentrate completely on the spot until you've cleared your mind of any other thoughts," says Dr. Curtis. As you focus on the spot, notice the color, the shape and the size. Make that spot your reason for living. When your mind is so riveted, let it rip. "With your mind no longer focused on the weight, you allow your body to take over," says Dr. Curtis.

Surprise yourself. "Usually I can curl 40-pound dumbbells. No more," says Dr. Curtis. "One day I was waiting for some guy to finish with the 40s. I jumped in and did my set. A tough set, but I did them. Later I realized they were 45 pounds. Had I known, I probably wouldn't have been able to do it."

The lesson is that sometimes the less you know, the better. To use this principle safely, though, you'll need a workout partner. Tell him before the workout that you'd like to move up in weight and by how much (make it only a few pounds). Then let him decide when to make the switch. Just make sure that he's someone you're on good terms with and who doesn't owe you a large sum of money.

Extend Your Running Limit

You've been running the same four miles after work for months. You know you can go farther. But just as you hit that familiar corner near the Home for Destitute Cheerleaders, your mind clicks. Two miles. You turn around. Maybe your legs and lungs are whispering, "Keep going," but your mind is screaming, "Enough already." To get your head in sync with your body, try these mental tricks.

Hum a show tune. About a quarter-mile before you hit the limit, begin humming a song you know well from start to finish. It might be Mel Tormé singing "Stardust," or a really rocking Gregorian chant. As you approach the usual four-mile limit, continue humming the tune (and running along) until it's finished. "By completing the song, you'll tune out that four-mile mental roadblock," says sports psychologist Joel Kirsch, Ph.D., director of the American Sports Institute in Mill Valley, California. "You might only go another quarter-mile, but what matters is that you've broken through."

Move back the start. Instead of tacking on the extra distance at the end, begin your run a few blocks ahead of your usual starting point. By the time you reach your regular turnaround, your mind has all but forgotten that you've actually gone farther than normal.

Control Any Situation

You've seen it happen to even the best of pitchers. He's hurling a shutout through five innings when suddenly, he gives up an infield single. Then a double just inside the line. Then he loads the bases

Act Like a Winner

So what if the guy on the other side of the net has a super-sonic serve and more tricks up his sleeve than the Nixon administration? You can still get the better of him if you remember one simple rule: Show no fear.

Research has shown that professional actors can stimulate physiological changes in their bodies (raising their own blood pressure, for example) by changing their facial muscles to mimic how they would look if they felt a certain, targeted emotion. "The physiological changes that occur in the acted-out emotion are no different than those that occur in spontaneous, genuine emotion," says sports psychologist James E. Loehr, Ed.D., president of LGE Sport Science Center in Orlando, Florida, and author of *The New Toughness Training for Sports*. "So wearing a mask of confidence actually turns you into a confident competitor." And you need not save this trick for the court or the ballyard. "Body language can actually make you perform more effectively, whether it's delivering a softball or a sales pitch," says Dr. Loehr. Here's how to act like a winner.

up with a walk. And then he serves up a pitch fatter than Roseanne's backside, which promptly lands in a pot of pasta in a restaurant across the street. All of this, hero to schmuck, happens in the span of a few minutes.

What happened was that the guy got rattled. "If a player makes a mistake and doesn't take the time to regain his concentration, the situation can only get worse," says Dr. Curtis. If you screw up, be it during the company softball game or the company sales meeting, you're likely to get flustered. And you're likely to compound your mistakes. Players regain their focus after screwing up by using part of a breathing method called the present-moment technique.

"As soon as you feel yourself losing control, take a deep breath and hold it for a count of one to five seconds," Dr. Curtis says. "As you exhale, feel the body slow down, letting go of tension and re-

- Keep your hands relaxed and loose. They should hang about four inches away from your side. "But avoid dangling your arms and hands—it makes you look less powerful," says Dr. Loehr.
- Keep your shoulders back and very broad.
- Keep your chin level with the ground, never letting your head drop.
- Keep a strong stride, on the balls of your feet.
- Don't let your eyes wander, even between points. Keep them focused on an object: racket strings, the ball, the ground. "Wandering eyes are an indication of a wandering mind," says Dr. Loehr.
- Keep up this confident front even at rest. "Any lapse provides enough stimuli to lose control," says Dr. Loehr.

If you like, have yourself videotaped while engaging in your sport. Pause on the sections where you're in peak form. "Try to re-create that image," says Dr. Loehr. Likewise, analyze your game face during bad spells. It could tell you something.

laxing. Do it until you find the tension slowly leaving your body." To get the most out of this technique, practice it whenever you're under stress (in other words, every day). Eventually, these tension-relieving breaths will become automatic—either in the heat of competition or after you've stumbled over a sentence in a speech.

Activate a Mental Rush

Remember that clown who copped your parking space this morning? Or the co-worker who stole your idea about edible paper clips? These creeps may be exactly what you need to give yourself a burst of energy on the playing field.

"Many pro athletes deliberately psych themselves up before games by thinking really angry thoughts of people who gave them grief in the past," says psychologist David Greenwald, Ph.D., player-relations consultant for the Philadelphia Eagles. "It's one of the greatest motivators I know." That's because the anger that you retrieve sets off the fight-or-flight response, unleashing adrenaline into your system. Unleashing it at the optimum time, say, moments before you're about to take the court, can be a performance boon. "That adrenaline burst may provide the extra energy to overcome the competition," says Dr. Greenwald. So even if the guy on the other side of the net is a perfectly nice chap, it might not be a bad idea to think of him as:

- The cretin in the nicer car who cut you off on the way to work
- The ex-girlfriend who denies ever dating you
- The boss who keeps referring to you by the wrong name
- Your ex-wife's attorney

But, afterward, just to show that there are no hard feelings, buy the poor defeated guy a drink.

Whack the Ball like Never Before

First-tee jitters. Any man who's tried to mix business with backswings has suffered from them. But the next time the guy with the bigger budget suggests that you tee off first, you can quell those nerves and put the onus on him if you take a few practice shots first. In your head.

"Jack Nicklaus never takes a shot without visualizing how he's going to hit it and where it's going to go," says Robert Weinberg, Ph.D., professor and chair of the physical education, health and sport studies department at Miami University in Oxford, Ohio.

"If research suggests imagery can cause beneficial changes in diseases," adds Dr. Curtis, "imagine what it can do for your golf game." Dr. Curtis recommends an imagery technique called mental recall—taking a past experience in which you performed well and mentally replaying it. "This builds confidence and allows you to practice the proper skills in your head," he says. Here's how.

Have a memory on hand. Remember it all in fine detail. Recall as many senses as possible: the sweat on your brow, the fabric of your shirt, the smell of the turf, the sound you heard when you hit the ball just right and the elation you felt afterward. "This creates a mental blueprint that can lead to actual physiological changes in how your neuromuscular system works," says Dr. Weinberg.

View the replay from your perspective. "It's common to replay events as though they're outside our bodies, as though we were spectators," says Dr. Curtis. Try to re-experience the event from inside your head. That makes it more vivid for the nervous system.

Recall in normal speed. This isn't the ESPN Play of the Day, so ditch the slow motion. "You're aiming for realism," says Dr. Curtis.

Make it part of your routine. "You should practice it at home 30 minutes before you're playing, build it into your preshot routine and do it any time that there are breaks in the action," says Dr. Weinberg.

Jettison the Jitters

It's the hour before a big game. Not only is the opposing team physically bigger, but they're also extremely hairy, boast elaborate scars and scoff at protective padding. This scares you. Whatever the occasion for dread, you have major monarchs somersaulting in your gut. Although a case of the nerves can help you get mentally prepared for an upcoming game, too many flutterings can disrupt your concentration, causing you to dwell too much on screwing up. To pluck the wings off the butterflies:

Be punctual but not early. Many Olympic athletes do this in order to eliminate any of the tension buildup that waiting around can cause. "This strategy short-circuits the mind by not giving you enough time to think," says Dr. Kirsch. It can also help ease the queasiness before a big meeting, a big date or a big root canal.

Stretch someplace else. Usually you practice on the field before the game. But instead, try practicing someplace nearby. You'll be away from all the tension and pregame jitters, and you'll show up looking like you don't need to practice—a sure sign of confidence.

Mix it up early. "Many athletes say that the most effective way to get rid of butterflies is to get into the thick of things fast," says Dr. Kirsch. It's like pulling an adhesive bandage off fast instead of peeling it off real slow. You don't give your head the time to think it over. That means handling the basketball as soon as you get into the game, getting in a few good shots early in a hockey match or charging the net during your first tennis volley. "The sooner you get into the action, the faster the butterflies will disappear," says Dr. Kirsch.

Block Out the Noise

In practice, you can do it easily. But suddenly, in the glare of the spotlight, you turn into Bill Buckner. You choke, you miss your shot, you blow the big one, and the guys at Nike stop returning your phone calls. "What happens when you try to perform in front of a crowd is that you start evaluating yourself as though you're a spectator, instead of focusing on what you're doing," says Darwyn Linder, Ph.D., psychology professor at Arizona State University in Tempe.

That doesn't mean that you can't perform a task well. It just means that you can't perform that particular task at that particular time in front of that particular crowd. "The definition of choking is when you fail to do something that you've done well many times before," says Dr. Kirsch. "So it's not your body that's the problem—it's your head." What you need to do is to short-circuit your thought processes and keep the pressure of the crowd from getting to you.

Here are a few ways to get your mind off your back.

Do a countdown. In one study, when subjects putted with bets placed on the outcome, those who counted backward softly as they putted were less likely to choke than those who didn't. "This simple task also helps reduce your chances of messing up by eliminating the opportunity for self-evaluation," says Dr. Linder. "You're too busy counting to think."

Imagine the crowd in their underwear. "Imagining a group of spectators as inferior is one of the best ways to get them out of your head," says Dr. Greenwald. You might imagine the entire throng, for example, wearing nothing but diapers; composed entirely of turkeys or, better, *Solid Gold* dancers.

"Most of us see the crowd as judge and jury," Dr. Greenwald says. "This imagery technique turns the crowd into something comical and ridiculous."

Act like a crowd is there. "This simply means re-creating the feeling of being observed in practice so that it becomes second nature," says Dr. Linder. One way to do this, he says, is with your handy camcorder. In a study, one group of golfers was asked to putt while being filmed, with the purpose of being judged later for technique. Another group wasn't filmed. When the cameras were removed and the putters performed under a different pressure (bets were placed on the outcome), those who had putted while being observed were less likely to choke.

"The initial scrutiny of being filmed got them used to performing under pressure later," says Dr. Linder.

Have a conversation with yourself. If, despite your best efforts, you feel a choke coming on and you're starting to lose your grip, use a technique called self-talk. "It's a form of internal dialogue that helps maintain focus on the task at hand," says Dr. Linder. In one study of golfers, Dr. Linder found that spontaneous, slightly negative self-talk used during the actual putting not only helped subjects putt better but also feel better after putting. And negative utterances were more effective than positive ones.

"This suggests that this process has more to do with attention than emotion," says Dr. Linder. So the next time you make a mistake in front of the crowd, say something like, "Man, that really stank," "You can do better than that" or "Don't mess this up." Don't put yourself down; just tell yourself that you've made a mistake, then move on. "The point is not to think negatively, but only to let off a little steam so that you don't think at all," says Dr. Linder.

Smarter Golf

How a Busy Man Can Lower His Links Score

To play golf well, you need to put in the time. Lots of it. Everyone believes this, and that's why most of us accept the fact that we're just not going to improve a heck of a lot . . . until retirement, maybe. There are simply too many other demands on our time right now—jobs, families, keeping the lawn in some state above disgrace.

But there is a better way. The plan that follows will not only allow you to play more golf and better golf, but will also make it possible for you to do so in a way that won't interfere with the rest of your life. The system is based on the same principles that a good businessman applies to his work, with big problems broken down into smaller, more manageable ones. Moreover, these smaller pieces are designed to fit neatly into a busy man's daily schedule.

Read the literature. You can learn a lot about the physics behind the golf swing by reading golf books and articles and studying the diagrams and illustrations in them. And the best part of this type of practice is that you can do it anywhere—on a bus, at the breakfast table or on visits to your in-laws when everyone else is watching TV. *Jack Nicklaus' Lesson Tee* and Ernest Jones's *Swing the Clubhead* are two excellent books. They'll teach you how to recognize your mistakes when your game goes awry and make mid-round corrections.

Time invested: 10 minutes, twice a week.

Hit the ball farther. To add power to your drives, build strength in your muscles. *Exercise Guide to Better Golf* by Frank W. Jobe, M.D., has a series of exercises for developing wrists, arms, shoulders, hips, legs and back. You can easily design a 45-minute strength workout for Mondays, Wednesdays and Fridays, and a 15-

minute stretch-only workout for Tuesdays and Thursdays.

Time invested: Strength—45 minutes, three times a week.
Stretching—15 minutes, twice a week.

Be an early riser. If those crazy joggers can get up at 6:00 A.M. to exercise before work, why can't you get up and play golf? Instead of playing a full 18 holes, tee off at the local course and play 5 or 6 holes before going to work.

On these abbreviated rounds, play two or three balls on each hole, and when approaching a green, drop a few extra balls in the deep rough and in the traps. You can't do this when you are playing with a foursome, so take advantage of it when you can. Playing these extra shots around the green will do wonders for your short game. You can finish your entire morning session and still be at your office at a reasonable hour.

Time invested: 1 hour 15 minutes, twice a week.

Golf with better players. Join a regular weekend group of golfers who play at, or close to, your target handicap level. It's the old theory that you'll play better if you play with better players.

Time invested: none.

Skip the cart. Shun the temptation of the golf cart and carry your bag and play on foot. Since most of the power in the golf swing comes from the legs, don't waste an opportunity to strengthen them.

Time invested: none. It's been scientifically proven that walking takes no longer than driving. Consider that the two players in the cart waste a lot of time driving to each other's ball.

Check out videos. You can pick up all sorts of useful tips by watching the pros on television, but it's a waste of time to follow tournament play. There you have to wade through hours of needless commentary to find the choice nuggets. It's more efficient to watch a good golf video. After reviewing several, we recommend *Golf with Al Geiberger*.

Fairway Favorites

We asked golf writer Dave Gould, former editor of *Golf Illustrated* magazine, to name a few books that should be on every golfer's shelf. Here are five slim volumes that have stood the test of time.

Getting Up and Down, by Tom Watson. The short game is not only the best place to begin improving your score but also the aspect of golf that you can truly learn from a book. Watson, a scrambler of the highest order, does a first-rate job on the stroke-saving art by offering specific, shot-by-shot instructions and useful drawings to go with them.

Golf in the Kingdom, by Michael Murphy. This is a rite-of-passage story in which a spoiled American kid learns Zen and the art of golf from a mythical Scottish pro named Shivas Irons. It's been a cult classic for years. Although it's fiction, you can pick up useful tips on swing action and the mental side of the game through the dialogue between student and master.

The Golf Swing, by David Leadbetter. The author has been teaching swing theory for ten years at $1,000-weekend golf schools. You get his expertise cheap this way. The book illus-

The best part about it is that you can watch a great pro golf swing over and over, in slow motion, so that you can study it. Mimic his swing in your living room until it becomes almost automatic. And, even better, that video is available to you any day, any time.

Time invested: 15 minutes, once a week.

Unwind with a ball, not a highball. Set up a rubber golf mat in your backyard and spend 15 to 20 minutes each evening hitting plastic golf balls. They slice and hook just like regular balls, so you can tell when you've made a mistake but they won't knock out your neighbor's windows.

Time invested: 15 minutes, five times a week—but more important, this is the same time slot that most men use to decompress

trates Leadbetter's classic crisscross drill, in which you plant your palms on opposite shoulders and rehearse your body movement without worrying about how you swing your arms. You'll see Nick Faldo occasionally doing this before he tees off.

How to Feel a Real Golf Swing, by Bob Toski and Davis Love, Jr. The authors show you how to feel your way to proper form through a series of exercises that involve golf clubs and other props such as yardsticks and handkerchiefs. For example, if you find that you're not getting enough speed with, say, your five iron, they suggest swinging the iron back and forth from hip to hip over a tee, aiming to clip it. (It gets easier as you learn to relax your grip.)

Harvey Penick's Little Red Book, by the late Harvey Penick. It took this sage Texan 60 years to compile his best-selling bedside reader. In humble tones, Penick advises us to "take dead aim" and "go to dinner with good putters" and that "the swing you bring to the course that day is the one you have to live with."

from work with the newspaper and a scotch on the rocks.

Record yourself. Every once in a while, position a camcorder next to the practice mat to record your swing. Compare your best swings with those of your golf video. It should be easy to spot where you need improvement, and that's where you can concentrate your efforts during practice and play.

Time invested: 15 minutes, once every two weeks.

BestVacation Ever

How to Really Relax When You Get Away

So there you are on the beach at Cape Cod with your Tom Clancy novel, your cooler of light beer and your bag of potato chips. The summer sun is melting your muscles, the waves are playing their lullaby and the goddess two towels down just ran out of cocoa butter.

But something is amiss. Although you can feel your toes curling in the sand and your hand reaching for that spare bottle of Deep Tropic, your mind is miles away, preoccupied with the work you left behind, a water heater that's been showering you with trouble and the nagging question of how you're going to pay for all this paradise. In short, your body is on vacation, but your mind is still working overtime.

Why can't you relax? Why does it seem as if your week's vacation is almost over before you finally start to unwind? What's the secret to achieving instant, worry-free tranquillity like that fat guy over there on the sagging beach chair?

The dilemma is that few of us know what true relaxation feels like because we experience it so infrequently. It's not the same as sleep or simple inactivity. There's much more to it than that. Think of it as the flip side of stress, a Slinky as opposed to a spring. And because we're much more familiar with tension, the key to learning how to relax is understanding how we get stressed.

Right now, your body is probably on low-level alert, poised for action. It's a biological response left over from caveman days, when a threat had to be dealt with by fighting or fleeing. The problem is that there's nowhere to run and no bogeyman to dispatch; the threat that your body senses comes from stress. Thanks to the job, the family, the commute and the evening news, here's what's going on in your tense body.

- Adrenaline, a potent stimulative hormone, is coursing through your veins.
- Your heart is beating 20 to 25 percent faster than necessary, and your blood pressure is elevated.
- Extra blood platelets are in your arteries, ready to speed clotting in case you're slashed by a saber-toothed tiger. That's bad, since these extra platelets also increase your risk for stroke and heart attack.
- Long-term muscle tension is causing fatigue and soreness as well as those headaches that you've been getting at the end of the day.
- Continuous shallow breathing is putting you in a chronic state of oxygen debt, depriving you of the fuel necessary for your body to operate efficiently and your brain to think clearly.
- Poor digestion, the result of blood being directed to more critical "emergency" areas, is turning your stomach into a "Queasynart."
- Mental preoccupation and physical fatigue are depressing your sex drive.

When you consider this semi-excited state that we live in, it becomes obvious why relaxation isn't instantaneous. "We're creatures of habit," explains Robert DeIulio, Ed.D., a relaxation specialist in Wellesley, Massachusetts. "You can't expect to go from a high-energy, high-power, high-expectation mode to one that is just the opposite overnight. You can't flip the switch off that fast."

There are quite a few things, however, that you can do to speed

JUST THE FACTS

With a 148 percent increase in participants from 1992 to 1994, in-line skating is the fastest growing sport in the United States.

the process. We talked to dozens of experts in a variety of fields who helped us draft a relaxation itinerary for your next vacation. Follow it as you would a checklist for packing, and we guarantee that you'll have the most rejuvenating, worry-free getaway ever.

Arranging the Getaway

Before you can actually take that long overdue vacation, you have to figure out where you want to take it. And what you want to do once you get there.

Think about what you want to do. Before you find yourself driving to Disney World with Cub Pack 666, think about the purpose of your vacation, says Gary Grody, Ph.D., a clinical psychologist in Lawrence, New York. If your job pushing decimals at the accounting office has become a bore, then the "Seven-Day/Seven-Country European Extravaganza" will probably be rejuvenating and relaxing. But if you work on the Wall Street trading floor and you need someplace to quiet your mind, then you'd better be headed for a palm tree and a piña colada.

Choose something relaxing. You're trying to relax, here. Don't go cruising if you're prone to seasickness, and don't go to a nudist camp if you're prone to unsightly skin rashes. A vacation for the purpose of stress reduction should be anticipated without trepidation. Save the challenge of heli-skiing for when you are feeling more energetic and in control.

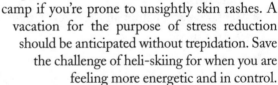

Take your vacation in pieces. If the idea of being in some Mexican beach hut without e-mail makes you uneasy, then vacation for three to four days instead of seven. Taking several extended weekends may be more soothing for some busy men than one to two weeks away.

Ease into your vacation.

It's impossible to relax on command. Instead, try to begin your vacation a few days early—not physically but psychologically. Dr. DeIulio suggests arriving at work a little later and leaving a bit sooner, getting a massage, listening to music, soaking in a hot tub or taking a walk. "Taper into the vacation," he says. "Take time to prepare for it as you would for anything else. Lay out the goods, the strategy. You can't do it overnight."

Okay, you've made the plans, bought the ticket and traveled across the face of the earth to your little private paradise. Now what? Relaxation is your goal, but if you're going to reach it, you'll need an itinerary.

The First Day

Instead of jumping headlong into your vacation, follow these steps to ease into a relaxing time away.

Just do nothing. Avoid making any specific plans for the first 24 hours, says Dr. Grody. You'll be stressed from traveling, the airline will still be searching for your bags and the last thing you need to worry about is making a 1:30 P.M. tee time. So take it easy. Acclimate. Sit on the balcony and enjoy your new view of the world. This is your transition period.

Clear your mind. In our typical stressed-out state, our thoughts are rattling inside our heads like monkeys in a cage. As Barry Sultanoff, M.D., a psychiatrist in private practice in Bethesda, Maryland, puts it: "The mind is jumping from subject to subject, worrying about the future or the past. It's very busy and very stressed."

The antidote is simple: "Take a walk," says Dr. Sultanoff. But instead of continuing to daydream, concentrate on the sensation that each foot makes striking the earth. "What you're doing by noticing

JUST THE FACTS

In a survey of 782 baseball umpires, 84 reported that they had been spat upon, punched, shoved, choked or hit with bats and balls by coaches or players.

that feeling is shifting your awareness and your energy downward and out of your head," he explains.

Tune in. Certain sounds, whether they emanate from nature or a set of speakers, can have a profound calming effect. Any rhythmic sounds, such as drumbeats, will manipulate heart rate and breathing, says Steven Halpern, Ph.D., composer and expert in the psychology of music from San Anselmo, California. Harmonious frequencies can cause cells and organs to vibrate as if they were tuning forks, resulting in a kind of inner musical massage.

"Take 20 minutes, close your eyes and go into the music," says Dr. Halpern. "Don't do anything but that. When you're outdoors, breathe deeply and listen to the sounds of nature. It's an aspect of 'being' rather than 'doing,' and it's very relaxing."

The "Stream" of Your Vacation

Check out your surroundings. Now is the time to schedule that golf game, pick up every brochure at the concierge desk and delicately inquire about the possibility of tandem naked parasailing. Take a drive or a bike ride to get to know the area. Locate the shopping center, a restaurant or two and the all-night topless go-go joint. Make some plans for the week, but don't try to do everything.

And don't think that you have to do certain things. Just because you're in New Orleans, that doesn't mean that you have to hear a jazz band. "Relaxation is very individualized," says Dr. Grody. "What relaxes some people will stress others."

Avoid "fun" instruction. Whether it's in scuba diving or windsurfing, taking lessons entails a pressure to perform. If you're not trying to outdo some muscle head, then you're frustrated because you can't stand up on this surfboard for more than three seconds. Instead, do what you feel comfortable doing and save the lectures for your staff when you return.

Let it all hang out. Did you ever notice how relaxed you feel after a yawn or a sigh? That's because it's the body's natural way of venting tension, says yoga expert Lilias Folan in *The Big Book of Relaxation*. Unfortunately, we stifle our yawns and sighs because they're considered impolite. But who cares about manners when you're on vacation? Get vocal with those yawns. Stretch when you feel the urge. Emit a long, eyebrow-raising "a-a-ahhh" when you push back from the bouillabaisse.

Cut back on the Zzzs. While it's natural to be tired the first few days of a vacation, if you continue sawing wood 10 to 12 hours a night, you're going to be one dull blade. "When all you do is sleep, it increases fatigue," explains Dr. Grody. "The human body is not designed to be sedentary."

Without setting any alarms, try getting out of bed earlier and taking a short afternoon nap, if necessary. In most cases, just listening to music or sitting quietly for 20 minutes will sufficiently refresh you.

Get physical. Don't try to get back in college shape in one week, but do try to break a sweat. Exercise at a level that's slightly above your norm. If your Norm has the last name of Peterson, then at least go for a walk before breakfast. Dr. Grody says that this will raise your metabolic rate so that food will burn faster, plus it'll trigger the release of endorphins, the so-called well-being hormones that aid relaxation.

Make love. Okay, maybe we should have prescribed this sooner, but with all the pressures involved with getting here and getting situated, why introduce one more?

What you want here is not just sex. You want vacation sex. This means letting it happen spontaneously. "Many men think that because they're on vacation, they'd better have sex and it had better be great," says Louanne Cole, Ph.D., a San Francisco–based sex therapist. "But if having sex becomes a must-do, like catching the sunrise over Haleakala at 4:00 A.M. when you're in Hawaii, then it's no different from any other week at home. It's just another duty." Linger in bed in the morning, cuddle in a hammock in the afternoon and see where it leads.

Let it be. Regardless of how stressed you were, by this time in the vacation you've probably already limboed and bought at least one outrageous hat. It's clear that relaxation is happening.

"Already you're into what's called the stream of the vacation," says Dr. Grody. "You're almost forgetting about work and the house, and you're accepting this as your primary environment. You're going deeper and deeper. Muscles relax, facial tension eases, your mood lifts. . . ." Surrender to it.

In the Depths of Your Escape

Here are some tips to really enjoy yourself once you've become completely immersed in your getaway.

Laugh like a child. Toddlers laugh about 400 times a day, compared to just 15 for adults. As we age, we're conditioned to become serious individuals because that's mature (and safe) behavior. But according to mirthologist Steven Sultanoff, Ph.D., when we lose our ability to laugh, we sacrifice a potent tranquilizer.

"Physiology is changed through laughter," he explains. "After a good, strong belly laugh, there's a reduction in stress hormones; muscles relax and heart rate slows. Call it laugh therapy."

Dr. Steven Sultanoff says that no matter how humorless you've become, you can always relearn how to laugh, and vacation is the perfect opportunity. Forget serious books and movies you wanted to catch up on; skip *Schindler's List* and re-rent *A Fish Called Wanda*.

Learn the relaxation response. Here's an exercise that you can practice now that'll help you better deal with stress later. It's called the relaxation response. According to Aggie Casey, R.N., who teaches it to heart patients at Deaconess Hospital in Boston, you need to find a quiet environment, sit or lie in a comfortable position, close your eyes and recite a repetitive word or phrase to keep your mind from wandering. A short prayer works, as do words such as "one," "calm," "relax" or anything else with a neutral meaning. Twenty minutes a day is all that's needed, either as a peaceful start to the day or just before bed if you have trouble sleeping.

Okay, we can't fool you. This is meditation, a form of self-hypnosis. But don't worry about what the guys down at the garage will say. "You don't have to cross your legs, burn incense, chant out loud or look like a freak," says relaxation expert Donald Morse, Ph.D., from Philadelphia. "Think of it as taking a nap. But the repetition of that word is important. That's what induces the meditative state."

If that's still too weird, try active meditation. Dr. Morse says that there's evidence that sports involving repetition, such as cycling and running, where the pedal stroke or stride becomes the mantra, can induce the same relaxed state.

Junk the java. Other than that morning cup, you're probably not drinking as much coffee as you do at home. That's because there you use it as a caffeine crutch to get through the day. Here, where you live in the valleys, there's no need to scale as many peaks.

Since you're already being weaned, why not go all the way and gradually swear off that last cup? Caffeine is a major contributor to stress and just as large an impediment to relaxation. Whether it's in coffee, cola, chocolate or tea, caffeine revs your body much like adrenaline does. Take it away, and you'll have a more even temperament and energy level.

Ignore your voice mail. Yeah, you're in paradise, but chances are that there'll be hell to pay when you get back. Maybe you can short-circuit one or two work-related crises beforehand?

Forget it. Your company is paying you to take a vacation. That's your job right now. Calling the office, checking the voice mail, giving out the hotel fax number—all these things work against the goal that you're being paid to accomplish by drawing you back into a work mode. So knock it off, will you?

Get a rubdown. Most upscale hotels have a massage therapist on call, while others in "knead" of work wander the beach with portable tables. Massage relaxes us by encouraging blood circulation, milking lactic acid from sore muscles, loosening knots in tissue and, perhaps most important, satisfying a basic male need for being touched.

"Men are touch-starved," says Dr. DeIulio. "The problem is that our society has identified touching with sexuality. Teachers are afraid to hug their students, even in a supportive sense, because of possible lawsuits. It's tragic. Being touched is a fundamental need, and massage fulfills that nicely."

Get in touch. Likewise, when we reach out and touch someone these days, it's usually over the phone. How long has it been since you held your wife's hand? When was the last time you hugged your child, or even a good friend? Do it now and feel how relaxing it can be.

JUST THE FACTS

Basketball accounts for more than 20 percent of all sports-related eye injuries treated yearly at hospital emergency rooms.

"This will sound so corny, but it's not," says Dr. DeIulio. "Hold each other. Walk hand in hand. Feel nature beneath your bare feet. Feed the birds. Follow the flight of a butterfly from bloom to bloom. Get back in touch with nature. Get back in touch with human nature."

Winding Down

Okay, it's finally time to think about going home. But there's no need to ruin the rest of your vacation with needless worry about what will be waiting when you get back. Follow these tips to smoothly re-enter reality.

Purge the panic. When does the vacation end? According to Dr. Grody, the instant that you confirm your return flight. That's when the adrenaline starts flowing, the muscles tense and your mood changes.

"Sure, you have to make that call," he explains. "But you can still avoid much of the anticipatory anxiety by making sure that you don't try to get the last ounce out of your vacation. Keep your agenda open and relaxed for the last day or two."

Ease back out of your vacation. Remember how you treated the first day as a transition period? Well, you need a similar buffer zone at the end of your vacation. In fact, it's best to return on a Friday night or Saturday, says Dr. Grody, so that you can savor that relaxed feeling at home for a day or two.

Likewise, try to taper back into work by going in later and leaving earlier on Monday. Or take a three-day weekend the next weekend.

Vacation a little bit every day. The relaxation tricks learned on your vacation can be adapted to any time and any place with the same results. It's simple therapy, but for some reason it's rarely used.

"A flaw in our culture is that we departmentalize everything," says Dr. DeIulio. "We think that things like this only happen during vacation. The result is that many men are out of touch with their souls. By this I mean what they really enjoy doing but somehow have become too busy to do. Whether it's music, massage, working out or walking, build some ways to feed your soul into every day."

PART 10

Ask Men's Health

Recent Headlines from Women's Magazines

There's no lack of advice being given to women about how to figure out men. Give us a beer and an occasional Sunday off, and we're happy as clams. By looking at the headlines below, though, it's obvious that women still have a lot of questions.

1. "Why I Share My Husband with Six Other Women" *First for Women*

2. "The Definitive Guide to Where the *Good* Men Are (and How to Meet Them)" *Cosmopolitan*

3. "Is He a Guy or a Man? And Which Is Better" *Glamour*

4. "Nice Guy, Terrible Clothes. Now What?" *New Woman*

5. "No More Dates from Hell: Forget Your 'Type' and Find Your Mr. Right" *Mademoiselle*

6. "Real Stories of the Night the Condom Broke" *Glamour*

7. "19 Lies Men Tell Women and 19 We Tell Them!" *Glamour*

8. "How to Get Him to Pick Up His Socks (He *Can* Change!)" *Good Housekeeping*

9. "Dating: Why Men Panic (12 Tricks to Calm Him Down and *Get Things Rolling*)" *Marie Claire*

10. "Why Bitchy Women Get the Best Men" *Marie Claire*

Ask Men's Health

Answers to Your Top 20 Questions

Keeping Those Muscles

Q I lift weights to tone my muscles. I don't want my muscles to get any bigger, but I also don't want to lose what I have. What kind of maintenance workout should I do? Must I keep increasing the weight that I lift in each exercise?
—*Z. O., Bangor, Maine*

A The rules of resistance training are pretty simple. As long as you keep increasing the intensity of the exercise (more weight, more repetitions, more sets), you'll keep going through clothes faster than the Incredible Hulk. To temper muscle growth but maintain what you've gained, back off on workout intensity.

According to strength-training expert Doug Semenick, director of the Wellness Program at the University of Louisville, two weekly 45-minute workouts are all that you need. The key is doing medium-intensity sets instead of the usual teeth-clenching ones. "With these, you aren't stimulating new muscle growth," explains Semenick, "you're just *reminding* the muscle where it's been."

Do two sets of each exercise in your normal workout but at an intensity that gives the muscles a "pleasant burn" without tiring them. "Find a level where your muscles are getting a workout but not getting worked on," says Semenick. And don't worry that your muscles will shrink because you aren't pumping more weight. "A moderate workout—8 to 12 repetitions—will keep your muscles stimulated enough to stay exactly where they are in terms of mass," he adds.

Shedding Light on Cigars

Q I think cigar smoking looks classy, and I've been tempted to start. Is it as dangerous as cigarette smoking?
—*F. C., New York, New York*

A In 1994, sales of cigars jumped 9 percent to 2.3 billion, the first increase in 24 years. Lighting the fire were hand-rolled heaters like the ones David Letterman, Bill Clinton and Rush Limbaugh puff. Sales of these premium brands were up 15 percent in 1994 and a smoking 28 percent in 1995. Like fine wine, mountain springwater, gourmet coffee and microbrew beer, stogies have suddenly become a trendy indulgence.

But even though you aren't supposed to inhale the smoke (it annoys people more if you release it directly into the atmosphere), cigars are still a health risk. Although death rates among cigar smokers from heart disease, lung cancer, emphysema and chronic bronchitis are not that much higher than for nonsmokers, according to the American Cancer Society, their mortality rates from cancers of the mouth and throat are about the same as for cigarette smokers.

This is because there's essentially no difference between cigar and cigarette smoke, explains Don Shopland, coordinator for the Smoking and Tobacco Control Program at the National Cancer Institute in Rockville, Maryland. Both contain the full complement of carcinogens as well as carbon monoxide and formaldehyde. In fact, some studies suggest that cigar aficionados may be *more* at risk of developing head and neck cancers—such as those of the oral cavity, larynx and esophagus—than are cigarette smokers. Margaret Barnes, M.D., an American Cancer Society adviser, speculates that this may be because carcinogens are allowed to pool in saliva and then are swallowed.

Nevertheless, many men argue that an occasional Havana won't hurt. And while this may be technically true (the previous research is based on men smoking four to five cigars per day), Shopland points out that cigars contain the same nicotine as cigarettes, so what starts as a weekend indulgence can easily become an addiction. Plus, do you really think she's going to want to kiss you after you've finished with that thing?

In our view, if you want to be classy, you should keep yourself healthy and fit. Nothing complements a tuxedo better.

Zapping Stress

Q I sit at a desk most of the workday, and by quitting time, my muscles feel really sore. My wife says that I'm too tense and should start looking for another job, but I like what I do. How can I get rid of the pain without abandoning ship?
—*B. R., Terre Haute, Indiana*

A Sitting in a chair all day can be much more stressful than it seems, says Christine Grant, Ph.D., research associate with the University of Michigan's Center for Ergonomics in Ann Arbor. And your wife may be right, too: Mental stress can lodge itself in your shoulders, back, eyes and head.

Here's a simple plan for adapting your work style to one that's better for your mind and body.

Be alert for bad habits. When you are on the phone, do you use your chin to pin the receiver against your shoulder? Do you hunch over the keyboard when you're typing? Do you use your legs to drag yourself, while seated in your swivel chair, across your office to get your mail? All of these unnatural movements—when repeated every day—lead to muscle strain and soreness.

Exercise your neck. This is often the first place you feel stress. Try this: Extend your right arm over your head and grasp your neck just below your left ear. Now gently pull your head toward your right shoulder and hold for a moment. Repeat with your left arm, pulling your head toward your left shoulder.

Move around. If your job requires you to stay in the same position for long periods, or if you repeat the same motion continuously, take 1-minute breaks every 15 minutes. Stand up, stretch, go for a walk—anything to get the blood flowing.

Lowering Cholesterol and Blood Pressure

Q I have moderately high cholesterol but healthy blood pressure. Do I have a greater chance of getting high blood pressure?
—J. S., Newark, New Jersey

A You can't get high blood pressure simply because you have larger-than-life lipids. While there's no direct connection between the two, however, they do have some risk factors in common, explains Edward D. Frohlich, M.D., of Alton Oschner Medical Foundation in New Orleans and editor of the medical journal *Hypertension*. Among them are being overweight and not exercising. So if you're trying to lower your cholesterol by losing weight and increasing your activity level, you're actually lowering your risk for getting high blood pressure, too.

Watching TV in the Dark

Q My mother always told me not to watch television in the dark because it would hurt my eyes. I'm all grown up now, but I'm still wondering if it's okay to turn off the lights.
—T. F., Santa Fe, New Mexico

A Mom was right about nice girls and always wearing clean underwear, but she's off base on this one. "Whatever lighting you find comfortable is fine when you watch the tube," says Andrew Farber, M.D., an ophthalmologist and spokesperson for the American Academy of Ophthalmology. After all, staring at a TV screen in a dark room is no different than staring at a movie screen in a dark theater. The light just isn't bright enough to cause any damage to your eyes. And while we're on the subject, here are two other myths you may have heard that are just that.

Don't sit too close to the TV, or you'll get radiation poisoning. Go ahead and sit where you like. One caveat: You may have problems focusing when your nose is only inches from the screen.

And don't read in dim light. Your eyes will tire more quickly reading this way, but it does not cause any damage.

Degreasing Your Hair

Q I have an oily scalp. By 4:00 P.M., it looks like I didn't bother to wash my hair that day. Is there anything I can do?
—*C. W., Warrensburg, Missouri*

A First, blame your parents, since oily hair is inherited. After that, try these tactics to deal with the problem.

Change brands. An all-purpose shampoo probably won't do enough to your hair. You need one that contains tar, says Jerome Z. Litt, M.D., assistant clinical professor of dermatology at Case Western Reserve University School of Medicine in Cleveland and author of *Your Skin: From Acne to Zits.* "The tar soaks up most of the oil," says Dr. Litt. "It's the best first option." Make sure that tar's listed as one of the primary ingredients.

Feel the tingling sensation. Apply the shampoo as soon as you get into the shower and leave the suds on your head for at least five minutes. Ignore the pounding on the bathroom door. You need to give the shampoo time to soak into and clean the hair.

Wipe down your scalp. Clear degreasing liquids such as witch hazel (found in many products made for oily skin) will also help remove excess oil. Try dabbing a little astringent on a cotton ball and wiping it gently against your scalp after you shower.

Go easy on the brushing. Brushing from the roots carries oil from your scalp to the ends of your hair.

Shampoo after working out. Sweating causes your oil glands to become more active. If you exercise during the day, make sure that you include a hair wash in your postworkout shower.

Polish to Perfection

Q I have polished my three-year-old dress shoes so many times that now there's a buildup of polish on them that is starting to crack. It looks really bad. Have I ruined a good pair of shoes?

—*J. E., San Antonio, Texas*

A Not at all. Just wipe the shoe with a fabric cleaning fluid— Afta and Carbona are two brands—and you'll get rid of the buildup immediately, says Ted Loucas, owner of Manhattan Shoe Repair and a man who's shined nearly half a million shoes during the last 40 years.

Once you've stripped the shoe, reapply the polish sparingly. "Guys think that the more polish they use, the shinier their shoes will look," says Loucas. "But exactly the opposite is true." Apply a dab of polish, smear it around until you've covered as much of the shoe as you can, then add another dab and smear that around until the shoe is covered with a light coating. Then shine the shoes as you usually would.

Staying Firm

Q During foreplay I am as hard as titanium. Once I put on a condom, though, I can barely maintain an erection. Why?

—*S. E., Bucksport, Maine*

A Your complaint is a common one. Consider the work that goes into donning a condom. First, you have to stop what you're doing to open the package, which usually requires fumbling and the use of your teeth. Then there's the physical barrier of the latex sheath encasing your penis, which can restrict blood flow. Throw a dose of self-consciousness into the mix, and it's easy to see how your ardor can take a detour.

William Hartman, Ph.D., co-director for the Center for Marital and Sexual Studies in Long Beach, California, advises that you try using a slightly bigger and less restricting condom. A lubricated one may give you a heightened sensation as well.

Also, keep the condoms near your bed and conveniently available. That means opening the box and separating individual packages beforehand. (One bachelor friend keeps several types in a candy jar. "It's festive," he says.) The point is that having to rifle through a drawer or walk across the room is likely to cause your sex drive to wane.

You can also try making the condom part of foreplay. Ask your partner to caress you or kiss your back while you're putting it on. Or have your mate put it on for you. Eroticizing the process will make it much more appealing.

Deflating a Puffy Face

Q My trainer says that the slight puffiness I always seem to have in my upper body and face is due to water retention. I thought that was something my mother had to worry about, not me.

—*N. S., Victoria, Texas*

A Granted, women are more prone to water retention, but it happens in all of us to some extent during a normal day, says Norman Staub, M.D., a professor in the Department of Physiology at the University of California, San Francisco. "Our bodies are constantly adjusting fluid levels based on what we drink and eat," he says.

Usually the human body does an admirable job of correcting

fluid balance. But sometimes the balance gets temporarily thrown off, often by too much salt or alcohol. To help clear these from your system, your cells release water into your bloodstream. This dilutes your blood, which helps your kidneys function more efficiently, but it also prompts you to drink more water to replenish your cells. Now you have water, water everywhere, and the result is some bloating. In any case, if buttons are popping, zippers refuse to budge and your watch is leaving an indentation in your arm, the following advice may bring relief.

Kick the salt habit. Too much sodium in your blood—from hot dogs, popcorn, olives, salted nuts, pickles or pepperoni pizza—can waterlog the tissues. This fluid stays with you until your kidneys have a chance to excrete the excess salt, which can take about 24 hours. Beware of hidden sources of sodium, particularly salad dressings, cereals and canned soups.

Work it out. Exercise can relieve the body of excess fluid and salt through sweating, increased respiration and improved circulation. If you must sit still, though, there are other ways of getting your circulation going. Try this: Point your toes down, then raise them as high as you can, while keeping your legs still. This will pump your calf and foot muscles, getting the blood moving and helping you cleanse your body of salt and other fluid-retainers. Moving your arms up over your head once in a while helps, too.

Fill 'er up. You'd think that it wouldn't be wise to drink even more when you're feeling puffy. But water will dilute your blood, and the more diluted your blood becomes, the faster your kidneys can flush salt out of your body.

Put your feet up. Sometimes this is the simplest and best thing to do, Dr. Staub says. If you recline with your feet in a raised position, you allow fluid that's pooled in your legs to more easily make its way into the circulatory system and then to your kidneys, where it can be excreted.

In some cases, water retention signals something more serious. If your skin remains plump or your finger leaves an indentation when you poke your skin, you may have a problem with your heart, kidneys, liver or thyroid. Consult a physician.

Growing Muscles

Q I have a very physically demanding job, and I also weight-train every other day. Is this wise? What effect does this have on my body, since my muscles never get a day off?

—*G. G., Richmond, Virginia*

A Men with physical-labor jobs are going to build muscle faster by working out less than men whose jobs require them to hoist little more than a coffee cup. You might be better off lifting weights every 72 hours instead of the usual 48. And cut down on the sets while you're at it. For your muscles to grow, you need rest to allow muscle tissue time to repair itself so that it can come back stronger.

"Working out combined with a grueling profession may not allow the time needed for your muscles to rebuild," says Ellington Darden, Ph.D., strength-training researcher and author of *Living Longer Stronger*. "Reduce the frequency of your workouts and you'll get better results."

Drinking O.J. for Healthy Bones

Q Since I barely drink one glass of milk a month, I've been drinking calcium-fortified orange juice. Is it a good substitute? Is it doing me any good?

—*P. T., Milwaukee, Wisconsin*

A Dietitians and orange-juice companies agree that you get the same amount of calcium (about 300 milligrams) from a cup of milk as from a cup of calcium-fortified orange juice. And that's good for your bones, good for your cholesterol, good for your blood pressure and very good for all those farmers in Florida.

Have you met Liz Marr, R.D., spokesperson for the American Dietetic Association? Well, she's concerned about your nutritional health. "There are a lot of other nutrients in dairy foods that aren't found in orange juice," she warns. Here's what Liz says that you're missing without dairy in your diet: vitamin D, protein, magnesium, riboflavin—and she's just getting started. So if you don't like milk, then eat more yogurt and cheese and drink vanilla milk shakes. With a couple of servings of these dairy foods and a glass of your calcium-fortified orange juice every day, you can easily get your recommended daily dose of 800 milligrams of calcium and all the important nutrients.

Sleeping after Sex

Q Why do I fall asleep right after sex? I try to be good company before and during, but I'm usually down for the count once it's over. Is it a physiological or psychological reaction?

—Z. Z., Toledo, Ohio

A Sex is no different from any other vigorous activity. When you're finished, you need rest—and maybe a slice of pizza. But after intercourse, you experience an extra letdown because of the release of tension and a general relaxation response within your body's muscles that lends itself to dozing. This annoys our partners to no end. To offset this response and keep your bedmate from mutiny:

Get in shape. Exercising regularly will give you the stamina, if not to have more sex, at the very least to carry on a conversation afterward.

Rise and shine. You're exhausted from work, so give it a try before breakfast when you're well-rested. Plus, research suggests that the morning is when you may be at your sexual peak anyway. That's when your sex hormones are rising.

Load up on carbs. Make it a complex carbohydrate to keep your energy level up. A bagel, some cereal or a piece of fruit may be all that you need. Avoid sugary food, which can cause your energy level to rise and then fall quickly.

Dry-Cleaning Wool Suits

Q How often should you dry-clean a wool suit to properly balance both hygiene and wear?

—*G. G., Brooklyn, New York*

A Unless you engage in dirt-clod fights on the way to work, you don't have to dry-clean a wool suit more than a few times during the winter season. Any more often could be damaging. "Dry-cleaning chemicals wear the fibers down and wear out the suit," says *Men's Health* magazine's clothing and grooming editor Warren Christopher. Instead, have the suit pressed at your dry cleaner when you want to freshen it. "If you wear the suit occasionally, that's all you need," he says. Pick up cedar hangers or chips for your closet. "They absorb odor and give your suits a fresh smell," he adds. But once you've been drenched in a downpour and the suit smells like a dead ewe, all bets are off. Get it cleaned. It may not be dirty, but it'll stink.

Toning the Lower-Body Muscles

Q I just started using a stair-climber at the gym to help lose weight and tone my lower body. But I think that this machine is making my butt bigger. Is this normal?

—*K. L., Denver, Colorado*

A If the weight you gain tends to end up on your butt and thighs, then any stepping action is going to accentuate the problem. Building and toning the muscles of your lower body will simply push the fat deposits outward, and the effect will be to make existing bulges, well . . . bulgier.

"Guys with what I've termed a spoon-shaped lower body are better off reducing the time on the stair-climber and moving on to other forms of aerobic exercise, such as stationary cycling, jogging or a cross-country ski machine," says Edward Jackowski, author of *Hold It! You're Exercising Wrong.* And if you really want to reduce fat in that area, jump rope.

"This helps reduce fat around the buttocks and outer thighs better than any exercise I know," says Jackowski.

Generic versus Brand-Name Drugs

Q A year or so ago, there was a lot of talk about generic drugs, but I haven't heard much lately. Are they lower in quality than brand-name prescription drugs? They sure are cheaper.

—*T. S., New York, New York*

A Generic drugs are cheaper, not because they're ripping off an established product (like the "Rolex" you got for $15 outside the train station), but because the company selling them simply adapts the formula from the brand-name product without forking out the cash for research and development that goes into creating a drug. Generics are still required by federal law to contain the same active ingredient as their brand-name equivalents, though, so they're nearly identical.

We said *nearly*. Generics often differ from the original brand in their choice of binders (the substances that hold a pill together) and other inactive ingredients. While this would have no effect on a healthy person, a man with kidney or liver impairment might metabolize the drug differently, and that could cause problems, says Sandra Justice, pharmacist and trustee for the American Pharmaceutical Association in Washington, D.C. Also, if you're taking a brand-name drug and you switch to its generic equivalent (or vice versa), you could notice a change in effect. "Your body gets used to whatever you took first," says Justice. That doesn't mean that you *can't* switch. It just means that you should discuss the change with your doctor and pharmacist before doing so.

Sleeping Away Back Problems

Q I've developed a back problem, and my doctor says that it's aggravated by sleeping on my stomach. He recommends sleeping face up, but I can't fall asleep that way. How do I change?

—*L. H., East Lansing, Michigan*

A "The reason that you can't sleep on your back may be that your body's trying to tell you something," says Milton Erman, M.D., chief of the Division of Sleep Disorders at the Scripps Clinic and Research Foundation in La Jolla, California. For example, your airway may be collapsing when you're on your back, a common problem that results in snoring. Snoring is more than just a nuisance for your bed partner; it's been linked to more serious problems such as high blood pressure, irregular heartbeat, headaches and excessive fatigue, and often requires a doctor's attention.

Another reason that you might not be able to sleep on your back is chronic heartburn that's aggravated each time you're face up. Whatever the cause, your body naturally looks for the most comfortable position.

The solution is to try sleeping on your side. It's just as good for your back but easier to achieve, and it won't make you snore. Here's what to do: Delay your bedtime by an hour or longer, then go to bed and try to sleep on your side when you're dead tired. If you don't nod off within 20 minutes, get up and watch the late show and ride it out. It may mean dragging yourself into work each morning, but after a couple of weeks, your body should adjust.

Cross-Training Correctly

Q I like to go for a run and then lift weights immediately after. Is there a problem with doing this? Should I be lifting first?
—_J. R., Tallahassee, Florida_

A It doesn't matter which form of exercise comes first, as long as you don't push yourself to the limit on both. "If you can keep the intensity to less than 80 percent of an all-out effort on at least one of the activities, you'll be okay," says William Kraemer, Ph.D., director of research at Pennsylvania State University Center for Sports Medicine in University Park. If you're going to run at your regular intensity, that means lifting weights at least 20 percent lighter than those you'd normally lift. If it's your weight lifting that you want to concentrate on, take it easy on the road. Cover the same distance, but allow 20 percent more time to do it. Remember, too, that you still need 24 to 48 hours' rest between sessions to allow muscles to recover.

Okay, you're a tough guy. You want to go all out on both activities. That's fine, but you should split your workouts. In a recent study from Pennsylvania State University, researchers discovered that subjects were able to perform both forms of exercise at high intensities in a single day—with no adverse effects to either routine—when they waited four to six hours and ate a meal between sessions. An added bonus is that you'll keep your fat fires burning longer and lose more weight if you exercise twice in one day.

Nipping Fights in the Bud

Q It seems that my girlfriend picks the worst possible moment to nag me—usually when I'm stressed out or angry. Why is that? Do women somehow sense when our defenses are down?

—G. T., San Diego, California

A As much as you'd like to think that your girlfriend has a built-in radar system that flashes "Attack!" when you're down in the dumps, it's more likely that the real problem is the stressed-out mood that you're in. "When you're unhappy, your girlfriend changes her behavior much less than you change *your evaluation* of her behavior," says Michael Cunningham, Ph.D., professor of psychology at the University of Louisville. When you're in a bad mood, he says, you simply become more critical. So harmless behavior that you normally shrug off now sets you on edge, but only because stress has exhausted your usually well-stocked supply of tolerance. You develop what Dr. Cunningham calls social allergies, a syndrome where you can't tolerate behaviors that in other circumstances wouldn't be at all objectionable. She may be sitting silently reading the Koran, but in your head those page-turns are just too loud.

The trouble is that if you let yourself respond irritably to minor annoyances, you'll only end up looking like a jerk. "Better to calmly tell her what you're stressed about than to become disproportionately outraged over minor things," says Dr. Cunningham. "You might deflect a potential flare-up by simply saying that you're a little on edge."

If that doesn't work, head for the gym or the ballpark. "Research indicates that exercise is one of the best ways to bring yourself out of a bad mood," says Dr. Cunningham. "It takes your mind off what's bothering you and renews the energy that you might have lost to stress."

Softening the Morning After

Q Before going out for a few drinks, I'll take a couple of Tylenol tablets to reduce the morning-after hangover. I think that it works, but I'm wondering if what I'm doing is safe.

—S. Q., Fort Lee, New Jersey

A Let's just say that it isn't doing you any favors. Acetaminophen (Tylenol), aspirin or any analgesic is intended to deal with pain when it hits, not beforehand, so there's no proof that it actually works to defeat an oncoming hangover, says John Brick, Ph.D., executive director of Intoxikon International, a company in Yardley, Pennsylvania, that conducts research for alcohol and drug studies. And new research suggests that, under certain circumstances, mixing acetaminophen with alcohol can be harmful. In a review of hospital records, 30 percent of patients who experienced liver damage after taking acetaminophen had also consumed alcohol within the previous week, says David Whitcomb, M.D., Ph.D., of the University of Pittsburgh Medical Center. The patients were also fasting (which can make you more vulnerable to liver problems), though, and they had gone well beyond the recommended dosage of acetaminophen. No liver problems occurred in patients taking less than the recommended daily limit—regardless of alcohol intake.

But be safe anyway. Instead of popping a pill to prevent a hangover, "it's better to reduce the amount of alcohol you're drinking in the first place or, before going to bed, drink as much water as you can comfortably handle, which prevents the dehydration that helps lead to a hangover," says Dr. Brick. Save the painkillers for morning, when the alcohol has cleared your system.

Smelling Your Best

Q What is the best way to apply cologne, and is it okay if I use both cologne and aftershave?

—*T. B., Lafayette, Indiana*

A The thing to remember about cologne is that less is more. That's especially true if you have a date (or just a business lunch) with a woman. The female sense of smell is more acute than ours is.

Where you apply it is up to you, but we recommend a few small drops at no more than two or three of the following spots: the base of the throat, behind the ears, at the breastbone, the inner thighs or the abdomen. Since fragrance rises with your body heat, try choosing one spot above the neck (for now) and one spot below (for later). Another important point: Apply your cologne at least 15 minutes before you leave the house so it will have time to dry and won't be quite so pungent.

As far as using aftershave with cologne, it's not necessary. "I discourage patients from using aftershave, since it can dry out the skin (most aftershaves are alcohol-based) and cause allergic reactions," says *Men's Health* magazine adviser John Romano, M.D., a dermatologist at New York Hospital–Cornell Medical Center in New York City. A better choice is an aftershave balm, such as A+ from Aramis or Face Fitness from Polo Sport. The products generally contain a moisturizing formula as well as a sunscreen, both things most men can use.

Credits

"Super Sex" on page 151 is adapted from "The Big Bang" by John Poppy. Copyright © 1995 by John Poppy. Reprinted by permission.

"Fantasies Explained" on page 164 is adapted from "Mind over Mattress" by Russell Wild. Copyright © 1995 by Russell Wild. Reprinted by permission.

"Hot Spots" on page 184 is adapted from "Please Try This at Home" by Mark Roman. Copyright © 1995 by Mark Roman. Reprinted by permission.

"A Man of Style" on page 195 is adapted from "Everyman's Guide to Style" by Hal Rubenstein. Copyright © 1995 by Hal Rubenstein. Used by permission of Doubleday, a division of Bantam Doubleday Dell Publishing Group, Inc.

"Backstabbing Protection" on page 270 is adapted from "Double-Cross Training" by David Hume. Copyright © 1996 by David Hume. Reprinted by permission.

"Cool Careers" on page 281 is adapted from "It's a Living" by Rob Medich. Copyright © 1995 by Rob Medich. Reprinted by permission.

Index

Note: <u>Underscored</u> page references indicate boxed text.

Abdominal muscles, 100, 104, 108–9
Accidents, automobile, <u>124</u>, <u>278</u>
Acetaminophen
  alcohol and, 327
  fever and, 139
  indications for, <u>64</u>
Achilles tendon, 101
Acquired immune deficiency syndrome
    (AIDS), <u>124</u>
Acting, physiological changes during,
    <u>292–93</u>
Adrenaline, 294, 303
Adult videos, 174–75
Advil. *See* Ibuprofen
Aerobic exercise
  abdominal muscles and, 104
  bicycling as, 6
  in cross-training, 113
  HDL cholesterol and, 10
  jogging as, 6
  target heart rate and, 109
Affection, humorous expression of, 239
Aftershave, 328
Age spots, 212–13
Aggression, playful, 255
AIDS, <u>124</u>
Alcohol
  acetaminophen and, 327
  calories in, 5
  decrease in consumption, <u>145</u>
  heart attack and, <u>124</u>
  water retention and, 320
Ale, 25–27
Aleve. *See* Naproxen sodium
Alpha hydroxy acid, 206
Alzheimer's disease
  ibuprofen and, <u>124</u>
  sense of smell and, <u>45</u>
Anacin. *See* Aspirin
Anchor Steam Beer, 31
Anecdotes in public speaking, 234
Anesthesia, electronic, 135
Anger, 293–94
Ankles, 81, 95, 102

Antidepressants, 127
Antihistamines, 205
Antioxidants, 22
Antiseizure medications, 127
Anxiety, 139–40. *See also* Stress
Apologizing, <u>252</u>
Apples, 21, 24
Appointments, software for, 57
Arcade games, for stress relief, 279
Arguing, 55, 183, 326
Arm curl machine, 90–91
Arms, tingling in, <u>45</u>
Arm twists, 98
Aspirin
  consumption, <u>128</u>
  indications for, <u>64–65</u>
  Reye's syndrome and, 139
Assertiveness, 234
Astringent, for oily hair, 318
Athletes, professional, <u>40</u>
Audience, speakers' attitude toward,
    296–7
Automap Road Atlas (software), 57

Back. *See also* Spine
  exercises for, 138, 212
  injuries, 100, 138
  lower, 76, 81
  pain, 67
  sleeping position and, 324–25
  stress and, 315–16
Backstabbing, 270–74
Bad breath, <u>208</u>
Badminton, <u>87</u>
Bags under eyes, 205, 206
Bananas, 35–36
  banana split, 12
Banking, online, 56–58
Barley wine ale, 27
Baseball
  batting cages, 279
  calories burned during, <u>87</u>
  pitching, 291–292
  umpires, <u>305</u>

Basketball
    ankles and, 102
    calories burned during, <u>87</u>
    drills, 116–18
    eye injuries and, <u>309</u>
Beans, 18, 24
Beards, grooming, 212
Bed raise exercise, 97
Beds, injuries involving, <u>48</u>
Beef. *See also* Meat
    stew, low-fat recipe, 13
    vitamin B$_{12}$ in, 38
Beer, 25–31.
    flavonoids in, 21
    mail-order, <u>288</u>
    nonalcoholic, 31
    T-shirts, <u>288</u>
Belts, packing for travel, 202
Bench presses, 59, 83, 115–16, <u>116</u>
Benign prostatic hyperplasia (BPH), 143
Bent-arm fly machine, 92
Beta-carotene, 22–23
Betrayal, 270–74
Biceps
    arm curl machine for, 90–91
    brachialis anticus muscle and, 99–100
    curls, 59, <u>117</u>
Bicycling, 308–9. *See also* Mountain biking
    aerobic benefits of, 6
    calories burned during, <u>87</u>
    children and, 87
    running and, 71
Bill paying, 54, 56, 57
Bleach, for age spots, 212–13
Bloating, 319–20
Blood pressure, high
    caffeine and, 36
    cholesterol and, 316
BLT sandwich, 14
Bock beer, 30
Body language, 230, 257, <u>292–93</u>
Bok choy, 24
Bologna, 14
Bonding
    dental, 133–34
    male, 237–41
Books. *See also* Reading
    cassette tapes of, 53

about golf, 298, <u>300–301</u>
    online, 57
    reviews of, 53
    about sex, <u>150</u>
Boots, 203
Boredom, 85, 266
Bosses, 230. *See also* Work
Bowling, 279
Box drill, 117–18
BPH, 143
Brachialis anticus (rotator cuff muscle), 99–100
Breakfast
    fatigue-preventing, 80
    low-fat, 4–5, 9
    muscle-building, 6
    peak-performance, 33–35
    sandwich recipe, 16
Breathing
    refocusing using, 293–94
    sex and, 152
    sounds and, 306
    speech and, 233
    stress and, 66, 278–79, 303
Broccoli
    flavonoids in, 21
    phytomins in, 24
    vitamin C in, 38
Burning sensation in limbs, <u>45</u>
Business. *See also* Work
    attire, casual, 215
    etiquette, <u>252</u>
B vitamins, <u>28</u>, 38

Cabbage, 24
Caffeine. *See also* Coffee
    exercise and, 36
    eye twitches and, 66
    headaches and, 68
    long-distance running and, 106
    stress and, 309
Calcium, 37, 321–22
Calf muscles
    leg press machine for, 93
    raises for, <u>117</u>
Cancer
    fruit and, <u>16</u>
    oral, 128
    phytomins and, 21, 23
    skin, 129, <u>143</u>

Cancer *(continued)*
testicular, 129
tomatoes and, 22
vegetables and, 16
Candy corn, 19
Cantaloupe, 24, 38
Canthaxanthin, 22–23
Carbohydrates
in bananas, 35–36
energy level and, 80, 322
muscle-building and, 7
peak performance and, 33
post-workout, 37
runners' need for, 106
stress and, 278
Careers, unusual, 281–86
Carotenoids, 22–23
Carpentry, 246
Car phones, accidents and, 124
Carrots, 24
Cars, 179, 226
Casual business attire, 191–94
Catalog shopping. *See* Mail-order
shopping
Cataracts, 23, 42
Cauliflower, 24
Celery, 21, 24
Cereal, as a snack food, 8
Challenges. *See* Goals
Checkfree (software), 56
Cheese, 47
calcium in, 322
Parmesan, 18
protein in, 37
Chef Boyardee Beef Ravioli, 16
Chest muscles, 91–92
Chicken nuggets, 19
Child development, 232
Children
death of, 246–47
displaced worries and, 279–80
exercising with, 86
fathers' involvement with, 219–22
time with, 266–67
Chin, double, 206
Chocolate, 288
Chocolate milk, 13
Cholesterol
aerobic exercise and, 10
garlic and, 147

HDL, 10
high blood pressure and, 316
phytomins and, 20, 23
reducing, 124
Cigars, 314–15
Citric acid, 205
Citrus fruit, 21, 22, 24. *See also* Citric
acid; Vitamin C
Clams, 16
Clausthaler (nonalcoholic beer),
31
Clothes
casual business, 215
current fashions, 190
designer, 213
dressing according to age, 209, 211,
213
for exercising, 88–89, 225
salespeople, 198–99
sex and, 159
shopping for, 58–59, 193, 195–200
for travel, 202
Coffee. *See also* Caffeine
headaches and, 68
health effects, 50
heartburn and, 62
mail-order, 288
Colds, 45, 51, 126–27, 144
Cold sores, 128
Collards, 24
Cologne, 328
Comfrey, 147
Communication, with women at work,
253–61
Commuting, 277–78
Compound exercises, 83
Computers, 42, 187, 226. *See also*
Software
Concentration, improving, 292
Conditioner, hair, 209
Condoms, 318–19
Confidence, radiating, 292–93
Contact lenses, 202
Control, stress and loss of, 278
Conversation styles, 258
Cooking, respect and, 235
Corduroy, as suit fabric, 198
Cotton, as suit fabric, 198
Couch hang exercise, 101
Coughing, 136–37

Counting, in golf, 296–97
Couples, inseparable, 177–78
Co-workers, 231, 261–62, 271–72
Cranberries, 21
Croissants, fat in, 23
Crossovers, 104
Cross-training, 113–14, 325–26
Crowds, performing in front of, 296–97
Crow's-feet, 204
Crunches, 75, 104, 117

Daidzein, 23
Dairy foods, 322. *See also specific kinds*
Dating. *See also* Relationships; Sex;
        Women
    exercise and, 86
    people from work, 261–62
Deadlifts, 83
Decision-making, joint, 178–79
Dental health, 130, 210
    bonding, 133–34
    brushing technique, 132
    common questions about, 130–35
    fillings, 50, 135
    flossing, 131–32
    implants, 135
    sensitive teeth, 60–61
    video headsets during dental work,
        124
    wisdom teeth, 133
    x-rays, 131
Deodorant, 205
Desk, cleaning, 276
Desserts, 12, 38
Diarrhea, treatment of, 137–38
Diet
    low-fat, 4–5, 8–10, 13–15, 104
    muscle-building, 6–8
    tracking, 88
    weight-loss, 4–5
Diet Coach (handheld computer), 88
Digestion, stress and, 303
Diner-style food, 7
Dinner
    in low-fat diet, 9
    in muscle-building diet, 7
    in weight-loss diet, 4
Dip, hot beer, 17
Discount brokers, 56
Divorce, respect after, 232

Dogs, gaining respect of, 235, 236
Double chin, surgery for, 206
Double vision, 44
Driving, while sleepy, 278
Drugs. *See* Medications
Dry-cleaning, 323
Dumbbell rows, 59
Dye, hair, 214

Ears
    as erogenous zone, 186
    growth of, 124
Echinacea, for colds, 144
Egg whites, 8, 204
Ejaculation, 48, 52, 151–52. *See also*
        Erections; Orgasm
Eldoquin, for age spots, 213
Electrolysis, 206
Employment, termination of, 258–59
Endive, 21, 24
Endurance, in running, 105–6, 291
English muffins, 23
Ephedra, avoiding, 146–47
Equality, in relationships, 179
Erections
    condoms and, 318–19
    ginkgo for firmer, 145–47
    improving, 185
Erogenous zones, 185–88
Etiquette, business, 252
Exercise. *See also* Workouts
    caffeine before, 36
    clothes for, 88–89
    equipment for, 89, 90–95
    fun and, 105
    glycogen and, 37
    making time for, 83
    meal timing and, 32–37
    mood and, 327
    morning vs. afternoon, 80
    for neck, 63, 316
    outdoors, 89
    pain and, 141
    procrastination and, 79–89, 84
    reading while, 84
    results of, 87–88, 103–11
    simplified routines, 59
    vacation and, 307
    varying order of, 88
    water retention and, 320

Exercise *(continued)*
  while injured, 81
  at work, 277
Eyebrows, 206
Eye contact, 230, 257
Eyes. *See also* Vision
  bags under, 205, 206
  changes in color, 127–28
  detached retina, <u>44</u>
  injuries to, <u>309</u>
  puffiness, 128
  reading in dim light, 317
  self-examination, 127–28
  stress and, 315–16
  twitches, 66

Fabric, 198, 200
Face, care of, 201, 204, 206, 211
Family, 86, 272–73, 279–80. *See also*
      Children; Spouse
Fantasies, 161, <u>166–67</u>, 167, 170
Fashion. *See* Clothes
Fast food, 6
Fat, dietary, 4–5, 11–12, 82, 109
Fathers, wisdom of, 242
Fatigue, 36, 80, 106, 303
Feelings, sharing with women, 180
Feet. *See also* Ankles
  massage of, 66–67
  muscles in, 102
  sweat glands in, <u>118</u>
Feminism, <u>229</u>
Fetishes, 171
Fever, treating, 138–39
Fighting, 55, 183, 326
Filing system for important papers, 54
Fillings, dental, 50, 135
Film, photographic, 203
Finances, 55–58, 73, 246
Fingernails, 213–14
Fingers, as erogenous zones, 188
Fish, longevity and, 75
Fitness programs, 79–89. *See also* Exer-
      cise; Workouts
Flavonoids, 21–22
Flaxseed, 24
Flowers, 280, <u>288</u>
Fluids
  diarrhea and, 137
  exercise and, 33, 36, 106

fever and, 139
protein and, 35
retention, 319–20
role in muscle formation, 35
role in skin care, 201
role in weight loss, 5
Focus, mental, 293–94
Food
  additives, 50
  irradiation, 50
  low-fat, 4–5, 8–10, 13–15,
    104
  sex and, 159
  tasting, 46–47
  trends in, <u>2</u>
Football, watching, 178
Forearm extensors, 99
Forehead, wrinkles in, 204
Foreplay, 160–61
401(k) plans, 55–56, 73
Friends, <u>244</u>
  betrayal by, 271
  as business partners, 270
  firing, <u>258–59</u>
  insults between, 237–41
Frog's legs, 18–19
Front squats, <u>116</u>
Fruit, <u>16</u>, 21, 22, 24. *See also specific*
      fruits
Fudge, 12

Garlic, 24, 147
Garlic bread, 15–16
Gender differences in communication
      style, 253–61
Genistein, 23
German language, 235
Gingerroot, for nausea, 145
Ginkgo, for improving circulation,
    145–47
Ginseng, avoiding, <u>146</u>
Gluteus medius muscle, 101
Glycogen, 37
Glycolic acid, 214
Goals, 52, 82, 110, 268–69
  fitness, 112–21
Goiter, 129
Golf, 119–20, 298, 299
  backyard practice, 300–301
  books about, 298, <u>300–301</u>

exercise value of, 5–6
mental tricks, 294–95, 296–97
Gradient compression stockings, 215
Grant's Scottish Ale, 26
Grapefruit, red, 22
Grapes, phytomins in, 21, 24
Green beans, phytomins in, 21
Greens, phytomins in, 24
Grooming, 72–73. *See also* Hair; Skin
Guava, phytomins in, 22
Guinness Stout (beer), 21, 27
Gums, care of, 61
Guns, 226–27, 279
Gym, 224–25

Habits, 55, 267
Hair, 208, 212, 214
loss, 210
oily, 317–18
stresses to, 209
Hammer twists, 99
Hamstrings, exercise for, 94
Hand(s), 201
holding, 310
muscles in, 99–100
shaking, 225
washing, 51
Hand-eye coordination, 88
Hats, for sun protection, 209
Hazing, 238
HDL cholesterol, 10
Head, skin cancer on, 143
Headaches, 68, 146
Health. *See also specific health issues*
online forums about, 58
self-examination, 125–29
Health clubs, 109
Hearing, 43–46
Heart attacks
alcohol consumption and, 124
seeking medical care for, 139
Heartburn, coffee and, 62
Heart disease
diet to prevent, 8–10
flavonoids and, 21
Heart rate
laughter and, 308
stress and, 303
Heat treatment, for eyestrain, 63
Herbs, medicinal, 142–47

Herpes, 124
Hiking, for stress relief, 279
Hip joint, pyriformis muscle and, 100
Hobbies, 245
Home brewing, 28–29
Hot dogs, low-fat, 15
Hotel(s), 203, 281–82
Hot spots, sexual, 184–87
Houseguests, unwelcome, 203
Humor
gender differences in, 254
in public speaking, 234
self-deprecating, 254
Hydrocortisone, for rosacea, 215
Hydrogen peroxide, for age spots, 212–13
Hydroquinone, for age spots, 213
Hypertension. *See* Blood pressure, high

IBM, 192
Ibuprofen, 65, 124
Ice cream, low-fat, 12
Ice packs, for injuries, 81
Iditarod dogsled race, 249
Illness, 46, 250. *See also specific illnesses*
Immune system, diet and, 9
Impotence. *See also* Erections; Ejaculation
ginkgo for, 145–47
sildenfil for, 124
Impulse buying, 73
Incline hammer curls, 99
Income levels, 74
Infidelity, 243
Infraspinatus (rotator cuff muscle), 81, 97–98
Injuries
back, 100, 138
exercising with, 81
eye, 309
involving beds, 48
In-line skating, 87, 110, 303
Insults
accepting, 241
between friends, 237–41
Don Rickles and, 240
Intercourse positions, 154
Interval training, in running, 71
Intimacy, sex and, 185
Italian ice, 14

Jackets, suit, 199–200
Jaw, speech and, 233
Jeans, 193–94, 202
Jitters, pre-game, 295
Jobs, unusual, 281–85
Jogging, 6
Juggling, <u>121</u>
Juice, in muscle-building diet, 7–8
Jumping rope, <u>87</u>, 114–15

Kale, phytomins in, 21, 23, 24
Kaopectate, for diarrhea, 137
Kegel exercises, 153
Ketchup, phytomins in, 22
Kissing, <u>187</u>
Knees
    as erogenous zones, 188
    injury to, 81

Lager, 29–30
Lasers
    for age spots, 213
    for dental treatment, 134
Lateness. *See* Punctuality
Lavender oil, as sleep aid, 76
Leg press machine, 93
Legs, tingling in, <u>45</u>
Leg twists, 100–101
Lemon juice, for sunspots, 205
Linen, as suit fabric, 197, 198
Lingerie, as sexual turn-on, 157
Liposuction, for double chin, 206
Lips, chapped, 205
Listening, 43–46, 234, 255–57, 265
List-making as work management tool,
    52, 276
Liver (body organ), acetaminophen
    and, 327
Lobster, fat content of, 16
Longevity, habits that promote, 74–75
Lotus Organizer 2.0 (software), 57
Love map, 169–70
Lovemaking. *See* Sex
Low-fat food, 4–5, 8–10, 13–15, 104
    (*See also* Fat, dietary)
Luggage, 203
Lunch
    in low-fat diet, 9
    in muscle-building diet, 7
    in weight-loss diet, 4

Lutein, 22–23
Lycopene, 22
Lyme disease, possible vaccine for, <u>124</u>

Macaroni and cheese, low-fat, 12
Magnesium, in dairy foods, 322
Mail-order shopping, 53, 59, <u>288</u>
Manicures, 213–14
Manners
    in business, <u>252</u>
    underappreciation of, <u>249</u>
Mantras, 308–9
Marathons, running, 106
Marriage. *See* Spouse
Massage, 47, 63, 309
Meals, 9, 32–37, <u>34</u>. *See also specific*
        meals
Measurements, body, 88
Meat, <u>288</u>. *See also* Beef
Medical exams, pre-exercise, 82
Medications. *See also specific*
        medications
    generic, 324
    prescription, 324
    side effects of, 46, 127
Meditation, on vacation, 308
Melanex, for age spots, 213
Melanoma
    on head and neck, <u>143</u>
    possible vaccine for, <u>124</u>
    self-examination for, 129
Melon, phytomins in, 24
Mentors, 265–66, 269
Metabolic rate, 82
Microwave ovens, 2
Military press, <u>116</u>
Milk
    alternatives to, 322
    chocolate, 13
Milk shakes, 18, 322
Missionary position, 154
Moisturizer, 201, 205, 206, 211
Money. *See also* Finances; Income
        levels; Wealth
    investing, 55–56
    saving, 73
Monogamy, 74
Motivation, anger as, 293–94
Motrin. *See* Ibuprofen
Mountain biking, 106–7

Mouth. *See also* Teeth
    as erogenous zone, 186
    self-examination, 128
Mouthwash, 133
Movies, 53, <u>218</u>. *See also* Videotapes
Muscle(s). *See also specific muscles*
    age and, 211
    diet and, 6–8, 35, 37, 80–81, 108
    fatigue, 80–81
    lower-body, 323–24
    small, 96–102
    soreness, 141
    tension, 303
    weight lifting to maintain, 313–14
Muscle confusion principle, in weight
        training, 107
Museums, dates at, 86
Mushrooms, carotenoids in, 23
Musical instruments, children and,
        220–21
Mutual funds, 56, 73

Naproxen sodium, 65
National Institute on Aging, <u>244</u>
Nature, getting in touch with, 279,
        310
Nausea, gingerroot for, 145
Navel, as erogenous zone, 187
Neck, 129
    as erogenous zone, 186
    exercises, 206, 316
    extensor muscles, 97
    pain, 62
    skin cancer on, 143
Neckties
    in casual business attire, 194
    packing for travel, 202
    shopping for, 197
Nerve damage, exposure to cold and,
        48
Nervousness, 292, 295
Neutrogena cleansing bar, 201
New Year's resolutions, 105
Night vision, 42
Nipples, male, 187
Nose reshaping, <u>62</u>
Numbness, in extremities, <u>45</u>
Nuprin. *See* Ibuprofen
Nurturing, men's need for, 280
Nuts, vitamin E in, 37–38

Oblique muscles, 104
Odors, "phantom," <u>45</u>
Olympic records, <u>78</u>
Onion rings, 14
Onions, 21, 24
Online services, 56–57
Open-can raise exercise, 97–98
Optimism, longevity and, 74–75
Oral cancer, 128
Oral sex, 160, <u>171</u>
Orange juice, calcium-fortified, 321–22
Orgasm
    enhancing, 151–54, 185
    fantasies and, 167
    female, 160
    physical contact after, 159
Orthodontia, 210. *See also* Dental
        health
Overstimulation, sexual, of women,
        160

Packing for travel, 202
Pain
    medications for, <u>64–65</u>, 124, 139,
        327 (*See also specific medica-
        tions*)
    treatments for, 60–68
Palate, cleansing, 47
Pants, casual, 194
Paperwork, filing, 53–54
Paradoxical intention, for insomnia,
        75–76
Parenting, 232. *See also* Children
Parkinson's disease, <u>45</u>
Parmesan cheese, 18
Passivity fantasies, 170
Passports, 202
Paulaner Salvator (beer), 30
Pelvic muscles, sex and, 153
Peppers, sweet red, 22
Performance
    anxiety about, 296–97
    mind's effect on, 289–96
Perineum, as erogenous zone, 187
Periodization program in weight
        training, 70
Peripheral vision, 41–43
Peroneals, 102
Pessimism, effect on longevity, 74–75
Pete's Wicked Ale, 26

"Phantom" odors, <u>45</u>
Photographers, 282
Physical examinations, pre-exercise,
　　82
Physical fitness. *See* Exercise; Workouts
Phytomins, 20–24
Pilsner Urquell (beer), 30
Pistol ranges, 279
Pizza, 17, 22
Plaque rinses, 133
Pocket Personal Trainer (notebook),
　　87–88
Pollutants, effects on taste, 47
Polyester, 198
Pop-Tarts, 16
Porter (beer), 28
Potassium, in bananas, 35–36
Potato(es)
　　chips, 17
　　nutrients in, 38
　　skins recipe, 13
Prednisone, weight gain and, 127
Present-moment technique, for stress
　　relief, 292
Pretzels, gender preferences for, <u>161</u>
Productivity, workplace, 51–52
Proscar, for benign prostatic hyper-
　　plasia, 143
Prostate gland, 126, 142–43, <u>248</u>
Prostitutes, fantasies about, 171
Protein
　　in dairy foods, 322
　　in egg whites, 8
　　fatigue and, 80
　　muscle tissue and, 7, 37, 108
　　stress and, 278
　　water and, 35
　　in yogurt, 35
Public speaking, 234
Pudding, fat and calories in, 19
Puffiness, facial, 319–20
Pull-ups, 83
Pulse
　　baseline, 125–26
　　during exercise, 109
Punctuality
　　pre-game, 296
　　respect and, 230
Putting (golf), 296–97
Pyriformis muscle, 100

Quatratus lumborum muscle, 100
Quicken Deluxe (software), 57

Ravioli, canned, 16
Razors. *See* Shaving
Reaction time, peripheral vision and,
　　42–43
Reading. *See also* Books
　　in dim light, 317
　　while exercising, 84
Reflux, effect on voice, 129
Rejection, fantasies and, 170–71
Relationships
　　balance in, <u>266–67</u>
　　dependence in, 178
　　equality in, 179
　　honesty in, 181
　　maintaining, <u>180–81</u>
　　stress in, 55
Relaxation
　　nature and, 310
　　sexual arousal and, 153–54
　　sounds and, 306
　　television and, 178
　　vacations and, 302–9
　　walking and, 305–6
Relaxation response (exercise), 308
Requests, gender differences in
　　expressing, 259–60
Respect, 223–36, <u>229–30</u>
Retaliation, backstabbing and, 273–74
Retin-A, 213, 214
Retina, detached, <u>44</u>
Retirement, 73, <u>244</u>
Reverse arm twists, 98
Reverse crunches, 104
Reye's syndrome, 139
Rhinoplasty, <u>62</u>
Riboflavin, in dairy products, 322
Ribs, barbecued, 17–18
Rituals, for stress relief, 280
Robbery, response to, 226–227
Rogaine, for hair loss, 210
Rogue Old Crustacean Barley Wine,
　　27
Roller coasters, for stress relief, 279
Rosacea, 215
Rotator cuff muscles, 81, 97–98
Routines, for stress relief, 280
Rowing, as exercise, 86

Running
   in cross-training, 325–26
   endurance, 105, 291
   improving times, 71
   mental tricks, 291
   repetitive nature of, 308–9
   training for 10-K, <u>118–19</u>
   walking as part of program, 113–14

Salespeople, 198–99, 225–26
Salmon, longevity and, 75
Salsa, mail-order, <u>288</u>
Salt, 206, 320
Samuel Adams Boston Lager, 29
Sandwiches, 14–15
Saponins, 23
Sardines, fat content of, 16
Sausage-and-pepper sandwich, 14–15
Saving money, 55–56, 73
Saw palmetto extract, 142–43
Scalp, oily, 317–18
Scottish ale, 26
Seeds, vitamin E in, 37–38
Self-esteem, 171, 224
Self-hypnosis, 308
Self-talk, 297
Sensate focusing, 48
Senses, 41–48, 185. *See also specific*
    senses
Sex
   aids, 175
   books on, <u>150</u>
   drive, 9
   fantasies about, 161, 164–74, <u>172</u>
   fantasies during, <u>166–67</u>
   food and, 159
   frequency of, 55, 74
   intimacy and, 185
   in morning, 322
   in old age, <u>124</u>, 243
   oral, 160, <u>171</u>
   physical fitness and, 74
   recharging, 184–87
   sense of touch and, 46–47
   sleep after, 322
   sounds during, 157–58
   stress reduction and, 280
   talking about, 155
   unusual locations for, 159–60
   on vacation, 307

Sexual attraction, 156
Sexuality, 162–63
Sexual satisfaction, 156
Shampoo, 208, <u>215</u>, 317–18
Shaving
   between eyebrows, 206
   irritation caused by, 61–62, <u>200</u>, 205
   razors, <u>215</u>
Shirts, 194, 196
Shoes, 209–10
   in casual business attire, 193, 194
   polishing, 318
   at work, <u>268</u>
Shooting ranges, 279
Shopping
   for clothes, 58–59, <u>193</u>, 195–200
   for food, 20
   mail-order, 53, 59, <u>288</u>
   online, 57
Shorts, in casual business attire, 194
Shoulders, 91–92, 315–16
Shower, health checks in, 128–29
Shrimp, calories and fat in, 12
Side ankle lifts, 102
Sighing, relaxation and, 306–7
Sight. *See* Vision
Sildenfil, for impotence, <u>124</u>
Silly Putty, as hand exerciser, 99–100
Sinus infections, sense of smell and, <u>45</u>
Sit-ups, 75, 104. *See also* Crunches
Skating, in-line, <u>303</u>
Skiing, 102
Skin, 210–11, 214–15
   cancer, <u>124</u>, 129, <u>143</u>
   care of, 200–201, 204, 206, 211
   protection from sun, 209
Slacks, in casual business attire, 194
Sleep
   back problems and, 67, 324–25
   increasing time, 74–75
   position, 67
   after sex, 322
   on vacation, 307
   valerian and, 144–45
Small talk, with women, 254–55
Smell, sense of, <u>45</u>, 46
Smiling, 231, 261
Smoking, 243, 314–15
Snack(s), 4, 7–9, 38
   cereal as, 8

Snacks *(continued)*
   late-night, 38
   low-fat, 4, 9
   muscle-building, 7
Soap, 201, 206, <u>215</u>. *See also* Face, care
   of
Soccer, <u>87</u>, 222
Social skills, respect and, 225
Socks, with casual business attire, 194
Sodium, 206, 320
Software, 56–57
Soleus muscle, 101–2
Sounds, relaxation and, 306
Soup, low-fat, 5
Soybeans, phytomins in, 23, 24
Spam, <u>30</u>
Spas, 281–82
Special-effects coordinator, 284
Speech, 233–34. *See also* Voice
Sperm, <u>152</u>
Spinach, 23, 24, 37
Spine, 186. *See also* Back
Sport coats, 194
Sporting-goods tester, 283
Sports. *See specific sports*
Sports producer, 285
Sports psychology, 289–96
Spouse
   career of, <u>238</u>
   exercising with, 86
   respect for, 231
   sexual fantasies and, 168
   stress reduction and, 280
Sprains, 81
Spy-gizmo designer, 285
Squats, 83
Stair-climber, 323–24
Steam beer, 31
Stew, 13
Stockings, gradient compression, 215
Stock tracking software, 57
Stout (beer), 27
Strength training, 113–14, <u>116–17</u>
Stress
   anxiety and, 140
   caffeine and, 309
   minor causes of, 49
   mood and, 327
   reduction, 275–80
      breathing for, 293–94

   laughter for, 308
   massage for, 309
   stretching for, 277
   in relationships, 55
   vacations and, 302–9
   weight fluctuation and, 127
   work-related, 315–16
Stroke, <u>124</u>
Strollers, jogging, 86
Stubbed toes, 68
Style, personal, 195–200
Styling gel, 208, 209
"Styling stress," 208
Subscapularis (rotator cuff muscle), 81,
   97–98
Sugar, fatigue and, 80
Suits, 58
   double-breasted, 213
   dry-cleaning, 323
   expensive, 199
   fabrics for, 198, 200
   fitting of, 199–200
   historical role of, 191–92
   shopping for, 197–99
Sun exposure
   age spots caused by, 212
   cataracts and, 42
   protecting skin from, 88–89, 206,
      209, 211
   sunspots caused by, 205–6
   vitamin D and, 37
Sunglasses, 42
Sunscreen, 88–89, 206, 209, 211
Super-slow method (weight training),
   115–16
Support socks, 215
Supraspinatus (rotator cuff muscle), 81,
   97–98
Sweat, <u>118</u>, 318
Sweaters
   in casual business attire, 194
   packing for travel, 202
Sweet potatoes, 24, 38
Swimming, improving technique,
   120–21

Tanzen, 187
Target heart rate, 109. *See also* Pulse
Taste, loss of, <u>45</u>
Tattoos, <u>235</u>

Tea, 21, 24, 124
Teeth, 210. *See also* Mouth
  bonding, 133–34
  brushing technique, 132
  common questions about, 130–35
  fillings, 50, 135
  flossing, 131–32
  implants, 135
  routine exams, 130
  sensitive, 60–61
  video headsets during dental work,
    124
  wisdom, 133
  x-rays, 131
Television
  football on, 178
  relaxation and, 178
  viewing habits, 71–72, 316–17
Temperature, cold, 48
Temples, 185
Tendinitis, 101
Tennis, 5–6, 102, 292–93
Tennis elbow, 81, 99
Tension, sexual, 152–54
Teres minor (rotator cuff muscle), 81,
    97–98
Termination of employment, 258–59
Testicles, self-examination of, 129
Testosterone, 9, 185
Theakston's Old Peculier (beer), 26
Thighs. *See also* Hamstrings
  inner, 187
  leg press machine for, 93
  rotation of, 100
Three Finger Jack-Hefedunkel (beer),
    30
Threesomes, fantasies about, 170
Thyroid gland, 129
Ties. *See* Neckties
Time
  apart from partner, 178
  for exercise, 83
  with family, 86, 266–67
  for listening, 265
  for partner, 177–78
  wasted, 263, 267
Tingling, in extremities, 45
Tinnitus, 44
To-do lists, 276
Toes, as erogenous zones, 188

Toe walking, as exercise, 102
Tofu, 23
Tomatoes, 22, 24
Tomato juice, 206
Toothbrushes, 132
Toothpaste, 132
  chapped lips caused by, 205
  for sensitive teeth, 61
Touch(ing), 46–47
  during conversations, 225
  gender differences in sensitivity, 255
  relaxation and, 309
  sense of, 45
  sessions, 185
Trapezius massage, 63
Travel, 201–2. *See also* Vacations
Travel agents, 202
Tretinoin, for age spots, 213
Triceps extension, 116–17
Triceps pressdown machine, 92–93
Triglycerides, 148
T-shirts, in casual business attire, 193
Tumors, brain, 45
Twinkies, 14
Tylenol. *See* Acetaminophen

Ulcers, 124
Ultraviolet radiation, 42. *See also* Sun
    exposure
Umpires, injuries sustained by, 305
Underarms, 186–87
Underwear, 288
Upright row, 117
Urination, problems with, 126

V-8 juice, 206
Vacations. *See also* Travel
  avoiding lessons on, 306
  choosing, 304
  easing into, 305
  exercise during, 307
  need for, 260, 264
  relaxation and, 302–9
  sex during, 307
  short, 304–5
  sleep during, 307
Vaccines, 124
Vaginal containment, 154
Valerian, 144–45
Varicose veins, 215

Veal Parmesan, 18
Vegetables, 16, 21. *See also specific vegetables*
Vertigo, ginkgo for, 146
Video-game tester, 286
Video headsets, 124
Videotapes
    adult, 174–75
    golf, 299, 301
    mail-order, 53
Vision, 41–43, 44, 317. *See also* Eyes
Visualization, in golf, 294–95
Vitamin A, 22
Vitamin-B complex, 28
Vitamin B$_{12}$, 38
Vitamin C, 38, 80–81
Vitamin D, 37, 322
Vitamin E, 38
Vitamin supplements, 10
Voice, 128–29, 230, 234. *See also* Speech

Waffles, 17
Walking, 106, 113–14, 114, 305–6
Walnuts, vitamin E in, 37–38
Wardrobe. *See* Clothes
Warmups, pre-exercise, 81–82, 89
Water
    exercise and, 33, 36, 106
    protein and, 35
    retention, 319–20
    role in muscle formation, 35
    role in skin care, 201
    role in weight loss, 5
Watermelon, carotenoids in, 22, 24
Wealth, 246
Weather, exercise and, 88–89
Weight, body, 126–27
Weight lifting. *See also* Bench presses; Strength training
    cross-training and, 325–26
    mental tricks for, 290–91
    muscle mass and, 7, 70–71, 313–14
    periodization program for, 70
    results of, 107–8
    super-slow method, 81
    training rotation, 81
Weight loss. *See* Aerobic exercise; Diet; Low-fat food
Weihenstephan (beer), 31
Wheat beer, 31

Whipped cream, alternatives to, 12
Wild Goose Light Ale, 25–26
Wine
    flavonoids in, 21
    mail-order, 288
    phytomins in, 24
    tasting, 47
Wisdom teeth, 133
Witch hazel, 318
Women; *See also* Dating; Relationships; Spouse
    arguing with, 183
    cars and, 179
    communicating with, 253–61
    desire to change men, 176–83
    honesty in relationships with, 181
    listening to problems of, 182
    living with, 180–81
    negotiating with, 183
    sex and, 163
    smiling, 261
    at work, 253–61
Women's magazines, 312
Wool, as suit fabric, 198
Work
    betrayal at, 271–72
    boredom at, 266
    breaks from, 316
    bringing home, 276–77
    dating people from, 261–62
    etiquette, 252
    physically demanding, 321
    productivity at, 192
    stress related to, 315–16
    women at, 253–61
Workouts, 59, 83–84. *See also* Exercise; Weight lifting
Wrinkles, 204, 205, 214

X-rays, 131

Yawning, 306–7
Yogurt, 35, 37, 38, 322
    frozen, 12
Yohimbine, avoiding, 147

Zinc, testosterone and, 9